UNIFIED PHILOSOPHY

SECOND EDITION

UNIFIED PHILOSOPHY
INTERDISCIPLINARY METAPHYSICS, CYBERETHICS, AND LIBERAL ARTS

Michael M. Kazanjian
Triton College

cognella® | ACADEMIC PUBLISHING

Bassim Hamadeh, CEO and Publisher
Angela Schultz, Senior Field Acquisitions Editor
Carrie Montoya, Manager, Revisions and Author Care
Kaela Martin, Project Editor
Abbey Hastings, Associate Production Editor
Emely Villavicencio, Senior Graphic Designer
Natalie Piccotti, Director of Marketing
Kassie Graves, Vice President of Editorial
Jamie Giganti, Director of Academic Publishing

Printed in the United States of America.

ISBN: 978-1-5165-3792-1 (pbk) / 978-1-5165-3793-8 (br)

In my preface, I refer to the seeds from which this book grew. Those were the answers and outstanding teaching that my Lane Tech high school teachers, Mr. Arnold Began, Mr. Herbert Herman, and Mrs. Yvonne Childs, gave me regarding college admission and the role of liberal arts therein. They gave me advice that I was too immature, hasty, and unwilling to learn, until philosophy classes in college taught me.

I dedicate my book to those three instructors.

CONTENTS

ACKNOWLEDGMENTS

Acknowledging the many people who have made this book possible has been as difficult a task as writing it. An author helped me along those lines by noting that he had been forced to omit more names than he included and that many helped him at least indirectly whose names he never knew.

My friend and colleague Ralph Forsberg is responsible for making this book manageable. I originally had sixty chapters in mind. Publish a book with that many chapters, he warned, and I will not read it. How about fourteen chapters? So I brought it down to thirteen and made exercises of the remaining chapters.

I wish to thank Angela Schultz, Michelle Piehl, Carrie Montoya, Emely Villavicencio, Abbey Hastings, Berenice Quirino, Daniel Menard, and Dani Skeen from Cognella Publishing for their help in writing my book. Their openness and willing to discuss, negotiate, and otherwise assist me in my venture have been major contributions to the final product. I cannot forget to thank Arek for sending me my first check.

John Tobin, Raymond Pfeiffer, longtime friend and colleagues Kara Malenfant, Bob Lichtenbert, David Lafferty, and Doug Binckley provided more input over decades or at least years than I can count.

Donald Ritchie, Corina Schusheim, and Ellen Harrow, like so many of my other friends, are unaware of the insights I have gained from them.

Robert Wiar, Leke Adeofe, Eugene Muhammad, Daniele Manni, Gary Zimmerman, and other colleagues from Triton College have fingerprints throughout this book.

My students at Waubonsee Community College and Triton Community College have taught me much. My appreciation to colleague and friend Ed Forst for insights that are seen primarily by me in my three books.

However the people above have contributed to and are responsible for the final state of this book, the designation of it being "our" work has limits. The author, more frequently than he is willing to admit for refusing good advice, is responsible for the shortcomings.

A NOTE ABOUT THE EXERCISES

I had initially intended that this book have approximately sixty chapters. The chapters would flow from the first as a set to the second as a subset of the first, and every successive one as a subset of the former. Each chapter after the first was crucial as a subset and could not be eliminated. A colleague warned me he would not scan or read a sixty-chapter book. He advised me to have roughly thirteen chapters. Because I could not eliminate chapters, I decided to use the present thirteen chapters and change the remaining ones to exercises. I choose to retain what are now chapters 1 through 13. This meant relegating to exercises the remaining fifty or so chapters. Due to the flow between chapters, exercises appear after chapters 4, 6, 9, 10, 11, 13. These exercises are for students to complete as chapters, each as few three pages. If students complete all exercises, they will see the flow from chapter 1 through what was intended as chapter 60.

PREFACE

Some classroom actions in high school planted the seeds of this book. I attended the Albert G. Lane Technical High School. Lane Tech, as we called it, is a selective admissions Chicago Public High School. It became selective after the Soviets caught the world off guard with Sputnik, the world's first artificial satellite, and Lane Tech administrators turned on a dime to impose admissions standards. They wanted only the best and brightest in order to compete with the Kremlin. Lane Tech suddenly admitted only the top two percent or so of applicants.

It's students, all male when I attended, were to be self motivated, inner-driven. Their motivations showed in the incidents I mention. Most of us, including myself, were committed to enter college. In at least three classes, we occasionally took time to ask our instructors about the difficulty in being admitted to colleges and universities. Nor were we interested in just any of the 6000 colleges and universities. The Ivy League, especially Harvard, Yale, and Princeton, MIT, the Service Academies, on down were our primary interests. In Mr. Began's German, Mrs. Child's U.S. History, and Mr. Herman's English classes, our question was the same. And we received the same answer.

We asked how difficult it was to gain admission to Harvard, University of Chicago, MIT, and so on. The answer in any case was not pleasant.

The part about being difficult to enter, was disappointing. Admission was based on several things including good grades in the most difficult subjects. But confusion set in, at least for me, with a phrase the instructors used about being admitted to the major universities. I had never heard of this phrase. Asking the instructors about admissions, they repeat a phrase regarding a program of study. This was the first time I had heard of the term program or college of liberal arts and sciences, or general education.

My confusion involved why a student must learn general education or be liberally educated. I was to learn that specialization was insufficient. I started thinking about this. Why should a student majoring in physics study chemistry, math, or history? Why does the school require a student majoring in literature study biology, sociology, or psychology?

I would learn the answers somewhat in high school, but more articulated in college. Life is not separated into physics, chemistry, and sociology. These are all part of the whole. Each discipline emerges from a generic unity.

Ironically, as I decided to major in philosophy, that generic unity eventually emerged. The thoughts of Alfred North Whitehead were especially good on this. I did learn that Plato, Aristotle, and other thinkers touched on almost all subjects. But Whitehead spoke of unified learning. Then came general system theory, human factors engineering ergonomics.

Ergonomics human factors engineering made a particularly deep impression on me. Where society has all but ridiculed philosophy, ergonomics was tacitly doing philosophy. An engineering and therefore hard science article noted that we may have options in the degree to which to interface people with machines and automation. However, we will probably never have automation or machines without any human operator, or an operator without machines. That's a philosophical, not engineering issue.

A book on engineering, along these lines, said that ergonomics is not a choice between having and not having the user, but the extent to which we design technology for the user. That, too, is the philosophical issue.

From high school on, I started researching and writing about general education or liberal arts and sciences. Two previous books, Phenomenology and Education, and Learning Values Lifelong, were first attempts at putting together my views. But thinking is always a work in progress. This book is a result of that attempted progress.

INTRODUCTION:
HUMAN FACTORS ENGINEERING SUPPORTS METAPHYSICS AND PHILOSOPHY

Unified Philosophy is for the student and educated citizen, but not at the exclusion of the professional intellectual. It introduces students and the literate citizen to the subject matter's importance as foundations of all jobs. Philosophical options underlie technology, arts, and sciences. The following pages serve as a unified view of ethics, philosophy, hermeneutics, ergonomics, and metaphysics, is an ongoing introduction, a reintroduction, orienting and reorienting advances in knowledge.

This volume is for colleges and universities and theological seminaries. It is for the study of philosophy, metaphysics, ethics, theology of culture, ergonomics, and hermeneutics. A careful perspective discerns that its scope embraces an interdisciplinary view of theology and religion. Metaphysics allows the reader to appreciate how all remaining topics are derived reality. Religion and theology are more expansive than we think.

In colleges and universities, this book is for introductions to metaphysics, ethics, hermeneutics, human factors engineering, city planning. I debranch metaphysics and shows it unifying all chapters. I debranch ethics and show how it is interwoven with and underlies metaphysical options and all remaining chapters. I demonstrate that philosophy, as metaphysics and ethics, is an ergonomic or human factors text. The phenomenological movement is subjective-friendly objectivity as one of the metaphysical options. Institutions must be human-friendly to be ethical.

Philosophy starts in wonder (Hamilton and Cairns 1964). Whitehead (1958) tells us it starts in wonder, proceeds as a dialogue with wonder and analysis, and in the end, wonder remains. That dialogue involves thinking. Thinking is about doing (MIT Undergraduate Catalogue 1961–62; Leamnson 2000; Benesh 2002), data (Shallit 2005), ethics, reality, and other aspects of reality.

While this book introduces philosophy to the reader, it is also an ongoing reintroduction to the field. Its aim is to reorient readers as they learn more in school, at work, and in life itself. Specific knowledge that people learn each day needs context. This work reintroduces philosophy once the reader has read it the first time. Reintroduction is the ongoing development of the specific information within the context of philosophy's holistic, fundamental framework.

Philosophy reveals human factors engineering/ergonomics' technology-person interface and special cases in the field of what I call person-stability interface. The special case interface reverses the technology-person interface.

Debranching metaphysics, shows a new view of philosophy and metaphysics. Metaphysics studies reality or being, while philosophy is the love of wisdom. Yet, the wise person understands reality. Reality is prior to all topics, including wisdom. Wisdom must be real before, and for it to "be wisdom." In that sense, metaphysics and philosophy are interchangeable. Metaphysics is more than a branch among other branches in philosophy. Understanding metaphysics is the highest form of wisdom. I, therefore, move metaphysics from a branch to equate it with philosophy. If reality is prior to wisdom, and wisdom must be real to be "wisdom," one day philosophers may well want to consider replacing the field's label from "philosophy" to "metaphysics." Being wise is being ethical. Being wise and ethical is the ability to interpret reality, language, and other topics.

As foundations of technology, arts and sciences, and connections between secular and spiritual learning, philosophy (metaphysics) is theoretical and applied. Theoretical philosophy is the general framework of reality connecting all knowledge and secularity. Technology, arts and sciences are derivative realities.

Thus, I move metaphysics, the study of reality or being, from just another topic, to their theoretical foundations.

If we have a study of knowledge, and then ethics, and then social philosophy, that may be fine. But if we then have a study of reality, that is what Ryle calls a category mistake. It is a category mistake unless the study of reality is a study of a general theory of reality, and knowledge and all other topics are derived theories of reality. We do not have knowledge, and social philosophy, and ethics, and then look at the topic of reality. We have, instead, specifics of reality, and a general view of reality.

Of course, while philosophers will argue against my positions, non-philosophers will even more emphatically question the usefulness of philosophy, metaphysics, etc. My aim then is to bring in human factors engineering, ergonomics, for support. A student seeking a career in philosophy, will hear that he or she ought enter a useful, no doubt well paying, job. Among those jobs might be medicine, law, accounting, business. Engineering is one of those fields. I find major support in human factors engineering or ergonomics, for philosophy.

Human factors design technology to match anatomic abilities and limits of humans. It speaks of the technology-user interface. Technology changes (Kantowitz and Sorkin, 1968), and the person as user remains stable. Matching users with user-friendly technology is one thing, designing the machines to be safe and comfortable for the user. But in the age of increasing automation, more and more people wonder if machines will one day operate totally on their own, minus the person. Chapanis (Chapanis, p. 534) notes that human beings will always be part of the machine-person interface. Adams (p. 256) says that we ought choose only the extent to which, not whether, people will interact with machines. In *Nudge* (2009), Nobel Prize-winning economist Richard H. Thaler and Cass R. Sunstein speak of nudging people or users to choose, and want to have choices be healthy. Perhaps without realizing it, the authors are taking into account their human factor making choices easier for them. Consumers do not always take health and the human factor into account. Their work is therefore paralleling human factors. The factor that makes it easier to select the better food, is the one to use in nudging people to buy that product. Is the food shelved at eye level in the store, rather than on the bottom shelf? Eye-level products tend to grab attention.

The human factor is the technology-person interface. However, a special case of this is the reverse interface, which I call the person-stability interface. Examples include the (1) firefighter-fire interface, (2) police-bomb interface, (3) military-nuclear interface, (4) military biological warfare interface, (5) military-chemical warfare interface, and (6) student-career interface. Each interface is the reverse of the technology-person interface. Firefighters change through training/design to fight fires by taking the burning building's limits and dangers into account. Police take a bomb's limiting factor into account. They dare not just approach and handle the bomb casually. In the third, fourth, and fifth examples, military weapons experts change to take into account the limits of dealing with nuclear, biological, and chemical dangers. Students change and train for careers. Thus, persons change for the fire, bombs, and weapons careers. The fire, bombs, and weapons remain stable, limited or fixed as to their danger, or requirements of the career.

Whether people ought accept a technology is a question of values, of philosophy or metaphysics, not technology. Philosophy of engineering enters, and therefore philosophical inquiry itself is supported. Albert Einstein, addressing the California Institute of Technology, reminded future engineers and scientists to give priority to human problems and social issues, as they discover technological and scientific advances. MIT's Vannevar Bush points out that tomorrow's engineer must study economics and psychology, and not just learn about nuts and bolts. Another MIT official, James R. Kilian, notes the importance of "greater engineering" and not just "engineering" in shaping and designing cities. Ergonomics as historically developed is what I call "micro ergonomics" or "micro human factors": engineers design a car, pen, computer, chair, or any specific technology for the user. Design in micro ergonomics matches machines to people's physical limits and abilities. Ergonomics ought to be integrated within philosophy as macro and micro human factors. Micro human factors, micro ergonomics designs a particular object such as a table, process, or aircraft cockpit for the user's physical limits. This is functional ergonomics. Macro ergonomics or phenomenological human factors asks first of all whether this technology ought to exist. Should we have cars, steering wheels, pens, computers, and workstations? The question is not how to interface any technology with the user, but whether we ought to have that technology. A safe car is user-friendly. But we might not want cars. We may need bikes, buses, and trains. Micro ergonomics involves virtually all chapters in this book, except those for ethics (chapter 7) and societal reality (chapter 8). Those two are macro ergonomics: How ought we design a city itself containing the micro technologies?

Philosophy ought be a hierarchy of a general theory of reality (metaphysics), with remaining chapters concerning what I call derived realities. These have been the other traditional branches including epistemology, ethics, social thinking, and aesthetics.

To both the educated person and professional intellectual, the following pages demonstrate how the broad field of philosophy as love of wisdom, insight into reality and interpretation, can serve as a foundation for liberal arts and sciences. Philosophy deals with technology and professions (medicine, nursing, law, education, engineering), science and art inside which are sciences and arts (biology, chemistry, physics, math, ethics, sociology, economics, history, religion and theology, languages, literature, and other) disciplines. My effort is to improve philosophy's organization of topics or fields (branches). Improvement will debranch metaphysics toward a hierarchy where it becomes general theory unifying derivations in philosophy. Philosophy then provides unified foundations of general education or the liberal arts.

Philosophers acknowledge metaphysics, ethics, epistemology, and other branches as equal in stature. I disagree with their view.

I argue that a hierarchy exists where general metaphysics (philosophy) studies reality and wisdom, while ethics, epistemology and other "branches," are derived realities. This book makes explicit that hierarchy between metaphysics as general theory and its ethical and epistemological applications. That hierarchy is more than a list. Metaphysics talks of the subject-object relation. Interaction or continuum of this two fold theme is a major factor. Within interaction comes derivations of the subject-object relation: hermeneutics, prediction, ethics, and all successive chapters. Each derivation previous chapter contains the seeds of a succeeding chapter.

My present work revises non-Western and Western thinking on philosophy's divisions. Some non-Western philosophies talk of human activity without dividing philosophy into branches in the Western style. Generally, non-Western thought expresses itself in religions such a Confucianism, Hinduism, and Buddhism (Hopfe, et. al., 2009). Chinese emphasize ethics through *Analects*. Hindus have the *Laws of Manu* for ethics. Buddhists talk of ethics through four fold truths and Eightfold path. These civilizations do not see ethics, epistemology, and metaphysics as equal branches or in a hierarchy. non-Western thought tends to emphasize ethics, and sees divisions in philosophy as virtually mutually exclusive. These thinkers speak of what I call static metaphysics, ethics, and epistemology, but omit dynamics: change and stability and how these derive from the statics. Non-Western thinking tends to view change as illusion.

Western philosophical tradition evolves from nonhierarchical branches in the early Greeks. Preocratics talk of cosmology, Socrates of knowledge (Cornford, 1953), the world. Plato is more explicit. He speaks of the Cave involving cosmology and metaphysics (reality), epistemology as illusion and wisdom, and ethics primarily as justice. Aristotle divides philosophy into metaphysics or first principles, knowledge, and ethics, aesthetics and logic.

Neither Western nor non-Western thinking sees a hierarchy with general and derived metaphysics. In Western thinking, Plato and Aristotle are explicit about differentiating metaphysics, epistemology, and ethics, but do not refer to them as branches. The two thinkers do not see knowledge and morality as derived metaphysics. Aristotle refers to metaphysics as first principles, but does not allude to ethics or epistemology as derived from those basic ideas. Frederick Copelston (1993, p. 277) believes Aristotle saw philosophy as theory, practice, and poetry. Aristotle does not connect the branches, and fails to show how metaphysics is basic with the others derived reality. Western thought divides philosophy into branches but never notes a general theory and derivation. Determining who first used the word "branches," seems impossible. No Western thinker shows philosophy as static and dynamic metaphysics, and its derivations. I define statics as atomism, structuralism, interaction, dualism, and the existential or individual.

Modern philosophy sees branches but no hierarchy or derivation from static and dynamics metaphysics. I select Rene Descartes, Immanuel Kant, and G.W.F. Hegel to represent modern philosophy. Descartes derives a mind-body dualistic metaphysics based on the cogito after a dualistic epistemology degrading the senses. No explicit ethics or metaphysical dynamics exist in Cartesian thought. Kant (Audi, 1995, p. 398) has a metaphysics, epistemology, and ethics, with no clear hierarchy. However, Descartes and Kant omit what I call dynamics. On the other hand, G.W.F. Hegel shows a vast and holistic dialectical metaphysics implying knowledge and ethics. However, Hegelian dialectical metaphysics shows only a process unfolding a goal. The evolving whole all but absorbs the individual within thesis-antithesis-syntheses. No explicit hierarchy exists in Hegel. Descartes and Kant omit evolutionary or process thought, and Hegel ignores what I term static thinking.

Nineteenth and twentieth century philosophy looks at branches through movements. Thinkers comprise a spectrum of movements involving what I call the statics. The spectrum omits hierarchy, metaphysics as theoretical foundations of derivations, and reference to dynamics. Positivism and linguistic analysis question or reject metaphysics, clearly not putting it in, much less at the top of a hierarchy from which to derive other areas of philosophy. But they believe in atomic reality and knowledge. Phenomenology and existentialism react to positivism and emphasize a subjective metaphysics and epistemology. Neither phenomenology nor existentialism encourages hierarchy approach to the humanization. Most existentialists deemphasize reason, thus seeing mathematics as all but anathema. Husserl, founder of phenomenology, likes the subject-object continuum. However, he stops short for applying his initial career, mathematics, toward phenomenology or the lifeworld. None of the movements include an objective taxonomy of the statics and dynamics.

Process philosophy does not fare any better than other Western thought. A. N. Whitehead, frequently called "the" process thinker, gave us a metaphysics, and epistemology. His strength is what I am calling dynamic metaphysics and epistemology. But he neglects the statics, explicit ethics, and hierarchy with metaphysics at the top.

Philosophy is the love of wisdom. But if philosophy is theoretical and applied metaphysics (study of reality), philosophers love reality. The wise person loves the hierarchy of theoretical and derivative reality. Specifically, the wise person loves to think of what I term statics comprising reality: atomism, dualism, phenomenology, and existentialism as options. For my purposes, I omit reference to pragmatism, nihilism, solipsism, skepticism. The wise person loves also to think about deriving from the statics the four options of change alone, change-stability, change colored by stability, and stability alone. Derivation occurs within metaphysics as I derive change's relation to stability from statics. Outside theoretical metaphysics derivation occurs as I derive the applications from the general theory.

This book consists of thirteen chapters. Chapters three, six, nine, ten, eleven, and thirteen have exercises. These exercises were to be chapters, but a colleague and friend warned that would have resulted in sixty-four chapters, too long for the book. As general theory, the first chapter contains the seeds or essence of all remaining chapters. All chapters except the first arise from within a previous one. Thus, some chapters arise from within an exercise in the previous chapter. Readers may disagree whether a given exercise or chapter belongs inside a previous one. They are free to choose a different organization of chapters and exercises.

Chapter one is theoretical. It is a general theory of metaphysics. The general theory shows three sections: subject-object, change-stability, and problem-person conceptual framework underlie all remaining chapters. Many options exist in the subject-object relations. These include monism, phenomenology, dualism, existentialism, pragmatism, nihilism, skepticism, postmodernism, and solipsism. I restrict my book to the first four. Four options in change and stability include change only, change through stability, change and stability, and stability only. Finally, alertness/reactive problem solving, problem prevention, ignorance/reactive problem solving, and problem denial comprise the third metaphysical section. Readers do not necessarily understand subject and object, change and stability, automatically. Problems arise. Four options exist in dealing with problems. Are we to be alert and react, prevent, ignore and react, or deny problems?

Remaining chapters are the applications of metaphysics' four options. Chapter two deals with linguistic or hermeneutic reality in terms of simple and idiomatic language arising from within the subject-object interaction. Chapter three seeks whether truth always needs theories and justification. Chapter four concerns correspondence and consistency (coherence) theories. Chapter five deals with prediction through determinism and freedom. Chapter six asks whether society originated as communitarian or contract. Chapter seven examines ethics as a general theory integrating economics, sociology, ecology, anthropology, psychology, history, and all other arts and sciences encompassing previous and remaining chapters. Chapter eight inquires into worker and the family or I-Thou relation, analyzing the meaning of neighborhood. Chapter nine looks at property as public or private. Chapter ten reflects on God. Chapter Eleven deals with knowledge source as empirical or rational. Chapter twelve seeks the relation between disciplines and philosophy. And chapter thirteen asks about technology's relation to science and art. Chapter fourteen does two things. Inside or as a subset to science/art, it examines the relation between science and art. Within that same chapter, I look at what scholars term *philosophy of science*. Here, I analyze methodology as method and the a-method. Method involves induction, hypothesis, and community of scholars. A-method is an interpretation of Feyerabend and his view appearing to oppose method.

Epistemology, traditionally dealing with empiricism and rationalism, is concerned with what we term in modern knowledge nature and nurture. Nature and nurture, which epistemology books and chapters almost never mention, are major issues in education or psychology. Ethics does not generally allude to the topic, and psychology and education do not cite it as equal to or derived from metaphysics. Epistemology is within the academic context. But since I derive academic topics from those within metaphysics, epistemology automatically arises from previous chapters. Epistemology is not simply "another" branch. Nurture is derived knowledge origin objectivity, nature is derived knowledge origin lifeworld. Teachers nurture students from, and all people gain some knowledge through the outside. All individuals appear knowledgeable in some sense from within.

My book opens up existing orientations in colleges and universities. It orients incoming freshmen toward the unity of their studies. Humanities as philosophy shows the power of liberal arts and sciences. Philosophy unifies liberal arts and the student's major field of concentration. It then shows connections within liberal arts and sciences, and announces the existence of relations within a student's concentration. But the humanities do not end at freshman orientation.

I open up what higher education calls the capstone. The capstone "caps" what a student has studied during the past four years. My book re-orients the senior's freshman year orientation. This reorientation explicates what the orientation hinted. It then helps the student understand connections throughout graduate and professional schools, indeed, throughout life.

A brief word about terminology. Throughout this book I use terms like object-alone or object-only, subject-only or subject-alone. This usage departs traditional texts in philosophy. I have a reason for this. For example, Immanuel Kant says perception is organized by innate categories, so for him, the empirical and rational go together. Phenomenology says something similar. The empirical/rational are colored by values. And, dualism talks of the perception-reason dualism. Thus Kant, phenomenology and dualism use dual words in different meaning.

However, we say empiricists argue for perception devoid of categories or innate ability, and rationalists insist on innate ideas or tendencies alone. Notice that Kant and phenomenologists use dual or binary terms such as empirical-rational, but empiricists and rationalist are simply called empiricists and rationalists. Using one term while someone else finds two are more complete, suggests that use of on words is incomplete. Empiricists are actually empirical-only, rationalists are rational-only.

We are wise in seeing metaphysics as the basic theory or question of existence with its many options of what is real, and wise to then select and compare the options in metaphysics. Seeing theoretical and derived metaphysics or theoretical and derived wisdom, is wisdom.

People debate as to which college majors are useless. What will you do with art, history, literature? Majors such as chemistry, physics, math, accounting, engineering, and biology seem fine. Beyond the debate, even taking a course in philosophy appears nonsensical. But is it?

Philosophy is thinking. Classrooms are for thinking about doing in chemistry lab. Highest executives think about what the company is doing in production of goods and services. R & D is thinking and developing new products and services. Members of the legislative, executive, and judicial branches of government think about what the people have been, are, and will be doing. Workers think about retirement. At the workplace, meetings determine options for how to work better. Each time we are to have a meal, we think about what to eat. Doing vacation requires thinking about vacation. Thinking occurs many times daily. Whether educational institutions offer, merge, or eliminate a course or subject matter, is a philosophical action.

Holidays are holy days. People think about what they will do or ought to do on a regular work day due to historical figures, divine intervention, or historical events. The Sabbath is the weekend holiday.

As we think, people are selecting the best options for action. They are philosophizing. Do they merely act, act in certain ways, or refrain from acting?

In other words, do we just produce, produce in certain ways, or refrain from production?

Philosophy, says Whitehead, builds cathedrals before the workmen have moved the first stone into place (Whitehead, Alfred North, 1964b, p vii.). Build before is metaphor for select whether cathedral or other building, stone or other material, the best way to move the material, where to settle it for the building, and so on. Not just building, but type. Not just material, but type. Not just motion, but type.

REALITY:
UNIFIED GENERAL THEORY OF METAPHYSICS

KEYWORDS

hermeneutics: Wisdom obtained from interpretation of sacred and secular texts.

lifeworld (*lebenswelt*): In Edmund Husserl, our prereflective, lived, prereductive, preanalytic, pretheoretical approach to the world.

lifeworld-friendly city: The humane city or small town with homes, sidewalks, recreation, worship, hospitals, schools.

lifeworld-only: An emphasis on subjectivity-only.

lifeworld-unfriendly: A bedroom community, big city where neighbors do not know each other.

monism: One reality exists. *See also* objectivity-only.

objectivity-only: One reality exists totally independent of people; monism; no lifeworld.

subjectivity-only: Reality is primarily the self, or subject.

phenomenology: Reality is the object-subject continuum. Reality is objective, but colored by and involving subjectivity.

human factors engineering (ergonomics): The branch of engineering that designs technology to be user-friendly.

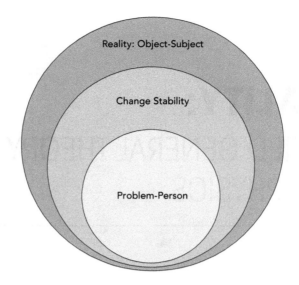

Fig 1.1

Chapter 1 is a unified general theory of metaphysics. But let me explain.

In this chapter and throughout the book, I integrate philosophy (love of wisdom), ethics, hermeneutics, human factors engineering, and metaphysics (study of reality). Wisdom must be real in order for us to deal with it. Understanding reality is the highest form of wisdom. Options exist in metaphysics, including reality, object embodied in subjectivity, object-subject dualism, subjectivity, and others. I restrict my book to the first four. We can understand right and ways and thus ethical views of reality, of wisdom. This chapter is derived ethics. Several interpretations of right and wrong, reality, and wisdom are present. Hermeneutics enters. Metaphysical options have parallels with human factors engineering. According to human factors engineering, those are homologous to the technology-user relation: Technology is the only reality, embodied in the user or user-friendly, dualism, and user-only. This chapter and book approach philosophy, ethics, interpretation, and metaphysics in terms of ergonomics or human factors engineering. This chapter is therefore a general theory of philosophy/metaphysics, derived ethics, derived hermeneutics, and ergonomics. For the sake of simplicity, I use "philosophy" or "metaphysics." Philosophy (metaphysics) is theoretical and applied. The remaining chapters discuss applied metaphysics.

General metaphysics is a unified general theory underlying all remaining chapters. It consists of general theory A of object-subject relation, general theory A.I of change-stability, and general theory A.II of problem-person. Each of these has many metaphysical options. I restrict my current work to four: monism, phenomenology, dualism, and subjectivity-only.

This chapter is a unified general theory of metaphysics (philosophy, hermeneutics). General theories occur in virtually all disciplines, but rarely, if ever, as that start of philosophy or metaphysics. Why do I call this chapter a unified general theory? My three sections in this and all remaining chapters are (1) object and subject, (2) process and stability, and (3) problem and denial (or person). Object and subject is the most general theory underlying the next two, and throughout the chapters. Process and stability is a derived general theory, inside object and subject. Finally, inside process and stability, problem and denial is a general theory applying to derivative problem and denial in remaining chapters.

Metaphysics is a unity of object and subject, inside of which is process and stability, inside of which is problem and denial. Thus, metaphysics is more than a general theory, for it unifies general theory of object and subject, of process and stability, and of problem and denial. Scholars are accustomed to general theory and its applications. But general theory is simplistic. In metaphysics it consists of object and subject, process and stability, and problem and denial. Therefore, it unifies the three general theories or dual themes.

STUDY QUESTIONS

- What five topics does this book, and this chapter, attempt to integrate?
- How can metaphysics (study of reality), philosophy (love of wisdom), ethics (right and wrong), human factors engineering (technology and person; objectivity and subjectivity), and hermeneutics (interpretation) be unified?
- Why does this book interrelate and nearly equate philosophy and meta-physics?
- How would you argue that philosophy, ethics, and metaphysics are separate and/or very much interrelated?
- What are a general theory and a unified general theory? How is the latter more comprehensive?

OBJECT AND SUBJECT: GENERAL THEORY A.I

Metaphysics comprises generally eight positions on reality: monism, phenomenology, dualism, subjectivism, existentialism, pragmatism, postmodernism, solipsism, and nihilism. Some philosophers may argue that subjectivity, existentialism, pragmatism, comprise the postmodern. As an introduction to philosophy, this book restricts itself to four positions on reality, but briefly alludes to the others. The four are monism, phenomenology, dualism, and postmodernism. These four serve as models for applying to each chapter. Each remaining chapter is a variation or derivation of the four options or positions. Pragmatism means what works, and does not take sides. Existentialism puts existence before essence and says each person develops their own nature. Solipsism says the self alone exists. Nihilism denies there is meaning in life. Skepticism doubts anything exists; usually it means we can know nothing.

Ethics sees each of the four as an ethical as well as metaphysical option. Philosophy tells us that wisdom means selecting the correct, ethical position. Theoretical metaphysics (the current chapter) is derived ethics. Chapter seven is theoretical ethics and derived metaphysics.

A future edition of my book will have a new chapter one. That chapter will be titled "Reality" and deal with metaphysics. However, its content will be more abstract than object and subject. The new content will be "part" and "whole." Part (cf. sum of objects) means reality is: the sum total of parts, parts embodied (in the whole), part-whole dualism, or a nonreductive, nonsummative whole. That whole (cf. subject) is not against reduction, but only non-reductive. Chapter two would be ontological reality. I see metaphysics as inquiry into reality, and ontology as what has been the content of chapter one: the spectrum from objectivity-alone to subjectivity-alone or postmodernism.

My reason for the new chapter one is to adjust my book so it will lay the foundation for what I call reverse human factors. Human factors says the designer must take into account the person. But reverse human factors involves police handling bombs; the military handling nuclear, biological, and chemical weapons; people dealing with weather (we take umbrellas in rain); and students preparing for careers. A general theory underlying micro and macro human factors, and reverse factors, would involve something more abstract that a human element. Wholeness, the nonreducible, and the like, probably fit that abstraction. Every chapter, then, will have the same topic, but will be moved forward by one. Chapter two becomes Ontological Reality (ontological positivism, ontological phenomenology, ontological dualism, ontological postmodernism), three becomes Language Reality, four is Truth Reality, and so on.

MONISM

Monism is the metaphysical position saying *one* objective reality exists devoid of subjectivity. For monism, reality is objectivity-alone or objectivity-only.

That one reality is *totally* independent of subjective or human existence. Subjectivity or embodiment does not exist, does not color objectivity. Objectivity here ignores human existence. Objectivity-alone is atomistic, or structuralist. Atomism means reality—including human existence—is totally reducible to the sum of atoms or parts. This is logical positivism (Ayer 1959; Carnap 1967). The Greek thinker Democritus was an atomist (Cornford, 1953). As an atomist, today we would probably call him the earliest "chemist" or "physicist." Structuralism denotes that reality is an undifferentiated whole, ignoring or overwhelming the person. Anthropology and sociology (Giddens 1984; Welsch and Vivanco 2015; Levi-Strauss 1963, 1969) tell us about structuralism. Both atomism and structuralism ignore human existence, dignity, and respect.

In the language of existentialism, which is the fourth position we will discuss below, the existential thinker might say monism denotes essence before existence. If this even suggests existence exists, a more accurate wording would say monism is essence alone, or essence without existence. The human factor does not exist; doctors treat the illness alone, not the patient. We are only social security numbers, passwords, and usernames. People are only fingerprints, optic security, and other means of protecting society.

The computer is an example of one reality or objectivity-alone. Talk with one or more human beings and you find it relatively easy. All you do is approach the person and either of you starts the conversation. This, of course, depends on the two or more of you speaking the same language. None of you present requires the others to identify themselves or use special code language. In a small town where everyone knows everyone else, conversation and identification is immediate. Even in a big city, strangers ask for directions or maybe the time of day, without requiring identification. The computer is different. A user needs to turn on the power, put in the username and password, and jump through other hoops.

In the language of human factors engineering, the computer is user-unfriendly. You do not merely start talking with a computer as with a human being, even as a stranger. Monistic communication, in atomism, is object-only. Imagine a world where you would need usernames and passwords when talking with people. Critics will argue that there is a place for usernames, passwords, and communications security. Bank and checking accounts, emails, and other forms of private communications are part of the real world, the critics argue. All this may be true.

However, life could be easier paying cash at the grocery, other daily shopping, at the gas station, and so on. Transportation on buses was once cash only. Taking a cab was cash only at one time.

Socrates (Hamilton and Cairns 1964) says "the unexamined life is not worth living." If Socrates implies the examined life alone is worth living, he is a monist. His statement does not appear to put examination into human context. For atomism, examination alone is valid. Life is composed of the sum total of simple atomic objects completely vulnerable to examination and the laboratory.

A monistic book might well mean reducing the arts, broadly speaking (social science, humanities, etc.), to math, physics, or chemistry. The book includes only numbers, symbols, and other quantitative writing. Religious implications exist here.

Jewish thought is among the foundations of Western civilization and Christianity. Its scripture is the Torah. Technically, the Torah includes the Hallakha or law, and Aggadah or story (Flohr-Mendez 1998). God relates law to humanity, through Moses, through story. This occurs through a personal relationship between God and the Jewish people. For monism, it would mean Hallakha and legalism without the Aggadah.

In human factors terminology, atomic objects and mere examination, monistic books, and Hallakha alone, are user-unfriendly. Existentialists would refer to the user-unfriendly as essence without existence. For human factors/ergonomics, it is existence unfriendly essence.

The monist sees object-only or object-alone as ethical and other options of reality as unethical. Atomism and structuralism are ethical under monism. Existentialism says monism is unethical because human beings are neither atoms alone, nor overwhelmed by structure.

Technology is quickly becoming dominant in society, especially in the workplace. Shoshana Zuboff (1988) explores the impact of machines replacing human workers. Sociological and psychology issues arise as society reduces human activity to mere motion. Machines replace people, and automation replaces traditional machines and employees. Society assigns to machines, computers, and automation the word *smart* as in *smartphone*. Corporate

America and manufacturers thus anthropomorphize—give human characteristics to—inanimate objects.

STUDY QUESTIONS

- What are the two kinds of monism?
- Compare these two kinds of monism and explain how they ignore persons.
- Who is Democritus, and why would we call him the first chemist?
- How would you feel studying chemistry or physics and finding that the early Greek philosophers laid the foundations of modern science?
- How can computers help us learn monism?
- How can a religion, say Judaism, be an example of learning monism in terms of engineering, logic, and Judaism?

STUDY QUESTIONS

- Why is ethics intimately interrelated and almost synonymous with metaphysics?
- Do you agree or disagree that ethics and metaphysics are related?

PHENOMENOLOGY

Phenomenology says *one* reality is *embodied or subjectively colored*. Reality is objectivity-embodied.

Reality is *somewhat* independent of subjectivity. Objectivity is continuous with and exists through subjectivity or embodiment. Where logical positivism and structuralism involve monism or disembodied, phenomenology speaks about embodiment. Some refer to phenomenology as continental thought (Audi 1997), where objectivity is subject-friendly. Human factors engineering is a parallel and talks of the user-friendly (Kantowitz and Sorkin 1968). Subjectivity is what Edmund Husserl (1970) and Alfred Schutz (1970) call the lifeworld. This is the prereflective world, where existence is irreducible to atoms. For existential language, this means existence. Essence, a fixed nature, an objective reality, an objectivity is existentially manifest. Embodiment says atomism and structure are embodied, or existential, essence.

Huston C. Smith (1966, 37) says Charles Hartshorne's (1991) *Logic of Perfection* does two things. In the book, Hartshorne "dissociates himself from the positivistic suspicion that such inquiry is misguided in principle and cognitively can come to nothing." On the other hand, Hartshorne "distinguishes himself from the dominant continental quests—Heidegger's, Jaspers', Sartre's, Marcel's—which, though engrossed with the problem of being, doubt that traditional tools (objective reason directed toward system construction) can effectively come to grips with it." Ricoeur (1966), Smith, and Hartshorne share much, objecting to disembodied atomism and subjectivity alone. Smith (1966, 37) says part and whole, prereflective and reflective, and reduction and generally irreducible, are together from the start.

Psychologists Francisco Varela and Evan Thompson (1992) tell us about embodied cognition; knowing and thinking are in a contextual, social situation, and artificial intelligence thus has limits. The ethical view can be that artificial intelligence may be technically possible, but morally invalid. Hilary Putnam (1992) says philosophy and reason are part of a social, ethical life, which Husserl would term the lifeworld. Paul Davies (1984) concludes his *Superforce* by saying that a universe by design is more than an objective reality out-there, independent of us; it "includes us." Studying the universe, reality, is inquiring into our social nature. A unified field theory is more than math and physics. It is sociological in the widest sense.

In Judaism, this would mean aggadah-friendly Hallakha. Story is the context for law. The Hebrew bible, which Christianity calls the Old Testament, is story after story. These stories contain propositions. The law or proposition is tacit or implied in most cases. Avigdor Shinan, Senior Lecturer at the Department of Hebrew Literature, the Hebrew University, Jerusalem, retired in 2012 as a full professor, tells us very concisely (Shinan 1990) that the Hallakha-aggadah relationship is that between the "stern" and "cheerful," the "strict" and the "forgiving," the "petrifying" and the "renewing." While scholars and laypersons analyze and objectify the Hallakha, everyone lives, does not analyze, add, substract, multiply, or divide aggadah.

Hans-Georg Gadamer (2013) says that our biases or prejudices color our actions and beliefs. Biases or prejudices can be good or bad. A person can be biased against tall or short people. That would be inappropriate. But the same person can be biased in that he or she comes from an engineering perspective, and may close a full garbage bag with perfectly crossed tape. Each bag might well have the same volume of garbage. Engineering has taught the engineer to be quantitatively precise and uniform in filling and closing the bags.

Unlike objectivity-alone, objectivity-embodied is humane. The computer does not negotiate with you if you lack a username and password. But go into a small, neighborhood store even in 2017, and certainly during the 1950s, and learn that you forgot adequate funds. The store owner might well have allowed you to take the grocery or other product home, and return as soon as possible with the money to pay for the merchandise. Humanity and negotiation are part of life.

In that store you are generally dealing with a living supervisor or cashier. You are not dealing with customer serviceperson who does not know you, or with a computer, especially in a self-service store. Shopping is as much as a social and cultural interaction, a community affair, as it is a commercial or business transaction.

Gabriel Marcel (2011) makes a seemingly sharp distinction between *having* and *being*. *Having* involves objectifying, while *being* denotes community, wonder, subjectivity." Whitehead (1958) says philosophy starts with wonder or being, proceeds through objectivity, and wonder remains. This suggests a Ricoeurian approach; we reintroduce having into being. This means a *having* and *being* dialogue. A Whiteheadian/Ricoeurian approach would then argue for game theory (Davis 1997) in the context of what I would term intersubjectivity. Game theory involves cooperative or competitive decision-making among participants. A future work of mine hopes to integrate human factors, game theory, cybernetics, phenomenology, government, and liberal arts. Human factors engineering might well be called 'independent variable factors engineering, stability engineering, or reference engineering, in that designing an environment varies in reference to the independent variable which could be human or an object.

STUDY QUESTIONS

- How does phenomenology differ from monism?
- How does phenomenology involve what we in 2017 call interactive?
- How does the self-service checkout or cashier in 2017 shopping differ from stores in 1950, when all businesses from groceries to gas stations employed workers serving the customer?
- How can studying businesses employing workers helping customers help in learning phenomenology?

Phenomenology is Cybernetic

I noted that phenomenology talks of embodiment. If phenomenology distinguishes and dissociates itself from positivism and Continental thought, it chooses between extremes. This brings us to the Greek term for steering, cybernetics. Norbert Weiner (1961) developed feedback cybernetics or control. Martin J. Cannon (1977) shows the integration of feedback and feedforward cybernetics or control. Feedback steers after waiting for information from the environment, feedforward is programmed to know in advanced how to steer in a changing context. Phenomenology steers between or rejects the atomistic and lifeworld-alone.

Adams (1989) talks of human factors engineering as neither training nor design alone. That is, steering between training alone (positivism) and design alone (being). Theoretical metaphysics involves phenomenology, and that movement is theoretical cybernetics. If theoretical metaphysics is applied ethics as I will say, applied ethics includes theoretical cybernetics. Cyberethics is steering between two bads, good and bad, good and two bads, and two goods. Cyber in 2017 means digital: cyberweapons, cybercrime, cyberwar. But why change meaning? Cybercrime is actually computer or digital crime. Ethics and economics become one, econ becomes cybereconomics. Cybercrime, cyberwar, and cyberweapons are misnomers. Two options for cyber exist. Either we give it two meanings: steering and digital epistemology (computers), or drop the second completely and return to the initial meaning of steering.

To repeat, cybernetics is steering from bad to good, or toward the better of two goods. Three options exist in steering: moderating from bad to good, bad to bad, and good to good. Steering is, then, a moderation between two extremes. For Aristotle, that steering is virtue theory of ethics (Aristotle 1999; Hursthouse 2002). In noting this, a link emerges between metaphysics and ethics. An existentialist, postmodernist, and pragmatist will well reject positivism as unethical. This is especially true of existentialism, which arose as an explicit rejection of positivism. The existential metaphysician argues that positivism is cold, human, sterile, and all but anti-person.

With all the talk about AI advances, predictions, and fears, Rodney Brooks' article in *The MIT Technology Review* (2017) assures readers that we have a very long way to go before AI, a presumably robotics, is widely deployed. Brooks steers between optimism and pessimism. We know a lot regarding AI, but it is not taking over the world in 2017. Paul Davies (1985) concludes *Superforce* by saying that a science explains the physical world, but human beings explain science; the unified field theory of physics is not independent of, but includes, us.

As moderation, virtue theory is a phenomenological ethic. Individuals in phenomenology do what positivism and existentialism do not. Positivism steers toward itself and away from others but not between extremes, or lesser of evils, or best of the good. It does not moderate. Existentialism does not moderate, dualism is not moderation. Only phenomenology is moderation.

But virtue ethics gives us a clue to ethical theory, on which I touch briefly for now. The chapter on ethical theory explicates the theoretical view. To identify theoretical metaphysics as derived ethics, and thus derived virtue ethics, persuades us to talk briefly of ethics in general.

Ethics involves virtue, egoism, divine command, natural law, duty, and utilitarianism. Typically these are said to be separate ethical theories. Indeed, they seem like the same thing. For example, by definition, we can integrate them. God can command us (divine command), to be egoistic (self-serving) in lessening pain (utilitarian), thus following natural law, by being moderate (virtue), as our duty.

For traditional ethics, in other words, any two theories are distinct and mutually exclusive. Divine command is about God commanding us, where natural law suggests we follow nature. But God can command us to follow nature, and a natural law can be to follow or obey God.

Judaism, The Lord's Prayer, literature, and economics give examples of cybernetics. "L'chaim," or "to life," is the Jewish proclamation that we choose or steer toward life and away from death. The Lord's Prayer (Matthew 6:9, King James Version) asks that the Lord "lead us not into temptation, but deliver us from evil," meaning steer us away from temptation and evil, and toward the good. In The Odyssey (Homer 1997), Odysseus steers between the dangers of Scylla and Charybdis. In modern history, economics (Mankiw 2015; Samuelson 1970) talks of choice or management of resources, duties, and general human affairs. Choice is steering toward the lesser of two evils or the better of two goods, from evil to good, or from two evils to good.

If, as James MacGregor Burns concludes in his huge volume Leadership (Burns 1979), that ability "lifts" a person from daily life to a better one, he is pointing to such talent as steering us from living as less than fully human, and toward a more complete humanity. His book defines the many aspects of leadership as causation, change, power, bargainer, and policymaker. I would add in all cases the leader is a cybernetic.

Phenomenology is Government

Few people associate cybernetics and phenomenology. Most political scientists will gladly define "government," but how many associate it with cybernetics? Not many. Most political scientists may not be aware that government is the Latin version of cybernetics. The Greek term *kvernete* became *gubernator*, and *government*.

Few political scientists will associate phenomenology, Huston C. Smith, Paul Ricoeur, and Charles Hartshorne with government or the state. But scholars ought not restrict themselves to governing meaning something aside from steering and cybernetics. A government steering committee is steering; therefore, by definition, government involves cybernetics.

Typically, the ordinary use of "government" includes a state or the rules. However, definition would persuade us to use *cybernetics* and *government* interchangeably.

PHENOMENOLOGY AND CONCRETE EXAMPLES

Ricoeur (1966) talks of objectivity within the subjective. His thought is consistent with that of J.L. Massey (1968) on the technical and human, Neils Bohr (Barnett 1965), Richard Bellman (1962), Massey (1968) on the numeric and metaphysical, and Daniel Kahneman (2013) on slow and fast thinking. Massey warns that technological development ought not to ignore the human element. Mathematician Bellman says the nonnumeric or metaphysical is the context for the numeric or reducible. Bohr notes that we are actors with and not just outside spectators of an independent reality. For Kahneman, logic and objectivity take time to calculate, where the intuitive or lived are faster because these are our immediate instead of mediate stance. While Norbert Weiner (1970) developed cybernetics, including feedback control (a device turns lights on and off after receiving or sensing the amount of light through feedback from the outside), Martin J. Gannon (1977) talks of progress where we now have feedback integrated with feedforward control (a device is programmed to feedforward turning lights on and off when it gets dark). Feedback acknowledges a reality objectively out there; feedforward is from a reality within the device.

Charles C. Ragin (2000) gives a detailed view comparing crisp and fuzzy sets. Crisp sets are those in which something or someone either is or is not a member. One set consists of Protestants, the other of Catholics. Only the intersecting set contains both Protestants and Catholics. Fuzzy sets are those where a member may be in both at the same time: one set consists of wealthy Protestants and Catholics, the other of lower-middle-class Protestants and Catholics. Life is never only crisp. Fuzziness frequently, if not most of the time, intervenes. Crisp sets alone are often unrealistic, positivistic, and atomistic in that they portray the either/or scenario. These actually emerge from a fuzzy world. Most people most of the time exist in a world where they are not completely healthy, never really hungry, and always generally busy. To design a city of crisp life, we would need to take into account the fuzzy, continuous nature of daily routines, health and illness, wealth, and the like.

The American Philosophical Association (APA) established the 2015 group "Beyond the Analytic-Continental Divide." With much of philosophy departments in the United States being analytically oriented, and only a handful following Continental thought, the APA has come to see a unity. Both analytic, by association, positivistic (Weitz 1966; Ammerman 1965; Ayer 1959), and Continental (Wild 1955; Spiegelberg 1984; Kaufmann 2004) philosophy are valid and contribute legitimately to the field we call philosophy.

The economist, Paul A. Samuelson (1973), remarks that quality of life is preferable over quantity. Governments once spoke of Gross National Product (GNP) as the barometer of economic well-being. Samuelson proposed Net Economic Welfare (NEW). This puts quality of life ahead of quantity of life. In 2012, governments practice Gross Domestic Product or GDP.

According to positivism, human beings are reducible to atoms, to flesh and bones. But sociologists (Hunter 1985; Barrows 2012) display a phenomenology position in speaking of social systems irreducible to atoms, and thus human beings being more than flesh and bones.

Ricoeur's (1966) idea is consistent also with military science's conventional and nonconventional war. Conventional war emphasizes uniformed combat, where the enemy is an object whose life we take. Nonconventional war emphasizes intersubjectivity in terms of civilians working along with the military's civil affairs teams (Robinson 2004; Cerami and Boggs 2007). During war, attacking the enemy's troops is one thing, destroying or disrupting its supply lines or the non-combat support, is another and perhaps equally effective effort (Levine 2008) and working with cultures to prevent future enemies from evolving. If we do not prevent war, the likely result is armed conflict and our killing the enemy. Ricoeur is consistent with Ludwig Wittgenstein (1961, p. 74) on (objectivity) speaking and (subjectivity) silence. Both thinkers argue that human beings engage in expression and nonexpression.

Steven W. Hook (2014) talks about American foreign policy. He points out the relation of hard power or military force, and soft power or diplomacy. In the field of foreign policy, integrating or reintroducing hard power into soft power is not so much a luxury, as it is a necessity in a future where nations with nuclear arms cannot afford to ignore diplomacy. Brigid Callahan Harrison, Jean Wahl Harris, and Michelle D. Deardorff (Harrison 2013) refer to Dwight David Eisenhower calling for the proper mixing of the military-industrial complex with peaceful objectives.

The views to which I refer compare with the profession of intelligence. Harry Howe Ransom (1958) notes that much intelligence results from academicians integrating (cf. reflecting on) data—which our spies gather covertly in another culture but do not analyze—into a coherent picture. Academicians do not need to blend into the culture in which they live and work; spies have to blend in because they are infiltrating a foreign sovereign nation. But analysts at the Central Intelligence Agency (CIA), as academics, produce the intelligence estimate.

Speaking of the CIA, the National Security Agency (NSA) has an interceptor's motto fitting into phenomenology. "In God we Trust, all others we Monitor" (Bamford 2002, on page after the book's table of contents), says the motto. Trust is our immediate acceptance ontologically, prior to analysis and monitoring. We trust God. The NSA trusts the Almighty but never human beings. Human beings may well hate each other, and national security requires monitoring and analysis of intentions. Allusion to God and "all others" seems like a distinguishing characteristic and thus dualism. This is not dualism if we consider theology of culture, trusting in some secularity, which I mention in my theology chapter. My point here is the seeming continuum in one agency. The motto is, of course, as poetic and proverbial as logical. The NSA trusts its leaders and employees, until evidence and suspicion arise as to traitors.

According to human factors engineering's machine-user interface (Kantowitz, Barry, H., and Robert D. Sorkin, 1968) and the body-consciousness continuum (Merleau-Ponty 1995), we develop a model for theoretical metaphysics by integrating ergonomics and phenomenology. The user or human being is only generally reducible to atoms. Subjectivity is only generally reducible to objects to atoms. Both say object and subject interrelate.

STUDY QUESTIONS

- How do some concrete examples show the interdisciplinary nature of phenomenology?
- Explain briefly how some additional examples can help people learn phenomenology.
- How is phenomenology relevant to the military and intelligence work?

PHENOMENOLOGY: MICRO AND MACRO ERGONOMICS

This book integrates ergonomics, or human factors engineering, within philosophy and metaphysics. Currently, human factors matches technology with the user's physical limits and abilities. But I call this micro human factors. The teacher-student relation, part of this book later, could also be ergonomic. Traditional human factors designs technology of the user, but a wider, philosophical view of ergonomics could mean designing people or authority for a person. Micro ergonomics is my term for designing particular objects, ideas, and processes for the person. Macro ergonomics is my term for first determining whether a technology and so forth ought to exist. That is the existential or phenomenological point as city planning, wherein every legitimate object or technology is to be designed. Macro ergonomics could well mean civil engineering as a whole.

Thus, philosophy can include general metaphysics as a general theory of ergonomics, with macro and micro ergonomics as part of applied metaphysics. Human factors (ergonomics) designs machines, work environments, and operations to match human ability and limits (Chapanis 1960). Matching human ability and limits means being user-friendly and avoiding user-unfriendly and user-too-friendly. Taking my cue from Phillips (2000), I call this the technology-user interface, where the technical are machines, work environments, and operations, not human beings. "User" refers to the human being with his or her limits and abilities to deal with the technological. "Technology" means the nonhuman machine, operation, or work environment in which the user functions. Such an interface, then, consists of two items: a human being with ability and limits and an artifact or operation to take account of those abilities and limits.

Generally speaking, the user is relatively "fixed" or stable (Kantowitz and Sorkin, 1968), orienting the way that engineers design the technological environment. Ergonomics speaks of the human factor or laws of work, instead of the mechanical factor. Design takes account of a person's limits, instead of a person taking account of technology's demands. Human factors calls for the technology-user interface and rejects two general distortions. One is sacrificing design for training, or the Procrustean approach; the other sacrifices training for design. Generally, ergonomics seeks a user-friendly balance (Adams 1989) instead of the either/or perspective. Philosophy (metaphysics), as with Wittgenstein (1968), can mean general human factors with subject as the "human" or irreducible factor for object. Micro ergonomics is the design of objects and processes, while the broader context, as with this book, is macro ergonomics: designing cities for people. Micro ergonomics includes what I term "reverse ergonomics," "reverse human factors," "person-person interface," or "person-technology" interfaces. Persons adjust to a "fixed" reference. These involve police bomb squads adjusting to bombs for diffusion, the military adjusting the nuclear/biological/chemical weapons, students adjusting to learning for careers, people adjusting to weather, doctors adjusting to doing surgery on patients, or people adjusting to playing a game (perhaps game theory). Theoretical, micro (including reverse human factors), and macro human factors integrate Wittgenstein's simple (1961) and holistic (1968) thought. The simple ought to adjust to the holistic.

Richard A. Johnson, Fremont E. Kast, and James E. Rosenzweig (1967) argue that workers, researchers, and supervisors cannot overlook the human factor in systems thinking without serious disruption in the workplace and society. Wittgenstein might argue that design in the workplace and society ought to involve silence-friendly speaking. Speaking quantifies and trains the person; silence is the personal or human factor that speaking, quantifying, and training must take into account.

If Wittgenstein's *Tractutus* is about simples, does Wittgenstein (1961) change his tune or contradict himself toward the end with his statement that we ought to speak, and whereof we cannot speak, we must remain silent? Yes he does. We speak of simples and are silent about emotive and other noncognitive topics, but he does not make that explicit. Speaking seems to require simples in his view; silence is more mystical and nonsimple. Phenomenology and human factors engineering see simples within the context of subjectivity.

Ockham's razor (Audi 1997) is relevant here. It admonishes us to simplify the irreducible to the extent needed. Leave room for the reducible. But the razor can also mean simplify the reducible. Simplicity applies to the numeric and nonnumeric. Ockham is possibly the modern world's version of Aristotle's (1999) golden mean. Another probable ally here is human factors engineering, with user-friendly design: Integrate the person and environment. Do not emphasize either the user or the machine. In other words, refrain from overreducing or underreducing people. Cybernetics might well inform us to integrate feedback and feedforward. Feedback says information or reality is outside (objectivity); feedforward tells us it is from the inside (subjectivity). In sum, the reflective must always integrate with and be in the context of the lifeworld.

Edmund Husserl's lifeworld is consistent with that of Alfred Schutz. Both thinkers say the lifeworld is prereflective. However, both are incomplete. Husserl (1970) says lifeworld is prereflective. Schutz (1970) says it is our *lived approach* to the subway, or any big city. Both thinkers see the lifeworld as subjective, or the way a person approaches the surroundings.

I argue that two kinds of lifeworlds exist. One is an object-, geographical lifeworld such as ahumane town or a humane big city without subways. The other is a subject-, approach-, or methodological-lifeworld, meaning how we approach or see an atomistic, atomistic-embodied, or embodied-only community (monastery). Thus, I see lifeworld as *object* (the living surrounding as small humane town, big humane city), and lifeworld as our prereflective *approach* to big humane atomistic city in 2016, small atomistic or humane town, etc. Education, procreation, criminal justice, church, medicine, and agriculture are among institutions. They can be either a lifeworld or reflective approach to gesellschaft or atomistic institutions, reflective-lifeworld continuum approach to the object life world, dualistic, or monasterial (lifeworld object, lifeworld approach). Our method and that geography we approach can be atomic (reflective) or prereflective. Husserl (1970) and Schutz (1970) talk mainly of our nonmathematical approach to the environment.

Husserl and Schutz imply what I term the object-lifeworld, as well as explicate the approach-lifeworld. However, they talk explicitly of our prereflective approach to the city or to any part of the world and society. They mention social institutions or structures without mentioning the objective nature of the lifeworld. Neither thinker says the lifeworld is "objective" and "subjective."

The institutions of the lifeworld are not just a list of social institutions or structures, as we find, for example in a typical phenomenology book (Stewart and Mickunas 1990). Stewart and Mickunas note applications of metaphysics, of the objective lifeworld as religion, moral codes, and economics. Throughout his *Crisis*, Husserl (1970) casually lists or mentions social structures (education, religion, military, etc.) without explicating a system of derived lifeworlds arising from the basic lifeworld. But my book has the applications emerge from within previous chapters, and ultimately from the first one.

Put another way, people approach *geographic* atomism (big city, bedroom community), geographic atomism-embodied or atomism within lifeworld (1950s city, humane small town), or the geographic lifeworld-alone (monastary) through methodological atomism-alone, methodological atomism-embodied (lifeworld), and methodological lifeworld-alone. Josef Pieper (1963) gives a brief but good accounting of method as objectivity, Matthew Crawford (2009) defends geographic body and manual effort, and Wolf (1993) is a classic regarding geographic community. Eugene T. Gendlin (1981) speaks of the living—which I would call geographic—body existing between objectivity alone and relativity alone.

STUDY QUESTIONS

- What is the difference between micro and macro human factors?
- How would macro human factors engineering help introduce engineering students to liberal arts and help students in other fields understand how engineering applies to general education?
- What do we mean by silence-friendly speaking?
- How can silence-friendly speaking impact on conversation, on using mobile phones?
- What are approach- and objective-lifeworlds?
- Which of those two lifeworlds seems to be Husserl's view of the lifeworld?
- How can someone argue that the objective lifeworld is an outgrowth of the approach lifeworld?

PHENOMENOLOGY IS METHODOLOGIC AND GEOGRAPHIC LIFEWORLDS

Lifeworld as method means embodiment as prereflection and thus preanalyzing. Prereflection is crucial and basic to reflection, theory, and systematization. Reflection, theory, and systematizion involve logic. The nonlogical is imagination, prereflection, or method lifeworld. I should point out that nonlogical simply denotes the nonrational, poetic, or awesome, while irrational or the illogical means the wrong thing to do. Putting water into an electrical outlet is irrational. Deciding to buy a car with some nonthreatening flaws, or that costs too much, is nonrational.

According to a letter (Dale no. 121) to the editor of *Philosophy Now*, Einstein spoke of imagination as the context for logic. Imagination can mean methodological lifeworld. Plato speaks of wonder (Hamilton and Cairns, 1964), as does Whitehead (1958), and Wittgenstein speaks of awe (Malcolm, 1967). Weinberger, (1990) notes that in foreign relations, the President of the United States, Ronald Reagan, began serious high-level diplomatic talks by socializing and telling stories before getting down to business.

Lifeworld as geography involves embodiment in terms of the body and culture. Body is vision, hearing, the anatomy or skeletal system. Books on human factors (Kantowitz and Sorkin, 1968) show vision, appendages, and hearing but never associate them with a lifeworld. Corinne Gilb gives a simple summary of culture (Gilb 1967): humans need "heroes, myths, festivals, dignity, love, belongingness, self-realization." Anthropologists may counter that this list is incomplete. It omits artifacts, and explicit mention of moral codes, social institutions or structures.

Dignity, love, and belongingness or community are part of medicine and therapy. Physicians treat the illness in terms of treating the patient. Claire Flower (2008), a music therapist, goes further; therapy must treat the family.

Intelligence agencies need agreement and working together: belonging, community (Odom 2004).

What I term the geographic lifeworld, David Kilcullen (2010) calls the social systems in combating counterinsurgency. *The U.S. Army and Marine Corps Counterinsurgency Field Manual* (Petraeus et al. 2007) deals with the social, political, and otherwise broadly cultural "spectrum of conflict" support of the military. Jessica Stern (2004) articulates as social systems in countering terrorism.

Integrating method and geographic objectivity and lifeworlds discerns our mental and sociobiological needs. Scholars do not associate utilitarian ethicists Jeremy Bentham and John Stuart Mill (Ryan 2004) as phenomenologists, but Bentham's emphasis on physical welfare and Mill's on cultivating cultural life and mental ability, show their combined affinity to the object embodied. Former Health, Education, and Welfare Secretary John W. Gardner (1962) argues well for integrating blue and white collar work. Both jobs are part of life: the objective white collar, and the lifeworld blue collar. Again, thinkers associate Abraham Maslow with psychology instead of philosophy and phenomenology. Yet, his *Psychology of Being* (1968) presents the pyramidal hierarchy of needs, which thinkers can interpret as (lifeworld) bodily-cultural, and (atomic) mental nature of method to study geographics, and the geographic itself."

PHENOMENOLOGY AS G-LIFEWORLD AND DUTIES

Rights are part of culture, the geographic or G-lifeworld, and seem to be the limits to which the state can impose duties. The state imposes duties on citizens to pay taxes, but it is within a person's rights to pay only a given amount. Taxation duties cannot and ought not hurt the taxpayer.

What are our duties? The Ten Commandments basic to Judaism and Christianity? Laws of Manu from Hinduism (Doniger and Smith 1991)? The Analects of Confucianism (Dawson 2008)? Are our duties in Lao Tzu's Tao De Ching (Johnston 2016)? Robert Nozick starts his *Anarchy, State and Utopia* (1974) with rights, Drucker (1974), his *Management* with responsibilities or duties. Immanuel Kant gives us duty ethics: people ought to do the correct or ethical out of obligation regardless of what happens to them (Kant, 1927. 220). The Federalist Papers (Miller 2017) argue for a strong federal government and the citizens' and states' duties to agree to such a central power.

In human factors terminology, rights and duties may well be inseparable. We are part of a social group: family, state, etc. The group may or must impose duties on us. Our rights are the limits to which we are responsible to do duty.

Duties are the centripetal force keeping society together. Taxation, food, clothing, shelter, obedience to the government, being good to others, driving safely, are among our duties.

Human factors language would say phenomenology and the G-lifeworld, theoretical metaphysics design duties to take into account individual rights. Defining duty denotes, *ipso facto*, articulating rights.

Taxonomically, duty without rights becomes almost inhuman. Duty through rights sounds more humane. A dualism would mean we have duties one day, time, or place, and rights another time and place. Rights without duties can be anarchy, libertarianism, chaos."

PHENOMENOLOGY AS G-LIFEWORLD AND RIGHTS

Human factors talks of the human dimension of environments. Engineers, indeed society, impose duties and training on users, taking into account the user's limits and abilities. Phenomenologically, this is the human or subjective factor of objectivity. Objectivity must take into account subjectivity as human rights. These rights are the body's limits as in human factors, but also in culture.

But are these the Bill of Rights? Which country's bill of rights? Are these the UN Declaration of Human Rights? Would they involve the U.S. Justice Department's documents and laws regarding civil rights? Do rights include the Miranda rule in law enforcement, of the suspect or person under arrest having the right to remain silent? Indeed, nations have the right to just war (Walzer 1977), and criminals and suspects the right to appropriate coercion (Kerstetter 1985).

Readers might be justified in saying that studying at least an overview of all the above goes into the idea of rights. Duty concerns taxation, obeying the government, the state allowing us to have food, clothing, shelter, and the like. But rights are the person's limits to which he or she pays taxes and obeys the government.

We have the right to food, clothing, and shelter. The group or state has a duty to help or allow us to acquire through work or welfare, the food, clothing, and shelter. However, the duty must acknowledge neither too little nor too much of these rights. People ought have sufficient food, clothing, and shelter, instead of too much or too little of these needs. In having rights and limits, individuals and rulers need steer between acknowledging atomistic and no food, clothing, and shelter. Such steering to avoid too much and too little or no obedience to the rules may be a duty of what we call government, taking individual rights (limits) and abilities into account. Virtue ethics, broadly speaking, underlies moderation in duty and rights.

PHENOMENOLOGY AND RELATIVITY THEORY

The lifeworld is more than a series or list of institutions and our prereflective approach to them. These institutions exist within each other. Positivism and analytics are a hairbreadth from mathematics, but Continental thought can also be intimately associated with mathematical method. Each successive institution or application is a notion within the previous institution. For example, reality is fundamental. Inside the chapter on reality is the idea of linguistic hermeneutical reality as an interpretation of words we use. We eventually come to social origins, inside of which are church and state, inside of which is ethics as a general theory of right and wrong institutions, inside of which are neighborhoods, and so on.

Husserl (1970) would question the systematizing of the lifeworld. He seems to reject systematization of philosophy and the lifeworld. For him, the lifeworld is monolithic. It is our prereflective approach to the world. However, a "theory" of the lifeworld is implied in that specific applications are not explained. Each application has four options in object and subject, change and stability, problem and person: (1) atomism and structuralism only, (2) phenomenology, (3) dualism, and (4) subjectivity-alone. Thus, society involves gesellschaft as atomic, the atomic within gemeinschaft as lifeworld (cf. Martin Buber's *I and Thou* in Kaufmann, 1970), a gesellschaft-gemeinschaft dualism, and gemeinschaft-alone. Atomic (gesellschaft) society can be the geographical area or people through the gemeinschaft/lifeworld approach or the reflective approach. Gemeinschaft (Tonnies 1957) community can be the geographical area through the lifeworld, or the reflective approach. In metaphysics, atomicity is reflective, and subjectivity is the lifeworld. In a given chapter, derived institution can be atomic or reflective, the derived subjectivity or approach can be lifeworld, or atomic. In theoretical ethics, we live in the big city or anonymous small town lacking sidewalks (gesellschaft). Therein, we can approach the big city or anonymous small town prereflectively or reflectively. The phenomenological option is that we live in a prereflective small town (gemeinschaft), where we approach events prereflectively or reflectively.

The lifeworld as object or approach is always relative to the institution. We do not have just one thing called the reflective world and another called the lifeworld. Husserl's (1970) *Crisis* suggests that the lifeworld is a monolith or absolute: our prereflective approach. If he means institutions can be part of it, his meaning is more implicit than not. His writing encourages the reader to believe that reality consists of "the" lifeworld and "the" reflective (theory, science). The lifeworld is one of two aspects of reality, the other being analysis or summative. Derivatively, it is the irreducible, lived, or human context of institutions and applications.

This view reminds us of what I call a theory of lifeworld relativity. When asked about the lifeworld, I respond with "which one, the theoretical one in metaphysics, or one of the derivations?" In other words, a given interaction of lifeworld and objectivity may consist of a derived lifeworld and reflection. Similarly, a given reflection or object may consist of a derived object and lifeworld. I see lifeworld as the prereflective context of reflection, and thus bridge the Continental-analytic separation.

In short, embodied objectivity claims that a city or town can be a lived community or neighborhood that people can approach through a lived or a reductive method. This rejects a totally reductive neighborhood accessible through either a lived or a reductive method, a dualistic view of a lived and a reductive neighborhood, each of which can be understood reductively, or a lived and an almost totally irreducible (lived) neighborhood approached through the lived or the reductive methods.

The APA has created the Beyond the Analytic-Continental Divide group. This group, by its definition, attempts to bring together phenomenologists, existentialists, positivists, and analytic thinkers. In so doing, the APA is doing what Huston C. Smith meant. In commenting on Charles Hartschorne's work, Smith (1966) points out that the Whiteheadian thinker is bridging the gap between those who advocate systematic, objective reason and the existential efforts to discern being.

Where Abraham Maslow (2014) talks of the hierarchy of needs from physical to self-esteem, sociologist Herbert Spencer (2015) notes the integration of the physical, emotional, and intellectual. Human beings are more than just physical or positivistic, according to Spencer.

Objectivity embodied involves propositions within the context of stories and human drama. Phenomenology can mean stories and cultural activities whereby propositions emerge. A book on positivism needs to be phenomenological, pointing out positivists and their reasons for emerging as members of a movement.

Within Judaism, God gives the Torah to Moses by a burning bush, on a mountain. This tells us that the law is more than a legal document or even divine scripture. The law is divinely inspired, but a person, God, speaks with and gives the law to Moses. To paraphrase Immanuel Kant (1987), objectivity without subjectivity is blind, and subjectivity without objectivity is empty. Judaism, where law or Torah integrates with story, would, in human factors' terminology, mean Haggadah-friendly Hallakha.

Heidegger (1966), Teilhard (1965), and Whitehead (1964b) speak in various ways of the generally irreducible whole within which the parts or reduction make sense. Unity for all three thinkers is irreducible to the sum of parts. It is a set meal instead of a la carte. Heidegger see Being as unity, human beings as DaSein or the "there of being," and beings as things in the world. Teilhard emphasizes sacred unity evolving, Whitehead says evolution is the becoming or evolution of a secular unity.

STUDY QUESTIONS

- What is relativity theory in phenomenology's object-subject theory and derivations?

- How does saying that the object-lifeworld relation is relative compare to Albert Einstein's notion of time relativity?

- Does this suggest that relativity theory can unify philosophy (broadly speaking) and science?

- Compare the lived and the analytic approach to the analytic-only culture, the lived and the analytic culture, the dualistic cultures, and the lived-only culture.

- How can religion, say Judaism, be an example of learning phenomenology, human factors engineering, or metaphysics?

STUDY QUESTIONS

- How can phenomenology be an integrative view of the six major ethical theories?

- If ethics is fundamental to metaphysics, including phenomenology and monism just discussed, what can this imply for the typical, separate course on ethics?

DUALISM

Dualism is the metaphysical position meaning two realities exist. Scholars typically call it the subject-object dualism.

Dualism can be Platonic (Hamilton and Cairns 1964), or Cartesian, following Rene Descartes (Haldane 1968). Plato's Allegory of the Cave argues that two worlds exist, one material, change and illusory where we now live, and the other the ideal world of unchanging forms. He attempts to reconcile (Cornford 1953) Heraclitus' view that reality is change alone, and Pythagoras' belief that stability is real.

Plato argues that the world is dualistic. Two worlds exist, one ideal and one material. He attempts to reconcile Heraclitus on change and Parmenides on stability (Cornford 1953). Why Plato stops at dualism and does not go as far as Aristotle with integrating form and matter is a mystery. The dualist finds that monism, phenomenology, and existentialism are unethical. Cartesian dualism is the more popular version, perhaps because it all but initiates modern thought or concentrates on a "this world" position of thinking and doing instead of discussing and arguing for material and formal worlds.

Plato's Allegory of the Cave (Hamilton and Cairns 1978) tells about his dualism. This allusion to Plato is relevant here, in subject-object dualism. The allusion is also relevant as we shall see later in this chapter, under the section of change and stability. Imagine a cave, at the bottom of which are prisoners or slaves. They are chained sitting in chairs looking at the wall or end of the cave. Their situation is involuntary, and represents all humanity born in this world. Behind them is a fire. Behind the fire is a demon manipulating puppets. The fire casts shadows of the demon and puppets on the wall at which the prisoners are forced to look. They look at illusion, not wisdom and stability, which are outside the cave.

The cave is a journey, a painful one, from ignorance to wisdom. A prisoner appears to have freed himself and liberated from the cave. This person, now a philosophy kind, has exited the cave and seen the sun, which Plato calls wisdom. He or she must now return to the cave and free the others.

Plato's Allegory of the Cave is a good example of the Socratic dialogue. Socrates is the Greek thinker who taught Plato. We know of Socrates only through Plato. Socrates rejects humans as passive learners requiring lectures, and the totally active student requiring no mentoring. For Socrates, dialogue brings out a student's hidden talent. In Socrates view, we are "pregnant with knowledge." What is needed is a mentoring or midwifery whereby the teacher asks questions and the student answers.

Descartes says mind and body are two realities (Haldane 1968). Where Plato sees two worlds (Hamilton and Cairns 1964), Descartes argues for two realities within this world (Haldane 1968). Ironically, in this material world, Cartesian dualism posits the material body but a nonmaterial mind. That may be because Descartes finds that the senses, part of the material body, deceive us. It appears reasonable that two realities, virtually unrelated, are grounds for two kinds of knowledge. One is sensory, the other cognitive. This dualism creates problems and has critics.

Objectivity-alone (positivism, some analytics), objectivity as a function of subjectivity, dualism, and objectivity embodied all have problems. Each position—including pragmatism, solipsism, postmodernism, and others that I do not mention—has critics. Velasquez (2014) shows positions and their critics.

Dualism has the problem of relating distinct realities. Materialists can say matter alone is real, and we do look around and see material things. Existentialists have the right to argue that human beings are irreducible. Phenomenologists argue for nonmaterial reality, which often has an uphill fight. Dualism presents a strange situation. How can two distinct realities exist? Matter exists. The nonmaterial might exist. But how can two different realities exist? How can the atemporal and temporal relate? The next section tries to answer these questions.

Phenomenology, through Ricoeur (1966), answers. He argues against Descartes and attempts to overcome Cartesian dualism. For Ricoeur, Descartes started with embodied mind. That is, embodied mind existed before Descartes's reflection on that philosophical option. Then, according to Ricoeur, Descartes did what he ought not to have done: He emptied mind from the body. In emptying mind from the body, Descartes developed a notion of dualism. Specifically, Cartesian thought brought about mind-body dualism. The question in dualism is how can two realities exist? More precisely, how can the human being be mind and body dualism? Ricoeur's response to Cartesian dualism is that "to overcome this dualistic situation, we must reintroduce mind into body" (1966, 217).

Ricoeur's perspective is holistic, taking the unified social context into account. Mind and body are inherently unified. Mind or objectivity is embodied. The objectifying ability of human beings, our analytic capability, is always there embodied. Human beings are one reality, the mind-body continuum. According to Ricoeur (1966), Descartes disembodied the mind.

That Ricoeurian view means that mind-body dualism is a Cartesian invention instead of a natural position. Such dualism does not and cannot occur in nature. Every human being is inherently essentially a unified person. Each individual is a thinking body. No person is a thinker juxtaposed to a material substance called the body.

STUDY QUESTIONS

- Who does Plato attempt to reconcile?
- What are the two main kinds of dualism?
- Explain how you would justify or resolve Platonic dualism.
- What is Cartesian dualism?
- How would you resolve or justify Cartesian dualism?
- How does Ricoeur's response to Cartesian dualism seem nearer human nature than does Cartesian dualism?

DUALISM: SIAN BEILOCK, RICOEUR, RYLE

Sian Beilock (2015) makes a good case for thinking-body unity. The mind or thinking is an embodied process. What we do with our bodies, physical actions, and senses directly impacts our thinking and emotions. Thinking and the body are not and cannot be two different substances. Studies show that actions and physical abilities that a youngster displays at a very early age can generally predict the child's intelligence as he or she grows older.

Making a distinction between people's bodily behavior and mental activity or thoughts is a wrong move. Our anatomy, broadly speaking, including bone, muscles, and movements, is directly related to and affects how well we think. Ricoeur would concur with Beilock, a psychologist, that reintroducing mind into the body's physical context is the correct way to proceed in overcoming Cartesian dualism.

We can say human factors, using Ricoeurian language, reintroduces technology into the user, rejecting machines without the user and user without machines.

At a philosophy and then sociology conference, I presented papers on how Gilbert Ryle compares with Paul Ricoeur in solving Cartesian dualism. Ricoeur (1966) reintroduces mind into body, while Ryle (1984), in the analytic tradition, reduces mind to body. But Ryle has a flaw. He tells of a visitor to Oxford or Cambridge who sees the buildings and then, through Ryle's "category mistake," seeks the "university" (1976, 16).

The "university," says Ryle (1976), is just the way the buildings already seen are organized. It is not another category. In other words, mind is body, not something else. Ricoeur would argue that we reintroduce buildings into the lived world of people: students, administration, staff, and faculty. This is the human factors approach. Building organization is designed or organized to take people into account. Ryle says buildings are organized. But they are not "just organized." They are organized according to the best ways people use the buildings. The best ways reject, for ergonomics, only buildings "out there." The organization also rejects one long, linear structure devoid of many buildings organized in a human, typical campus design taking people's limits and abilities into account.

STUDY QUESTIONS

- What is Sian Beilock's position on the mind-body or thinking-body problem?
- Compare Beilock and Ricoeur on resolving the mind-body problem.
- How do human factors engineering, Beilock, and Ricoeur compare in resolving the thinking-doing problem?
- What is the "category mistake"?

- Who is Gilbert Ryle, and what is his contribution to resolving Cartesian dualism?
- Compare Ryle and Ricoeur on resolving Cartesian dualism.

DUALISM AS MORE GENERAL A THEORY THAN TRADITIONAL ETHICAL THEORIES

In ethical language, this dualism means the following:

- Dualistic egoism (seeing people as dualistic is in our self-interest)
- Dualistic utilitarianism (helping people as dualistic realities)
- Dualistic divine command (deistic God distinct from a world of dualistic people)
- Dualistic virtue (the virtuous person is dualistic)
- Dualistic natural law (some laws to one part of humans, some to another reality in people)
- Dualistic duty (we have duties as thinking and as physical individuals)

STUDY QUESTION

- As with monism and phenomenology, how is dualism a more general ethical theory than the traditional ethical theories?

POSTMODERNISM

Postmodernism is the belief that many realities exist (Natoli and Hutcheon 1993). This is subjectivity without objectivity, or **subjectivity-only**. In existentialism, Sartre (1993, 2007) points out that human existence precedes essence. Objective essence does not exist. Each person is their own, free, existing self. Indeed, Donald Hoffman (Gafter 2016; Mark et al. 2010), suggests that thirty years of research with neuroscientists and quantum physicists, reveal that reality is what the observor perceives, instead of a public object existing independently outside the mind. Where objectivity as atomism disregarding subjectivity virtually eliminates the person, objectivity as primarily a function of subjectivity means the subject all but generates reality. Subjectivity is all but generating the objectively real and sees subjectivity as the primary or only real. This is subjectivity disregarding objectivity. Here, subjectivity almost exists alone, or deemphasizes objectivity. The existentialists emerged as they reacted against positivism and linguistic analysis, both monists, as unethical for reducing people to atoms. For existentialism, it is also unethical to be dualist and phenomenologist, though a great many pieces of philosophical literature may imply that phenomenology and existentialism are virtually the same. Existentialism is perhaps the largest single group of subjectivism.

Jean-Paul Sartre, Albert Camus, Martin Heidegger, and for some, Gabriel Marcel are existentialists (Kaufmann 1975). To repeat, historically, existentialism emerged as a reaction to positivism. The positivists—Moritz Schlick, Rudolf Carnap (2005; Ayer 1959), and others—were so inspired by scientific advances that they believe in a scientific philosophy. Philosophy for them was to be a mathematical, systematic logical-empirical way of thinking. But many others rejected this. Those rejecting it were existentialists. Positivists believed in essence before existence. That is, a fixed structure was ontologically prior, fundamental to human and all existence. Existentialists argued the reverse as true: Existence is before essence. Structure does not exist but is objectivity created by subjectivity. Ergonomics says this is to be rejected as user-too-friendly.

Each person creates his or her own structure, meaning, and reality. Variations of objectivity as a function of subjectivity, or subject-alone, show that this position is not monolithic. Objectivity as a function of subjectivity can mean at least three things. One is **existentialism**.

Existentialism is by no means monolithic. This philosophical position is interestingly inclusive with a range of interpretation. Atheistic existentialists deny God exists. These include Jean-Paul Sartre (1969), Friedrich Nietzsche (2014a, 2014b), Ayn Rand (1996), and Albert Camus (1983). However, theistic and Christian existentialists believe individuals serve and reveal God. These include Paul Tillich (1957, 1965), and Søren Kierkegaard (2003). Existentialism shows a revolt against positivism, as well as an anarchist attack against authority or a whole that seems to overwhelm the individual. Such attacks are seen in Kierkegaard against Hegel, and by Rousseau's (not usually placed with existentialists, but …) opposition to urban society; Nietzsche's criticism of the herd, state, and institutions; and in Rand's speaking against authority.

Here, subjectivity is overwhelming and prior but is not totally disregarding objectivity as real. Where objectivity-alone can mean "essence before existence," subjectivity-alone usually means existence before essence (Sartre, 2007, p. 20). Human beings, reality as such, are not structured. Objective meaning or reality may not exist. Instead, people make their own meaning.

Nihilism is a second variation of subjectivity-only. I will refrain from detail and will say only that nihilism finds life or existence as meaningless even more than does existentialism. Existentialists create meaning. Nihilists might say meaning is not possible. Finally, we can see **solipsism**. This view has its roots in those thinkers who vehemently react to positivism. Where positivism and empiricism find reality and knowledge external to us, many thinkers such as Husserl and Descartes argue that knowledge is subjective. That is, knowledge is subjective roots underpinning objectivity.

Where G.W.F. Hegel (2003) says truth is in the whole, Soren Kierkegaard argues that truth is subjectivity (Kaufmann 1975). Existentialism's main point is "existence before essence" (Sartre, 2007, p. 20). Truth for the positivist is almost completely independent of the subject. For the phenomenologist it is colored by subjectivity. Dualism says two truths exist. Subjectivity maintains that truth and reality are almost completely within us.

But this subjectivity can be dangerous. If subjectivity is sufficiently powerful, then it implies a reality that is far more, if not exclusively, within the person. If that is strong enough, then the mind or brain generate reality. Other selves or subjects do not exist. The world outside disappears. Subjectivity-alone is real.

With subject-alone in itself an extreme form of solipsism, two things are gone. One is the other self or subject. Our social nature no longer is valid. The second is the outside world. The external world no longer exists as nature devoid of other selves.

Human factors engineering rejects both the object-only and user-only. Ergonomics sees both as extremes to avoid. Put another way, human factors, or ergonomics, rejects both positivism and existentialism. Positivists are user-unfriendly in that human nature and reality are not totally reducible to atoms and propositions. Existentialists are user-too-friendly, because people and all reality are not almost completely irreducible.

STUDY QUESTIONS

- How did existentialism emerge?
- How are existentialism and ethics intimately related?
- If subjectivism-only, as existentialism, argues that monism is unethical because it reduces people to atoms, how can a medical example for phenomenology counter that refusal to reduce people to analysis is also unethical?

- What is existentialism's main point?
- What philosophical movement is existentialism opposing, and why?
- How is existentialism justified in being derivative ethics in metaphysics?
- How does human factors engineering respond to subjectivity-only?

STUDY QUESTION

- How is subjectivity-only a more general ethical theory than the traditional six ethical theories?

PROCESS AND STABILITY: GENERAL THEORY A.II

The previous section involved reality as object and subject. I restricted my discussion to four options: monism as objectivity only, phenomenology as object-subject continuum or embodied objectivity, subject-object dualism, and subjectivity-only from existentialism through solipsism (objectivity as only a function of subjectivity). Traditional philosophy suggests that the spectrum from monism to existentialism differs from the relation of process or change and stability is another. I disagree. Reality is on the one hand atomism through existentialism, and then within this context, process and stability. Claiming that atomism through existentialism (and finally pragmatism and solipsism) is one thing and that process and stability are something else is wrong. Process and stability are inside atomism through existentialism, and not something different.

Traditional "process philosophy" often seems to imply that some thinkers believe in substance, but that reality is more accurately process. That does not make sense. Substance can move, change, and so on. Substance does not need to disappear and become mere change or process. Process as process does not make sense. Process is the process of something. Atoms, structure, objectivity embodied, dualism, subjectivity-only. Some may argue that mind or thought in Cartesian dualism is atemporal or aspatial and cannot change. But "thinking" is a process, however intangible.

Most philosophy books have sections on metaphysics or reality, involving the spectrum from atomism through solipsism. To my knowledge, no philosophy book gives equal time to process and stability. This is particularly intriguing since the movement explicitly called "process philosophy" has made an impact throughout knowledge. Process philosophy influences, for example, theology and education. Ironically, process philosophy seems to start with A.H. Whitehead (1979), and not necessarily with Hegel (2003), or even further removed, with Aristotle (McKeon 1966), Heraclitus (Cornford, F.M., 1953), and others. But process cannot just be "process."

My point is that "something" changes or remains stable. "Change" or "stability" by themselves are meaningless. Objectivity and subject can change only, change within stability, can be stable or change, or be stable only.

Inside objectivity and subjectivity, reality is the relation between change and stability. Object and subject change only, change within the context of stability, change at one point and are stable another time, or are merely stable. Change means that a reality is transitioning from place to place, or form to form, or even state to state outside space and time. The movement goes from here to there, or at least from one situation or another. In the broadest sense, this is a goal. Moving from here to there is the goal, or mere goal.

Human factors engineering would defend change embodied in stability, avoiding both change-only and stability-only. This differs from philosophy taking a neutral stance and allowing the reader to decide which metaphysical is correct in change and stability.

STUDY QUESTIONS

- What is traditional philosophy's notion of the relation between objectivity-only through solipsism, and change and stability?

- How does seeing change and stability within the context of object-subject relationship clarify and give more detail to objectivity and subjectivity?

- Why is "process philosophy" misnamed?

- What does it mean that process or change is that of something, some substance?

CHANGE MONISM

Change Monism or **change-only**, is the position of Heraclitus (Velasquez 2014; Russell 1972), the Greek thinker. He says reality is change. We can include doing-without-people, or automation. This is dynamic atomism, movement from place to place, time to time. Such change is totally external to, and unrelated to, human beings.

The association of change-only is with Heraclitus. Heraclitus speaks of change as reality (Cornford 1953). But in the later, modern, more "technical" term, reality is process. Yet it is probably not until Hegel and Whitehead that philosophy acknowledges a process philosophy. For Charles Darwin (2003), Daniel Dennett (1996), and Marjorie Grene (2004), change and process generally mean evolution.

For ethics, change-only egoism, utilitarianism, virtue, divine command, natural law, and duty mean subjective and objective positions of these change for change's sake. We are ethical when changing our thinking constantly instead of as needed, that reality is atomic, structural, embodied, dualistic, or subjective. We are ethical if and when we change from one ethical theory to the next, for its own sake. Someone never always follows egoism or utilitarianism or divine command or natural law or virtue or duty.

Change-only or change-alone is exemplified in academia by awarding tenure to a college or university assistant professor not deserving that job security. Academia changes the assistant professor's status for political or personal reasons, instead of for professional reasons.

STUDY QUESTION

- How does change-only show us that derived ethics is an integral part of, perhaps synonymous with, metaphysics?

CHANGE PHENOMENOLOGY

Change Phenomenology or **Change-embodied** is the position of the Greek thinker Aristotle (McKeon 1966). He says change is the unfolding of stability. This denotes nonhuman activity of unfolding, and also doing through human beings. It is dynamic phenomenology, or stability-change interaction. In a sense change embodied and a purposeful or teleological human act is

Socratic (Cornford 1953). Cornford (1953) says that before Socrates, the Greek thinkers talked of reality in terms of nature only. Nature was either stable or changing. Socrates introduced the idea that change must be within stability (Cornford 1953).

Change embodied in Socrates means the Socratic method or irony. Socrates teaches by questioning students. He appears to not know the answer; ironically, he is smarter than the student. The Socratic method, some will say, is the means of dialogue whereby a philosopher king helps a prisoner struggle toward exiting the cave. Lawyers often use the Socratic method in court trials. Educators use it in terms of the R. L. Moore method of teaching. The teacher does not lecture, but provides students with material to learn (Zitarelli 2000, 2004; Wilder 1984; Fitzpatrick 1997). As the student comes to class, the teacher asks questions to see how well the student has learned the material. The R. L. Moore method is similar or along the same lines as the Flipped Classroom (Bergmann and Sams 2012). Instead of students listening in class and doing homework at home, they listen at home, and discuss and do homework in class.

In academia, too, the issue of tenure can involve phenomenology. Here, awarding tenure is embodied in the stability of the assistant professor from the time the school hires him or her (Nelson 1997). The school can interpret Nelson as saying that competent hiring denotes that the college or university hires the correct person and gives them job security from the start. At some point, a celebration occurs because the tenure is completed, not just suddenly decided. The school ought to go from some to fulfilled job security, not from zero to total security. A brief piece in *The Personnel Administrator* (1978) puts it as process vs. outcome, or summative evaluation. Outcome evaluation occurs at the conclusion of a process or project; process evaluation takes place while something is occurring.

For Socrates, my legs are not just changing in terms of walking motion. The walking motion or change expresses a telos, or purpose, a stability toward which the moving legs are "changing." Pierre Teilhard de Chardin (1965) tries to reconcile evolution with God and Christian belief. Management thinker, Herbert G. Hicks (1972) says change and stability are related, and cannot be mutually exclusive. Consider change as serial or linear thinking, and stability as the human or unifying thought. To repeat my earlier statement, this has implications for corporate and government (*government* derived from Greek *cybernetic*) leadership management. Robert Wrubel (1991) and Preston Smith and Donald Reinertsen (1991) speak of simultaneous management teams (SMT) replacing what is called serial management alone in corporations. John

Hanson (Michael 2011), talks of unified government instead of what I would call serial government, or what the Constitution says is separation of powers.

John Searle (2001) talks of actions through intentions, and Talcott Parsons (1967) of action through values. Both thinkers, starting from philosophical and sociological points and converging to a common destination of integrating process with being, discuss embodied action. Action, process, change, and doing cannot or ought not to be mere behaviorist doing.

Paul Ricoeur (1966) talks about actuality as a process, moving from potential to actual. His ideas sound very much like Aristotle, for whom change is good, and the very unfolding of a stability. In Ricoeur, each moment of a process is an aspect of the actual, and not something illusory or apart from the actual. With process or change, each moment reveals a portion of the real or actual from the start. The actual is increasingly visible as time goes on.

We will see in the next section of this chapter that change embodied is preventative activity. There we will talk of preventing, reacting, and denying problems. These can include preventative medicine, crime or fire prevention, terrorism prevention, and the like.

The previous section, mind and body, showed Ricoeur and Ryle overcome Cartesian dualism in each one's own way. Now, change embodied is a teleological interpretation of Ricoeur and Ryle overcoming what I term "time dualism" of stability occurring at one time and change during a second time. Ricoeur would say to reintroduce change into stability. Ryle would argue that stability is the way we organize change or telos. This interpretation assumes, of course, that he would accept the reality of change and stability, though rejecting mind in the mind-body problem.

We are ethical by changing from one ethics theory to another as needed. Our ethical position changes as we find it necessary to do so. Our option in the object-subject relationship changes as needed. To paraphrase Kant (1987), change without stability is blind, and stability without change is empty.

STUDY QUESTIONS

- How does Socrates's notion of change or process differ from that of the pre-Socratics?
- How is Socrates anticipating the Aristotelian change-stability continuum?
- What do Searle and Parsons say about change and stability?

- How do Searle and Parsons compare with the thoughts of Aristotle on change and stability?

- How is change embodied different from change-alone? What is an economics/ethical implication of change-alone and change embodied?

STABILITY-CHANGE DUALISM

Stability-change dualism means two realities exist. Plato says change and stability are two distinct realities (Hamilton and Cairns 1964). For Plato, the two realities are dual worlds (Hamilton and Cairns 1964). Our material, changing world is illusory, while the ideal world is one of stability, permanence, and reality. The material world is one of time and space. Temporality and spatiality are illusion, whereas timelessness in the ideal world means stability and reality. Only timeless, unchanging truths are real. Platonic and Cartesian dualism differ. Cartesian dualism speaks not of two worlds, but simply of thinking and the body as two distinct realities (Haldane 1968). But dualism is more complex than just coexistential, or Platonic and Cartesian dualisms.

Plato's Allegory of the Cave (Hamilton and Cairns 1964) exemplifies his dualism. Plato's dualism is relevant now for the idea of change and stability, as it was also for the previous section on subject and object. Prisoners are chained to chairs facing a wall opposite the opening of a cave. A demon stands behind them, manipulating puppets. Behind him is a fire casting shadows on the wall, of the demon's actions. The prisoners see only the shadows. This is illusion and change. Outside the cave is the sun, wisdom, stability. A philosopher king is outside. Plato does not say how he got there. The philosopher-king descends into the cave, struggles to free the resisting prisoners accustomed to illusion, and helps their struggle to leave the cave and into the sun light.

The question of college and university tenure again emerges. This question emerges again because it is relevant in phenomenology and now in overcoming dualism. It was seen in change-alone, and change phenomenology. Change phenomenology tenure claims to correct the typical and traditional ideas of stability-change dualism in granting tenure. Such dualism in academia means that schools hire someone, possibly incompetent. There is a time of many years during which the instructor, through assistant professor, has no job security. Then the assistant professor applies for tenure. He or she is going from no, to complete job security. Nelson (1997) criticizes this as we just saw.

STUDY QUESTIONS

- What is Plato's position on dualism?
- How do Platonic and Cartesian dualism differ?
- How are Platonic and Cartesian dualism the same?

STABILITY-CHANGE DUALISM FROM COEXISTENCE TO TIME DUALISM

In our material world of time, stability and change can mean the existence of two notions of time (Kazanjian 2002). I call this time dualism, compared with Cartesian substance dualism, or Plato and cosmological dualism. Where static dualism denotes mind and body as substances coexisting, or existing together, time dualism means two "times" exist. These include an initial time devoid of a goal, and then a second time where we see a goal devoid of human context. In other words, time dualism means human activity day-by-day devoid of goals, followed by a problem and solving it by goal without humanity.

For example, take health. Stability-change dualism is the theoretical basis of what I will present in later chapters as ignorance-reactive dualism. This can mean ignoring and then solving a problem as in any chapter. An initial time occurs when we ignore a potential or actual problem. The problem becomes or erupts into a crisis. Or the problem evolves into a serious one that we must then solve as quickly as possible. The initial time of stability, a time when we ignored the problem, suddenly ends.

Now a second time erupts as the crisis hits us. We now need to acknowledge and solve the problem. We ignored the goal initially and now must reach the goal regardless of human cost. Time dualism can mean health topics. We ignore good health habits during an initial time, until we become ill to the extent that we either could not control events, or indeed sickness was under our ability to avoid. Once people become ill after ignoring good health lifestyles, they suddenly acknowledge the need for professional medical assistance. They see a doctor.

During this second time in time dualism, the doctor may prescribe medication to solve the problem of illness. Individuals practicing time dualism may not have consciously thought of such dualism. They were merely not paying attention to their health. They might get professional help and hopefully return to good health. Individuals thus recover from instead of having prevented illness.

STUDY QUESTIONS

- What is time dualism?
- How does time dualism occur in health?
- What is the difference between time dualism and preventative medicine?

Ricoeur and Ryle deal only with substance dualism in Cartesian thought. However, interpreting their Continental and analytic efforts for overcoming time dualism is possible. According to Ricoeur and phenomenology, we overcome time dualism by reintroducing the goal (which I term "second" time) into the process (preventative or "first" time) of prevention. From the perspective of Ryle, we can resolve time dualism by accepting only the first time, and claiming that the second does not exist.

Any of the four positions on reality are ethical in one situation and unethical in another.

STABILITY POSTMODERNISM

Stability postmodernism is the metaphysical option saying stability is real. Parmenides (Velasquez 2014) says stability is reality. Change is a function of stability and thus an illusion. Stability is the independent variable; thus, change is not real and the dependent variable is stability. According to a widely accepted human factors engineering principle, the human being or user is "stable," and designs or changes the technical environment to match the person.

The four positions of reality never change as to their being ethical. We are ethical if we always hold to a certain view of reality.

Stability-only is exemplified in academia when colleges and universities eliminate tenure. One major concern about tenure is that professors work too hard for it, and they then have job security when tenured. The schools believe a problem exists with incompetent tenured professors. But problems with tenured professors would most likely disappear or be minimal, if schools hired the correct person and monitored them. It makes little to no sense to tell faculty they will never have job security.

PROBLEM AND PERSON: GENERAL THEORY A.III

Inside change and stability is reality as problem and person. Dealing with problems derives from the general theory of change and stability. At one extreme, solving problems involves mere change through reaction in situations. At the other extreme, stability means no problems exist. Between the extremes are problem prevention and problem-person dualism. Knowing and doing object and subject as change and stability never occurs in a vacuum. Problems can arise as we attempt to know and do. Dealing with problems involves ethics. Hence, ethical or moral issues enter in and are part of metaphysics. A general theory of ethics appears in chapter 7. But that chapter applies to this chapter and all remaining ones as well. Each chapter involves an ethical approach to that chapter's topic.

Ethics is a moral or nonphysical constraint on what we do. It asks whether there is right and wrong. But if we "do," we ought to do right instead of wrong. Doing right will enable us to act in a good manner to accomplish goals, preventing wrong. If we do wrong, problems will emerge. Right and wrong are a matter of doing and not doing. We are wrong when doing wrong but also when refraining from doing right. Problems will occur when we are wrong, whether doing wrong or refraining from doing right.

Doing right means acting correctly at the start. Such action generally means doing instead of refraining. Aristotle (1999) and St. Thomas Aquinas (2001) point out that "time" is as important as anything in deciding what is ethical. "When" we do right is as crucial as what we do. Thus, do we do right before or after the wrong? We do the right thing at the right time. Problems arise if we do wrong. We ought to do right before the problems emerge. Ethics tells us to do right before problems come about, according to Aristotle and Aquinas. Four options exist in dealing with problems, each believing that its position is ethical: being alert and reacting to solve problems after they occur, preventing problems, ignoring and then reacting to solve problems after they occur, and denying problems exist.

STUDY QUESTIONS

- What is the relation between attempting to know object and subject, and change and stability, and the issue of problems?
- What do Aristotle and Aquinas say about time and dealing with problems?
- How is dealing with problems an ethical issue?
- Why is problem solving inadequate?

PROBLEMS AND LESTER THUROW

Massachusetts Institute of Technology's (MIT) Lester C. Thurow (1993) concludes his *Head to Head* with a note on problems. "America's tough problem," he warns, "is realizing that problems exist that must be solved" (1993, 299). Thurow continues, "without that realization, nothing can be done" (1993, 299). According to Thurow, "minor problems that remain unsolvable in the present, create major problems that are difficult to solve in the future" (1993, 299). Replace "solve" with "prevention," and we are able to give nuance and detail to Thurow's insights about dealing with problems. Problems will exist or occur. Any minor obstacle we do not prevent will become or escalate into a major problem, perhaps a crisis or disaster to which me must react and resolve.

Are we alert and react to solve problems? This is alertness to and putting out fires. Do we prevent them? This prevents fires. Ought we to ignore and react to solve problems? Here, we ignore and then put out fires. Should we deny that problems exist? We can deny that a fire is occurring. According to the fire prevention view, prevention of problems is ethical, while responding or reacting to problems by problem solving, putting out fires after they occur, is wrong and unethical.

STUDY QUESTIONS

- What is Lester C. Thurow warning us about regarding problems?
- How can problems with which we do not deal now become major crises in the future?

PROBLEM MONISM

Problem monism means alert-reactive problem solving whereby we are alert and react to solve problems after they occur. Alert-reactive problem solving sounds good to people. Individuals feel delighted when talking about and promoting problem solving. This position should not surprise us. Problems are obstacles. They get in the way of progress and everything we consider acceptable for a civilization. This view is alert-reactive problem monism. We assume problems will *always* occur and that we ought to be alert to them. Being alert and reacting to existing problems is ethical.

In alert-reactive problem solving, an assumption exists that problems are natural, normal events that people ought to solve. That is, people tend to say that, yes, problems will occur, and we need to solve the issue. However, if problems occur, the possibility exists that danger will occur. A problem is, by definition, something causing harm in some way. Thus, simply being alert and waiting for problems to occur, and then reacting to solve them, could result in a crisis or disaster. This is an ethical issue. Should we wait for a problem to occur and harm us before we react to solve it?

If object-only, object-embodied, dualism, or subject-only involve problems, individuals are alert to and preparing themselves for confronting the obstacle to overcome it. Alert-reactive problem solving is the metaphysical stance that people are preparing to first be hurt, even fatally, before solving the bad situation.

A generalized ethical view can be made of alert-reactive problem solving. Ethical action can mean alert-reactive egoism, utilitarianism, divine command, virtue, natural law, and duty theories. This means egoistic, utilitarian, divine command, virtue, natural law, and duty alertness-reaction problem solving. God, duty, virtue, natural law, egoism, or utilitarianism tell us to be alert and react to solve problems after they occur.

Being alert and reacting to solve problems after they occur is ethical. The six ethical theories tell us to be alert and react to problems. We also accept an ethical theory only after alertness and reaction to a problem.

John Douglas, an FBI profiler, initially trained as a SWAT sniper (1995). But sniper sees the human as an object, a target in the cross-hairs. Law enforcement snipers are concrete examples of alert-reaction. They are constantly alert to a criminal act where it might be necessary to shoot at someone committing a crime.

STUDY QUESTIONS

- What is alert-reactive problem solving?
- How can alert-reactive problem solving be unethical?
- How is alert-reactive problem solving a more general ethical theory than the traditional ethical theories?

PROBLEM PHENOMENOLOGY

Problem phenomenology or problem prevention means individuals or groups prevent problems before they occur. Preventing problems is the ergonomic position. Ergonomics experts analyze a situation and determine where a problem can and might occur. They then design a machine such that the person will use it safely. In macro and micro ergonomics, which is my interpretation of philosophy, we ought to design any authority or person, as well as technology, whereby society can prevent problems. We assume problems can always occur, and our task is to prevent them from doing so. Problem prevention is ethical.

B. Aaron Johnson (2018) gives a good example of problem prevention in terms of fire prevention. Fire houses most exemplify the visible aspect of a fire department in any city. People walk, bike, bus, or drive past the generally red brick buildings and, if doors are open, see the fire trucks. This is evidence of alert-reaction to fires. But unseen are the fire prevention activities, usually, by the same fire-fighters who are working in the fire houses.

In preventing problems, individuals are not waiting and preparing to get hurt. They are not waiting or preparing for crisis and fatality. The effort to foresee a problem to the extent that that is possible is an attempt to avoid crises. Problem prevention attempts to avoid instead of solve problems that exist. Kant (1987) would say reality problem without person is blind, and reality person without problem is empty.

We prevent problems because divine command, egoism, utilitarianism, virtue, duty, or natural law tell us to prevent problems. Thus, we have preventative divine command, egoism, utilitarianism, virtue, duty, or natural law.

Criminology gives good concrete points about prevention. Crime prevention is one of the most talked-about items.

As Douglas experienced profiling and the psychology of the killer, he eventually realized that being a sniper, being the shooter, was losing its appeal. He wanted to reach the person before they became killers. The sniper is on the reflective, atomistic level where we reduce the person to the criminal and object. In the real world, alert/reactive police work requires crime scene investigative expertise (Svensson and Wendel 1965). But prevention involves broader cultural contexts. Negotiation and psychology are on the approach lifeworld level, where we study and reach the person as a nonreducible human being (Douglas 1995; Gaines and Miller 2012). Indeed, the American Bar Association (1973) and John Conklin (1995) talk about crime prevention as a wide-ranging, interdisciplinary issue. A borderline issue may be protecting the president of the United States. The United States Secret Service reacts to adults trying to or attacking the president. Yet, retired Secret Service Agent Joe Petro (2005) makes clear that protecting the commander-in-chief is more *preventing* than reacting to an attacker's actions.

STUDY QUESTIONS

- What is the difference between alert-reactive problem solving and problem prevention?
- How can problem prevention be ethical and alert-reactive problem solving be unethical in the larger framework?

PROBLEM DUALISM

Dualistic problem solving means we initially ignore problems, then there is a problem to be solved. Where alert-reactive problem solving prepares for a crisis, which it must then solve, dualistic problem solving accepts the position that we can ignore and then react to solve a problem.

Pearl Harbor, the Normandy invasion, and September 11 all exemplified ignorance-reactive problem solving. In Pearl Harbor, the US government was generally unaware of Japanese intentions and preparation to attack the US naval base in Hawaii. The Normandy invasion was a massive effort to prepare our nearly dormant military to suddenly emerge on a scale sufficient to attack the Nazis. The September 11 attacks woke the nation to acknowledge vulnerability to an enemy who wishes to harm the United States on its soil. It is ethical to ignore and then react to solve problems after they occur.

People suddenly find that egoism, utilitarianism, divine command, virtue, natural law, or duty tell them to solve problems after they have ignored problems. We can have dualistic problem-solving egoism, divine command, virtue, natural law, utilitarianism, and duty ethics.

John W. Gardner, in his *Self-Renewal* (1965), warns that society is often stubborn about needed change. Any organization may well have to undergo a financial crisis before being forced to make necessary reform. For much of civilization, innovation is not natural, or something people voluntarily seek. They prefer to react after ignorance and crisis, instead of preventing problems.

William E. Burrows (1986) gives a good account of how the United States ignored, then reacted to Pearl Harbor and foreign relations. The American government has, in several ways, mostly ignored and then reacted to a crisis in foreign affairs and science. Sputnik, Pearl Harbor, and September 11 are good example of ignorance-reaction dualism.

STUDY QUESTION

- How do world and US wars exemplify ignorance-reactive problem solving?

PROBLEM DENIAL

Problem denial. We deny problems exist. This is an isolationist view. It denies that bad things can happen. According to problem denial, obstacles cannot occur. Nothing exists or can occur that will harm us or be fatal. Buddhism states that pain is desire. Indeed, eliminate desire and ego, and we see that pain vanishes. Christian Science will say that pain is bad thinking. Think good thoughts, and you deny pain exists as a problem.

Problem denial is the subjective extreme in dealing with problems. Where dualism is initial ignorance but awakens to react to solve a problem after a crisis, problem denial is the most subjective and isolationist stance. This position denies that a problem exists, and generally continues that state of isolation even after a crisis hits. A nation may deny an enemy's existence even if the adversary is harming other countries. If the hostilities finally come to the denying nation's shores, an adamant isolationism could well insist that a crime instead of an act of war has occurred.

STUDY QUESTIONS

- What is problem denial?
- How does problem denial become an ethical issue?

CHAPTER TWO

LINGUISTIC REALITY:
SIMPLES AND IDIOMS

KEYWORDS

deflation: The philosophy position that we do not need theories of truth.

linguistic reality: That variation of existence which is wording about existence.

simple language or **simples:** Words and symbols requiring no interpretation.

idioms or **idiomatic language:** Words and symbols requiring interpretation.

metaethics: Analysis of ethics' language.

existential: The philosophical movement emphasizing human existence, or life, over a merely scientific approach.

Inside objectivity and subjectivity, change and stability, and dealing with problems, linguistic reality means simple and idiomatic language. How important is hermeneutics, or interpretation, in this book? What role does it play in any book? Should we use the words we use in this chapter and book? Does their meaning change or remain the same? Is language or its meaning atomic or subjective? Start with the previous chapter.

Chapter 1 interpreted reality (monism, phenomenology, dualism, existentialism or subjectivity). But we express reality in words: "monism," "phenomenology," "dualism," and "existentialism" or "subjectivity." Linguistic interpretation is fundamental to literacy. Without understanding the meaning of words, photos, and symbols, we cannot proceed with reading a book. Starting would probably be impossible. Literacy means knowing the language in which the author writes, but also the meaning of the words. Whereas chapter 1 interpreted reality, chapter 2 now interprets words about that reality. Language reality is a variation of reality. Linguistic hermeneutics is variation of hermeneutics (general metaphysics).

In many philosophy books, interpretation usually is in a chapter toward the end. Interpretation is certain not associated with metaphysics or other branches. That does not seem correct. Putting hermeneutics toward the conclusion of the book is like saying that we will read the book through to the end and then will see about the meaning of what we have read.

Deflation, from the chapter on truth (chapter 3), would tell us that interpretation is not necessary. If we accept as true what someone writes or says, perhaps no reason exists for an interpretation for the meaning. The meaning is clear because we hear or see something, and we need no further proof.

If we need proof of a statement, there is also a probability that a statement needs interpretation. By "interpretation" here, I do not mean the typical career or profession of the simultaneous or serial interpreter or translator working in foreign languages. That is the context of translating, or interpreting from one language to another.

The point in philosophy as hermeneutics is different. It discusses interpretation even if only one world language existed. This chapter, along with the one on ethics (chapter 7), is unique from the remaining chapters. Both interpretation (hermeneutics) and ethics are derived reality. It would seem from the traditional path of general theory to applications that any chapter after that theoretical one is only an application and cannot apply back to the one from which it is derived.

But consider the following. A general theory only sets up the framework or foundations for applications, for derivations. A hermeneutic derivation, while derivatively real, nonetheless tells us about how we interpret every topic. If so, chapter 1 on general theory becomes, ironically, one of the chapters or topics we ought to interpret. Metaphysics is a hermeneutic regarding reality. Likewise, the chapter on ethics is derivative theory. Yet it is telling us what is ethical, including metaphysical and hermeneutical options. If the general theory consists of several options, then each of the options sees itself as ethical. In the sense that hermeneutics interprets a meaning, a general theory of metaphysics (philosophy) is general hermeneutics, interpreting reality. Remaining chapters, as applied metaphysics, are applied hermeneutics.

This chapter, then, is broader than those on hermeneutics in typical philosophy books. I am discussing linguistic interpretation. My effort in this chapter is to explore and give a "general theory" of linguistic hermeneutics as to which words to use in any chapter, including the one on general theory (chapter 1).

In that sense, readers can ask themselves some questions after reading this chapter. They might reverse and go back to my chapter on a general theory of reality. Is wording about reality totally objective, objectivity embodied in subjectivity or my views, dualistic, or subject-alone (what I say it is)? Readers, after reading the chapter on ethics, can go back to this and the chapter on general theory. They would then ask, what aspect or position in linguistic and of general hermeneutics seems ethical? What position in the general theory seems ethical?

I look at meaning (1) without reflecting a person's bias, (2) somewhat reflecting the individual, (3) distinct from the person, and (4) almost totally mirroring the person. The first deals with simple language needing no interpretation. The second means bias or prejudice is part of human nature. Third, distinction from the person denotes a dualism where something is to be interpreted, while something else needs no interpretation. Finally, the fourth denotes that everything is idiomatic and requires interpretation.

A human factors engineering approach is that simple-only (idiom-unfriendly) and idiomatic-only (idiom-too-friendly) positions are wrong. They are extremes. Only simple-language embodied is correct, for it is what ergonomics calls "user-friendly." It takes into account the person's limits and abilities to be simple in language.

STUDY QUESTIONS

- What is linguistic interpretation?
- How does linguistic interpretation differ from general interpretation of reality?
- What does it mean that an applied chapter may apply back to a general chapter, whereby the general one is now also derivative?
- How does human factors engineering, or ergonomics, explain linguistic hermeneutics?
- Try to predict the consequences if meanings of words always need interpretation or never need interpretation.

SIMPLE AND IDIOMATIC LANGUAGE B.I

CLARITY MONISM

Clear or simple language can mean linguistic monism, simple or clear language-only. In linguistic hermeneutics, simple-language reality monism means words—a language—ought to be such that readers need no interpretation of their meaning. The previous chapter was on metaphysics as general hermeneutics, the interpretation of reality (monism, phenomenology, dualism, subjectivism). Linguistic reality as linguistic monism means language is totally reducible to the sum of linguistic atoms or parts. These are logical, rational, or empirical atoms with only one meaning.

Imagine the world speaking one language. People living in different parts of the world, even in separate nations, might not need foreign language interpreters or translators. Individuals in Germany would speak the same language as those in Japan. Suppose, however, that whether the world speaks one or one thousand languages, the meaning of a word remains the same in one language or across languages.

Imagine words in different languages having only one meaning. "Chair" always means something on which to sit. We might need translators or interpreters to hear or read French and translate or interpret this to Italian or Chinese. However, the different languages would have words with the same meaning. "Door" in Chinese never would need interpretation to another Chinese. It would have a different word in English, but that word would need no interpretation among English-speaking people. Another possibility is that interpretation involves the same word in one language, "fire," having a different meaning in another language.

Analytic and positivistic thoughts advocate a "scientific," "mathematical" language. A word means the same thing everywhere and cannot have two or more interpretations. The philosopher Ludwig Wittgenstein (1961) proposed such a simple language in his early efforts. Later he learned, reluctantly, that people are idiomatic and that this prohibits the existence of a simple, mathematical language.

Simple-language-only in interpretation denotes the total absence of the need for interpreting. A word is completely objective reality. This would be the opposite of the approach of Thomas Kuhn, for whom a subject-matter, science in his case, is "what the scholars say it is" (1970, 5).

A totally objective approach to a subject matter follows a very mechanical path. This could be Karl Popper (2002). A theory exists for a long time, but eventually a new and better one emerges. Indeed, the old theory is wrong, the new one correct. Popper argues that science, and perhaps any other subject area, involves thinkers immediately, objectively, dropping the old for the new.

Thomas Kuhn (1970) disagrees. Language arises from within a human, "dramatic" context. People do not just jettison the old for the new. Emotions play an often decisive role. The section in this chapter on subjectivity-only addresses Kuhn's idea.

We are ethical in holding to a simple language when speaking about any of the six ethics theories. This is simple-language-only egoism, utilitarianism, and so on. These theories always mean the same thing and are never idiomatic or change in meaning.

An example of simple-language-only, as the early Wittgenstein sought, are computers. Consider "enter." "Enter" means to go into a room, car, building, and so on. But "enter" can mean jumping to the next line or space on a computer when typing, or clicking or pressing a button or space on a cell phone or smartphone to perform an operation. The early Wittgenstein can insist only one meaning for "enter." If it means to "go into," then other gestures, operations, and so on for computers and phones will require another term (Wittgenstein 1961).

Analytic philosophy (Ammerman 1965; Weitz 1966; Corrado 2008), seeks to clarify language, and arose from what it saw as the weeds of metaphysical thinking, where philosophical arguments seemed endless and going nowhere. Someone has complained that analytic thinkers merely analyze and never live, while Continental philosophers only live without analyzing.

A criticism of clear language monism might be that clear or simple wording may be irrelevant, or that we do not talk like that. The sentence "I am walking home" can mean the same as 'I am walking the dog.' But I am not walking the home as I am walking the dog. Some might argue that 'I am walking home' could mean toward someone else's home. The most explicit way to say I am walking home may be 'I am myself walking toward my own home.' However, people do not talk that explicitly.

Analytic thinkers Bertrand Russell (Stevens 2011), Gottlob Frege (Geach and Black 1980), Saul Kriptke (1991), and Ludwig Wittgenstein (1958) believe that philosophy is the analysis of language. Our theological and philosophical problems, according to them, are due not so much, if at all, to legitimate questions about reality, knowledge, ethics, and other aspects of philosophy. The issues are language. Scholars ought to use clear, simple, logical words to discuss the real world. Such usage will, according to analytic philosophers, help eliminate what they perceive as the inadequacy of metaphysics.

STUDY QUESTIONS

- How can computer language such as "enter" help us understand meaning that is simple?
- How can the meaning of "enter" help us understand that "enter" is not simple and has come to mean going into a room, clicking a computer key, and so on?
- Can you can think of how to simplify other computer words?
- How may linguistic hermeneutics show ethics?
- Explain a world in which we have only simple language.

STUDY QUESTIONS

- What does simple-language-only mean?
- Explain or predict the implications of simple-language-only, requiring no interpretation.
- Why do you believe Wittgenstein failed to find a simple-language-only?
- How would you proceed to find a simple language requiring no interpretation?
- How would you explain a compromise between Kuhn and Wittgenstein?

CLARITY PHENOMENOLOGY

Phenomenology is simple-language embodied. Linguistic reality here is generally never completely reducible to linguistic atoms. These linguistic atoms are embodied in idiomatic context. Embodied or interacting simple language means that language and meaning should remain roughly or exactly the same throughout time. "Chair" should always mean furniture on which to sit, though we could place something on it as we would on a "table."

Embodiment suggests that precision and simplicity should exist as much as possible, though idioms are part of life.

Psychologists and computer scientists seem to concur with clear language embodied, or language phenomenology. George Lakoff and Mark Johnson (2003) argue that language embodiment in terms of metaphors reflects the social context in which we communicate. It is likely that no person, not even a monk in a monastery, communicates outside a social or cultural context. Qi Wang (2017) and Hans-Georg Gadamer (2013) find that truth from psychological and philosophical thought, respectively. Rejecting society does not mean the world rejecting ascetic lives literally outside a physical, social, environment. The cloistered monks live outside what we call a society as cities of families and workers producing goods and services. But these monks nonethelss reside within a social milieu consisting of other monks, however cloistered. The metaphor is not a literal meaning. A literal meaning for much of reality may be impossible. We may interpret metaphor as idiomatic in that it talks about a reality by referring to a physical event, object, and the like. Use of metaphor implies the need to employ idiomatic, non-clear language in life.

David Priess (2016) points out that old assumptions might well color intelligence analysis. Analysts can collect intelligence on foreign nations, especially those with whom we have no formal relationships and who are not friendly to us. Yet, collection is not mere gathering of data. Outdated theories and beliefs about a given nation can underlie intelligence conclusions. The President's Daily Brief can thus be partially flawed or deceptive.

Five forms of idioms may exist. These suggest that even a simple literal sentence might be fundamentally nonliteral, idiomatic. First, the sentence "I walk home" looks the same as "I walk the cat." The meanings are different. Technically, to be as clear as possible, I am saying I am myself alone walking toward my home. Normally, it would be strange for me to be that specific.

Second, I call words like Cal Tech, MIT, University of Chicago, and Harvard University social idioms. Readers know that each is the name of a university. That knowledge is universal. The names are idioms in that each university refers to itself in different spellings. Total clarity demands that we refer to them perhaps as CIT, MIT, UC, and UH. Indeed, we would replace CIT with UCPA (University of California at Palo Alto), and MIT with UMEC (University of Massachusetts in East Cambridge). Third, phrases like "kick the bucket" are idiom phrases where the sentence meaning is different from that of each constituent. Finally, the meaningless word *Ardwa* could mean a person's own spelling for anything, maybe *water*.

Simplicity embodied acknowledges that we can and ought to be as simple as possible with interpretation. In that way, simplicity need not be an end in itself. Meaning would be generally idiomatic so that minimal interpretation is necessary. Human beings are generally idiomatic, with phrases and words to be used metaphorically instead of strictly scientifically. The simple must be in the context of the idiomatic. Kant (1987) would argue that simple language without idioms is blind, and idioms without simple language are empty.

R. Kenneth Jones and Patricia Jones (Jones and Jones 1975) remind us that people are part of the social, human world. To that extent, interpretation is our method of approaching any discipline and taking action. If, as Bohr has stated (Barnett 1966), we actors as well as spectators, then we are interpreters as well as passive observers of a totally objective reality. Everyone resides in some social milieu, a human setting, and that context colors what we see, hear, think, and do.

At a church dinner I attended one fall in Chicago, a common topic of conversation was raking leaves. The dinner organizer told a friend that his brother-in-law was an engineer. The engineer did more than collect, bag, and dispose of the leaves. As an engineer, he made sure each bag was equally full and the opening taped crosswise. The engineer's background and training was a bias as to how he put the leaves in bags and taped them shut. Here, bias orients action. But bias or hypothesis also orients perception.

Popper (2002) argues that hypothesis always orients perception. We do not just perceive or know through induction. Simplicity embodied could be perception or induction embodied. According to Popper, individuals do not just gather facts. They gather what they believe are facts in terms of hypotheses, questions, theories, or cognitive orientations.

Kant (1987) says that categories orient our perceptions. His view would mean that innate abilities exist for us to interpret words and reality. Of course, Kant means our abilities are universal, whereas romantics disagree, arguing that innate abilities are culturally dependent.

Huston C. Smith (1966) has argued for analytic and positivist thinking embodied. His position defends simplicity that takes the idiomatic or nonreductive into account. He would be elated by the APA's recent move to establish the group Beyond the Analytic-Continental Divide. His views directly parallel human factors engineering, calling for what phenomenology notes as embodied objects, objects designed for users.

In Kenneth Boulding (1968), the nonreducible image colors our perception. This can be interpreted as meaning that our image of something compels us to interpret that reality in certain ways. We are not looking at words purely objectively. The perceiver or observer is always part of the perception or observation. Reality is never totally independent of the observer.

According to Kahneman (2013), simple-only language takes time to pin down. Analytic thinking, logic, and systematization take more time than idioms. Using analytic methods involves taking time and thinking slowly to determine how precise we can get in carefully describing something as literally as possible. Idiomatic language, as fast thinking, quickly uses a phrase and pictorial language to describe that same reality. Precision is not the goal in idioms; emotion and pictorial images are more appropriate.

Hans-Georg Gadamer (1976); Moss (2005) tells us that all human beings are biased or prejudiced. We are all interpreters. Our cultures color perceptions and meaning. Wealthy people, especially those isolated from interaction with the middle class and the poor, have certain images, biases, and prejudices about life itself. At the other end of the socioeconomic spectrum, someone born and raised in the inner city or a ghetto has other images or biases about human existence.

Niels Bohr (Barnett 1966), tells us that we are "actors and spectators" in life. Language is neither objectively clear, nor subjectively idiomatic. Both are involved. If Bohr is correct, language is a combination of many factors: the author's objective meaning according to Aquinas (Clark 1972), Fredrich Schleiermacher (Audi 1997) and Wilhelm Dilthey (Audi 1997); the text's more flexible impact for the reader (Wittgenstein 1968), and the reader's own cultural context (Gadamer, 2013).

While Bohr is not technically a phenomenologist, his perspective is that of phenomenology. That view, from Bohr's perspective, says interpretation is frequently necessary. A text, voice, picture, are always prone to mean what the author intended, how communication influences readers, and the cultural heritage which a reader brings to the words and pictures. Language is clear and idiomatic. It is neither merely external to a reader and listener, nor simply the reader's invention or cultural context. This integrated view of interpretation takes us back to Kant. Bohr can add to Kant. For Kant, knowledge is of the thing-in-itself which we cannot know, and the thing-for-me, which is the only item a person can know (Kant, 1987). Taken seriously, the former may be something requiring no interpretation, because its meaning and impact are completely independent of the perceiver. Bohr would say we are mere spectators of the item, if indeed we are even able to be spectator of the unknowable (Barnett, 1966).

On the other hand, Bohr might well say the thing-for-me, because it is for me, could be purely idiomatic, and have no shared meaning. A perspective of Bohr could tell us that Kant needs a thing-for-us. Such a social position would then mean interpretation is always possible. Three views emerge: the thing is independent of us as spectators seeing meaning requiring no interpretation; meaning or impact with interpretation necessary based on cultural understandings in which we act; also bringing in personal context unique to individuals as mostly actors.

STUDY QUESTIONS

- Illustrate or draw a way to match image, categories, hypothesis, and fast and slow thinking with the thinkers who use those terms.
- How would you argue that Popper, Kant, Smith, Boulding, and Kahneman present an interdisciplinary view of phenomenology as simple-language embodied?

CLEAR LANGUAGE PHENOMENOLOGY IS CULTURE

Following Gadamer, someone has suggested that children of wealthy suburban parents experience coping issues in life's difficult times. They think life will be easier than it is, because of their more "cushioned" upbringing. On the other hand, youngsters from the inner city may have experienced bad times much of their lives. These have immunized them with the bias or prejudice that life is very hard. They have developed a view of some self-reliance and working independently to achieve their goals. Culture colors our expectations and abilities.

Human factors engineering points out that we have limits and abilities influencing how we use machines (Kantowitz and Sorkin 1983; Chapanis 1960). This ergonomic position is engineering's interpretation of the human dimension. In what I call macro and micro ergonomics, human factors would design cities (macro) and specific technologies (micro) in urban areas, taking into account whether the city and technology ought to exist, and then how to match human ability and limits.

Where simple-only is positivistic and eliminates or minimizes emotional language, embodied simplicity reflects messy life. People can say that every home has at least a front door, maybe a rear door. Indeed, every building has at least one door. The door allows individuals to enter and leave. This is a literal meaning of "door." On the other hand, people also talk of someone opening doors for someone's career. That interpretation is metaphorical. A literal wording would prohibit talking of "opening doors for someone's career." Instead, such opening of doors could well be put in words such as "someone has given me an opportunity for work, for a job." To eliminate or minimize metaphors, idioms, and the nonliteral interpretation possibly goes against the existential in life.

Phenomenology argues that our brain, mind, body, and social context color or influence perception, actions, thoughts, and thus language (Gadamer 2013). Where simple-only language argues that language reflects the objective world completely, phenomenology and the existential disagree. According to phenomenologists, our bodies and brains are contexts making us part of objective reality. We are related to and influence what we perceive.

Even a very basic understanding of biology tells us that the body or brain color perception. The color-blind person looks at green and sees brown, for example. Our backgrounds, heritage, and initial culture all orient our language and actions. Thus, language cannot be, according to phenomenology, something requiring no interpretation.

Simple-language embodied is somewhere between a subject matter as completely asocial, totally objective reality, and Thomas Kuhn's (1970) sociological orientation as more subjective than not. When simple-language embodied looks at the arts and sciences, it sees objectivity within the social or subjective context. The subject matter is generally objective regardless of author or researcher. But the author's biases could be involved, and readers must exercise caution as to what they read.

STUDY QUESTION

- How does human factors engineering contribute to interdisciplinarity when appearing in the same section as Gadamer, a philosopher, regarding embodied language?

CLEAR LANGUAGE PHENOMENOLOGY HAS HIGHER EDUCATION ROLE

College and universities can take the lead in simple-language embodied. Among the best courses to study at any institution of higher learning is the course that is transferable. Physics is, or ought to be, the same at Podunk and MIT. Sociology is and ought to be the same at Stanford, Yale, and a community college in Long Island.

Instruction and methods can differ. Instructors can teach with different styles or idioms in the same academic department or same school. However, instructors ought to teach the same topics. Simplicity of words ought to acknowledge idiom of pedagogy. Chemistry, economics, art, and music cannot be that different in two or more colleges and universities. Teaching methods, while varying, cannot be that distinct with two or more instructors.

We are ethical if acting with any of the theories as though their meaning is simple within the idiomatic context. Bentham (1987) believed utilitarianism means lessening pain by feeding hungry children, while Mill (2005) responded with a utilitarianism of providing intellectual opportunities to children, not just food. Simplified through embodiment, we can see levels from the physical in Bentham to more intellectual and cultural in Mill (Ryan 1970).

STUDY QUESTION

- How are simplicity and course transferability in colleges related?

STUDY QUESTION

- Explain how hermeneutics can be a theory of ethics.

CLARITY-IDIOMATIC DUALISM

Language dualism means that simple-only language has a specific time and place, while idiom-only language has another time and place. Put in other terms, a certain time and place requires language having no interpretation, while another time and place is for purely idiomatic language requiring continual change in meaning.

Imagine that on Mondays and Tuesdays no interpretation is necessary for communications, study, or other forms of literacy. Celebrations, rituals, and ceremonies have words and gestures needing no interpretation and having only one meaning. Then, all remaining days of the week require interpretation in all ceremonies and other events.

Or think about school, work, or play. One course of study in school, one area of work, one moment or kind of play has no need for interpretation. Another or other courses of study, other areas of work, and other times or places of play require different meanings for the same words and gestures.

Dualism is different from simple-only language because of the precision factor. Meaning does not just differ, and interpretation is not simply necessary at one point and not at another. The different times and places are distinct. One meaning occurs on a specific day, at a specific time and place. It is different on another specific time or day.

Simple-idiomatic-language dualism presents difficulties. A simple-only language needing no interpretation works one time during a given day, or one or a few distinct days, and not other times or days. The other times or days necessitate idiom-only language.

STUDY QUESTIONS

- What is simple-idiomatic-language dualism?
- Predict what could happen if people use simple language requiring no interpretation in certain times and places, and in other times and places idiomatic language needing interpretation.

STUDY QUESTION

- What are the implications of a simple-dualist theory of ethics?

IDIOM POSTMODERNISM

In ethics, the issue of standards inquires into whether ethical behavior is the same everywhere and every time in a given place, same embodied in all places and times, dualistic, or never the same in any given location and the times there. Thus, ethical behavior in idiomatic-only would mean that morals differ not just in different locations, but also at different times in the given location. What is ethical depends on where we are, but it depends also on yesterday, today, and tomorrow. Idiom-only language is linguistic postmodernism.

The ethical is only idioms. Any of the ethical theories can be stated according to a person's idiomatic interpretation.

This idiomatic situation applies also to law. The legal becomes illegal, and the reverse.

Idiomatic-only linguistic hermeneutics is a postmodern, deconstructionist perspective. All idioms are equally valid and real. Each culture and time within a culture practices its own linguistic and general behavioral idioms. The French thinker Jacques Derrida (1976) emphasizes subjectivity, and American political theorist Nozick, Robert (1974), a libertarian or anarchist, proclaims all contracted realities, cultures, and idioms as valid.

However, a modernist could dare them to walk into a store and declare shoplifting is valid. In addition, a government agency would take the modernist approach by setting limits on exceptions. For instance, The Internal Revenue Service (IRS) will allow you to extend a deadline for tax payment. But the IRS does not extend the tax deadline indefinitely. There is an expiration date for the deadline. Exceptions to the rule, however idiomatic, cannot be indefinite. The IRS will not consider valid the extending of deadlines to any times the taxpayer wants. If the IRS becomes thoroughly postmodern, revenue collection stops, and the federal government comes to a halt.

Similarly, idiomatic-only language means that interpretation depends on where we are, but also on when we are there. That would seem to pose a problem of incredible proportions. As you converse with someone, your words will take on different meaning at certain times. Within a five-minute period, theoretically, interpretation may be necessary ten times. Indeed, a word or phrase could require interpretation each new time people use it. For example, chaos would result if the word "stairs" changed meaning each time you enter a new building where stairs are not in plain view and you need to ask their location.

The reader of this book can well imagine the consequences of idiomatic-only interpretation. Imagine that a word takes on a different interpretation with each use. Of course, no reasonable individual could expect such a practice or theory to exist. Society could argue that such a theory and practice are completely out of touch with reality.

This theory and practice approximate a hermeneutic Alzheimer's disease. In that condition, the patient suffers from chronic forgetfulness and memory loss. An individual with Alzheimer's may hear something and forget it immediately. Continuity and memory do not exist. Thus, idiomatic-only language or hermeneutics carries that shortcoming. If and when an idea takes on new meaning frequently, this means not only social and personal problems occur, but they happen to the point of aggravating culture.

I find it somewhat amusing when I use a phrase a younger person does not understand. The idiom was common, say, twenty or forty years ago. The wording either no longer exists or has taken on new meaning. This is another problem with idiomatic-only interpretation. The same words acquire new meaning. The idiom itself may disappear. A new idiom may appear. Another example is how a person carries a mobile device. I no longer see people carrying such a device in a small case attached to the belt. The devices are in a pocket. A colleague recently told me the belt case is no longer in fashion. So is society making a big deal out of how we carry a mobile device?

Thomas Kuhn tells us about the meaning of science. For him, science is "what scientists say" (Velasquez 2014, 405; Kuhn 1970), and no objective meaning of science exists. This prepares us for an extreme look at the sociology of science. Indeed, it would apply to the sociology of any subject. A subject matter is as much if not more a sociological reality as it is objective reality. A topic is the drama and human side of its meaning, from which we might try to discern an objective reality. Physics is as much a result of the interaction and drama among physicists as it is knowledge of time, space, matter, and other physical laws.

Idiomatic-only language interpretation parallels political anarchism. Anarchy means no government exists. Each person is his or her own government. Idioms can become linguistic anarchy. The idiom-language children may be a case in point. While no university case study appears to exist, a movie and several interviews are our only sources (*San Diego Tribune* 1977; Learning Channel 2007; *Time* 1979). In the 1980 film *Poto and Cabengo*, Grace and Virginia Kennedy, born in 1970, developed their own language. This development was because both parents worked and the two girls were left in the care of their German grandmother, who spoke no English and never interacted with them. The little girls were isolated from people and developed their own language (*San Diego Tribune* 1977; Learning Channel 2007; *Time* 1979). Social isolation can cause people to create their own idioms. On another front, regionalism involving normal adults can also result in local/regional idioms.

The problem here is that people live in different cities, parts of cities, towns, and so on. People living in one town may develop idioms useful and meaningful in their geographical area. For example, people living in the Northeast, Midwest, Southwest, and Southeast use various words—including "soda," "pop," and "coke"—to request the same beverage (Harvard Dialect Survey 2002).

When people speak with residents in another part of the city or town or in another city or town, they may well need other idioms. In the Southeast, customers might ask for a coke and then need to specify the kind of coke. In other regions of the nation, they might well receive a coke without further questions as to the kind of beverage. No universal, standard language or interpretation might exist. This linguistic anarchy has serious implications beyond geography. One family can have its own idioms; the family next door may have their own idioms.

Serious as that can be, communications can degenerate further. Suppose individuals in the same family, living under the same roof, each invent their own idioms. Simple language is one extreme and may be impossible as another extreme (Velasquez, 2014). Idioms taken too seriously and rejecting simplicity in general can be another extreme. Where Hans-Georg Gadamer (1975) speaks of "prejudice" (Velasquez 2014, 468) and implies "idioms," we might well need a neo-Gadamer idiomology. This can integrate simplicity within the context of the idiomatic and human.

The clarity-idiom, clarity-colored relationship just discussed, deals with the question of a word's meaning. Linguistic analysts (and logical positivists) seek only words which have cognitive meaning. Phenomenologists and thinkers like Gadamer acknowledge that all people live in context, have prejudices or biases which color the cognitive (Gadamer, 2013). Now, the change and stability relationship enters, with the next section. That section asks whether meaning, whether cognitive or biased/prejudiced, changes over time. This is the issue or topic of space/time hermeneutics, space/time interpretation. Theoretical hermeneutics in theoretical metaphysics (meaning of reality), then applied as linguistic hermeneutics, becomes a subset of language analysis in terms of space/time hermeneutics (do meaning of words change over time and culture?).

STUDY QUESTION

- Predict the implications of idiomatic-only language.

LINGUISTIC CHANGE AND STABILITY B.II

LANGUAGE CHANGE MONISM

Simple and idiomatic words are only communicated. Machines can do the same thing. People do not count or matter. And the relation between simplicity and idioms change only. People and stability are irrelevant.

If people do communicate the word, ought they to be using it, or is it unnecessary? The early Wittgenstein advocated a simple language (Velasquez 2014), which he later realized is not possible (Wittgenstein 1968). Whether we use a simple or idiomatic language, the world changes, and words reflect the change.

Language change-only means that words simply come and go. We produce a good or service and thereby introduce or eliminate a word. That change as an end in itself creates problems for people. Are they aware of a new word? Ought people be daily on the alert for a new word that emerges? Updating our language, our vocabulary and meanings, becomes a serious, frequent need in life.

The idiomatic-only view of language interpretation is comparable to Alzheimer's. In that disease, memory continuity disappears. Those with this illness cannot remember certain facts. Seconds after someone informs them of something, the individual will forget what he or she was told. In idiomatic-only linguistic hermeneutics, the constant change means that an idiom will be used one time and possibly change to another idiom soon thereafter. People need to be constantly told of a new idiom. The change would not be that dramatic with simple-only language. Chances are that a mathematical basis of the simple language means continuity of meaning and usage.

Linguistic hermeneutic change-only ethics says we can change interpretation of any the ethical theories for the sake of change.

- How does change-only mean that we merely communicate simple language, and what implications does this have for machine communications replacing humans?

- How would the world be if, adding a new word to our language, it would have to be either simple or idiomatic? What are the implications of adding words for their own sake?

LANGUAGE CHANGE PHENOMENOLOGY

Human beings communicate simples and idiomatics. Where language change-only involves change for its own sake, language change embodied changes simple, idiomatic, or any combination as needed. To paraphrase Kant (1987), language change without stability is blind, and language stability without change is empty.

First, language is something that human beings, not machines, need to communicate. Language or communication is a primary, not mechanical, enterprise. The urge to have a machine answer telephones when customers call a company reveals that clients do not necessarily need to talk to a live corporate employee. Language is reducible to sound, not an irreducible activity. But if language is generally irreducible, then simplicity means that the simple meaning is to be embodied in noncognitive contexts, and that a person, not just a machine, is to be the communicator.

Second, language change embodied also signifies that simple meaning ought not to stand alone, that a strictly mathematical language is not humane. Idiomatic language is part of human life.

Language change embodied involves new words and upgrading only as needed. New goods and services may not be needed. Thus, new words, however simple, may not be necessary. Embodied language change assures people that they may go on with their daily lives not worrying that, or whether, they ought to keep up with a new word. This worry usually occurs with a new technology. The term "user name" emerged with the computer.

Language hermeneutics says it is ethical to change interpretations of an ethical theory only as needed. No changing interpretation for its own sake. We ought to change our interpretation only as proper. Thus, we step in the same river twice.

STUDY QUESTION

- Explain how the world would be if we added new words, or eliminated old ones, primarily as need be.

LANGUAGE STABILITY AND CHANGE DUALISM

Language or word meanings are stable during one time and place, and they change during another. Imagine life divided into two places or times. One place or time is for language change-only, the other for language stability. In the former, new words are suddenly or even carefully introduced weekly or monthly, or older terms are discarded just as frequently. The latter is a time or place where new words are almost never inserted. Stability, taken too seriously, can mean that a good or service may become obsolete, but the word stays around.

STUDY QUESTION

- How would the world react if words and meanings changed for the sake of change in one time and place, and remained constant in others?

LANGUAGE STABILITY POSTMODERNISM

Imagine a world where words always remain the same. And imagine a world where no new words arise. That culture may be impossible. Change will occur, unless we totally disagree with Heraclitus (Velasquez 2011).

The world changes. Unless we are living in an ancient tribe, words will change over time. Stability-only denotes a world where change does not occur. Since language reflects the world, an unchanging culture will use an indefinitely stable language.

People in such a culture will always believe in and use words denoting a mind-set that has been their history. They may have always believed that the gods or devil cause illness. For them, the sun and moon are gods or expressions of spiritual realities. If the society is relatively modern, it has no automobiles, or the cars will always be the same type. Energy or power will always be coal, or oil, or wood burning.

Unfortunately, research into disease or medicine does not occur. Thus, diseases continue.

Poverty, wealth, and disparities among the rich and the poor would continue. Social classes and words reflecting injustice continue.

A stability-only linguistic situation forces that culture to become increasingly backward. The world as a whole seems to march onward, make progress, and advance scientifically and technologically. A stagnant society ignores advances in cosmology, space research, geography, history, and all the arts and sciences.

STUDY QUESTIONS

- Explain how people are ethical to never change our interpretation of an ethical theory or its wording.
- How would you see a world where meaning and the number of words never changes?

LINGUISTIC CHANGE-STABILITY: ETHICAL THEORIES

Philosophy does not associate hermeneutics—or as I note, linguistic hermeneutics—with ethical theory, except within the topic of metaethics, the analysis of ethical language. However, consider the following options in linguistic change-stability as ethical theories.

- Change-only linguistic hermeneutics: Word meanings in egoism, utilitarianism, divine command, virtue, natural law, and duty changing for the sake of change is ethical.
- Change-embodied linguistic hermeneutics: Word meanings in egoism, utilitarianism, divine command, virtue, natural law, and duty changing as needed is ethical.
- Change-stability linguistic hermeneutics: Word meanings in egoism, divine command, virtue, natural law, and duty changing in some places but not in others is ethical.
- Stability-only linguistic hermeneutics: Word meanings in egoism, utilitarianism, virtue theory, natural law, duty, and divine command never changing is ethical.

LINGUISTIC PROBLEM AND PERSON B.III

LANGUAGE PROBLEM MONISM

People are alert and react to solving a language problem after it occurs. They almost never consider preventing linguistic problems before these arise.

Two or more people might be arguing about a topic. They find that they cannot agree. Their problem is not the topic or a serious disagreement, but the semantics involved. Each is using a word in a different sense. If they stop and think about the different meanings they attach to a word, the two would stop disagreeing and arguing.

The traditional example of this is when people address someone as "doctor." That word, for most people, signifies a medical professional with an MD degree. Technically, individuals with a PhD, ThD, DD, and so on is a "doctor" because they hold the doctorate, or terminal degree, in that field.

Another example is when individuals argue as to whether everyone ought to go to college. People can argue yes or no until they are blue in the face. One of them may be defending the four-year college, while the other is arguing for the two-year college. So the person arguing for the two-year school is saying that everyone should have at least an associate's degree. Not everyone needs a bachelor's degree. However, if the two people simply use the word "college" without clarifying the meaning, they will yell at each other indefinitely. At the least, they will disagree endlessly without realizing that they are talking about two different things.

Alert-reactive-language problem solving believes that linguistic problems will necessarily always occur. Individuals holding this stance feel that life is one linguistic problem after another.

The movement in philosophy of linguistic analysis, or the analytic school, insists that philosophy is the clarification of language. If this movement is arguing that alertness and reaction to language problems are the way to approach understanding, then it will always wait for linguistic issue to occur, and it believes that words must be cognitively meaningful.

Analytic thinkers who argue that we wait until a linguistic problem occurs are not looking to prevent those issues. For them, hearing a word such as "spirit" or "spiritual" evokes a problem that they must solve by analyzing and perhaps cutting it from usage. Ockham's razor tells them not to needlessly multiply words (Audi, *Cambridge Dictionary of Philosophy* 1997). The analytic thinker then urges individuals to eliminate the words "spirit" and "spiritual" after they hear it, because these words are cognitively meaningless.

The analytic thinker frequently does not take into account what an ergonomic approach might consider. Human beings may well have a need for idioms and other words and phrases that are not cognitively meaningful, according to analytic thought. Or analytic thought may be wrong. The word "spirit" may not be a problem to solve after we hear it. Perhaps one day science or philosophy will show that that word is meaningful and does refer to something that exists.

STUDY QUESTIONS

- What is alert-reactive language hermeneutic problem solving?
- What are the implications if alert-reactive language hermeneutic problems are inevitable?

LANGUAGE PROBLEM PHENOMENOLOGY

People prevent language problems of simplicity and idioms before they occur. The linguistic analyst may attempt to prevent a language problem from occurring. Kant (1978) would argue a language problem without a person is blind, and a language person without a problem is empty.

Here, as above, analytic thinkers argue that certain words are purely emotive and have no cognitive meaning. They will, however, try to prevent such a word from being used instead of waiting to solve it after someone uses it. The question arises as to whether a word is indeed a problem. Ought we in fact to see the word as a problem and try to prevent it from usage? Preventing a word from being used is fine, and trying to avoid a problem from occurring is acceptable, if the word is unnecessary.

STUDY QUESTIONS

- What is language problem prevention?
- Predict a world in which language problem prevention all but replaces problem solving.

LANGUAGE PROBLEM DUALISM

People ignore and then react to solving a language problem. New simple words and idioms emerge. People immigrate or otherwise encounter new words and find themselves in a corner. Only when individuals have problems do they, or individuals in a position to help, react. Problem prevention would ask if the new words are needed.

STUDY QUESTION

- How is ignorance-reaction different from alert-reaction language hermeneutic problem solving?

LANGUAGE PROBLEM POSTMODERNISM

We deny that language problems exist. Assuming people need to learn new ideas and words, denial accomplishes little. Language problem denial believes that whatever our current stance on language, no further changes are needed.

Denial position believers live in a bubble. They use the same simple, idiomatic, dualistic, or phenomenological language they have in the past.

STUDY QUESTION

- Why should we be concerned about language interpretation problem denial?

CHAPTER THREE

TRUTH REALITY:
INFLATION AND DEFLATION

KEYWORDS

inflation: The philosophical position that we need theories of truth to validate statements.

deflation: The philosophical position that we do not need theories of truth to validate statements.

correspondence theory: A theory of truth that statements require facts for validation.

coherence (consistency) theory: A theory of truth that statements require only coherence with beliefs we already have.

Inside hermeneutics, truth reality involves the ideas of inflation and deflation. "Inflation" is my word as the opposite of "deflation," which many philosophers use to denote that theories of truth are not needed.

How do we know if words are true? Any communication including interpretation involves simple or idiomatic language. But only simple, atomistic words might require no theory of truth. Idioms most likely need justification. Thinkers deflate the need for theories. If they deflate the theories, saying we do not need them, the opposite is inflation. The existence of theories of truth is, as I see it, an inflation.

In general, thinkers engaged in truth theory and deflation seem to look at the situation as either/or. Either we use theories of truth such as correspondence and coherence, or we ought not. Whichever position we choose appears to be universal. We will either have theories all the time and in all places or deflate such theories from all times and places. I will explore alternatives or nuances to this in the text.

Two theories of truth with which I shall deal are correspondence and consistency theories. I will explore those two themes of inflation reality in the next chapter.

STUDY QUESTIONS

- What are inflation and deflation regarding truth?
- How can communications involve deflation?
- Can you explain and compare situations requiring inflation and deflation?

INFLATION AND DEFLATION C.I

TRUTH-INFLATION MONISM

Truth-inflation monism is inflation-only. To repeat, "inflation-only" is my term for the traditional perspective on truth theories. Truth reality monism says truth is totally reducible to truth objectivity, or inflation-only. We need theories of truth virtually all the time. Someone says "it is cold outside." Or we read in the newspaper or online that "it is 23 degrees outside." Truth theories attempt to verify those statements. We go outside to see if the statements are true; is the weather cold? Inflation truth says that a theory of truth is necessary because we should always, or almost always, analyze the statements for their verification. The statement by itself is insufficient.

Inflation-only says truth reality is totally reducible to inflation theory atoms or parts. Almost total objectivity is the basis of the "inflation-only" approach. This is not surprising since in statics and metaphysics, my first category or position is objectivity-alone, or objectivity disregarding subjectivity. Inflation is the effort to objectify or analyze a reality, even a derivative reality. We do not simply trust the statement, person, or other source of an expression. In inflation, the individual reasons out, thinks about, examines, or in some other scholarly, objective way tries to determine if the statement is true. Someone's utterance, or something written down, does not automatically verify the statement's truth. This logical, analytical, objective-only view takes time.

The City News Bureau of Chicago reportedly once had a motto for new, young journalists: "If your mother says she loves you, check it out." Or there is the phrase "I am from Missouri, show me." The unexamined life, said Socrates (Johnson 2011), is not worth living. These examples tell us that only analysis, objective methods, reasoning, or examination can help us reach the truth.

Presumably, a mother's love is clear. No one questions a mother's love. But the news bureau emphasizes objective reporting. Check out even a mother who says she loves you. Love cannot be true unless evidence for it exists. Even a mother's love requires objective reporting.

Inflation-only means that we ought to scrutinize every statement, or any given statement or situation. Theories of truth imply that life is the sum of a series of events where verification or analysis are needed. However, some may argue that life is more complex and not simplistic.

According to ethics, we are ethical when we use truth theories to justify statements or find their truth.

STUDY QUESTION

- How would you behave if you needed to analyze and seek factual verification for every, or almost every, statement you hear or read?

INFLATION PHENOMENOLOGY

Truth Inflation phenomenology, or embodied inflation, is the phenomenological view of truth that some statements require deflation. Some situations require inflation, but others allow for deflation. This is not dualism. It simply reflects life in its complexity. Inflation embodied does not mean that we need truth theories during a set time, say morning but not during afternoon. We can accept a statement as true without analysis when we hear or read it. With other statements that require analysis and truth theories, individuals should scrutinize events and statements. Such distinction is not permanent or set in stone as to time, date, and location. We do not say that statements during the morning are valid without analysis and afternoon ones are not. They are valid or invalid at the time we hear or read them. A Kantian (1987) view says inflation without deflation is blind, and deflation without inflation is empty.

One major distinction is between police work and someone telling us about the weather. If a person comes in a building where we have been inside for some time and tells us it is raining, we believe the person. We need no evidence. Take police work. When a criminal commits a crime and someone calls the police without having seen the crime take place, the officers who arrive at the scene must have evidence that a particular individual committed the crime. Let us say that no one saw the crime being committed.

The police will check for fingerprints and seek witnesses to identify any individual in the area who seemed suspicious. Neither the police nor any citizen can simply make a statement that a certain person was the perpetrator. That would show bias or prejudice against the innocent. Someone may be suspect, but evidence must exist that this person committed the crime.

That evidence would involve the inflationary theory, showing the truth of the charge that the individual committed the crime. Police require reasonable evidence or proof of guilt to charge the suspect with the wrongdoing, with breaking the law. They cannot simply arrest and charge individuals without evidence, take them to court, and have the judge or judge and jury convict them.

What constitutes evidence or proof of guilt depends on the law. Time and again, judges have decided whether an object, testimony, or witness is adequate evidence.

Using a theory of truth, inflation means society needs to be objective and analyze the situation when a criminal commits a crime. Such a theory may also work in many situations during a given or typical day. For example, these would not involve crime and criminals. The average interpersonal interaction is one. Two friends meet. One of them has always said he does not want to eat at a particular restaurant or does not like a certain food at an eating establishment. As they meet, the two decide to have lunch or dinner. The one who has expressed dislike for a certain restaurant suddenly suggests they go to that place. Or that individual unexpectedly wants to eat a food that he has never liked. The other friend, hearing this, asks why the inconsistency? Why did the first friend surprise the second by suggesting a restaurant or food that the initial person never wants? The second friend has the right to analyze the situation or statements that the first friend has made.

These two situations involve the need for inflation in truth. In criminal and in noncriminal cases, lawless acts and noncriminal inconsistent statements are times for analysis and verification. What of deflation?

Let us consider that persons are inside a building. Indeed, they are away from the window and do not know the weather outside. They have been inside for a while. When these individuals see someone entering the building, those entering could be evidence of the weather outside. If they enter the building with dripping umbrellas, wet raincoats, or were caught in the rain without any protection, the people inside may not need to ask the weather outside.

Another scenario is possible. People are in a room without windows. Individuals walk in saying they just entered the building. Those entering are not wet, because they saw the rain but ran fast enough to enter the building without getting wet. They then enter the room of people and tell them it is raining outside. Usually, this statement is sufficient to notify the people already in the room that it is raining outside. People inside the room do not need to scrutinize the statement about it raining; they do not have to apply a theory of truth. They accept the individuals' statement that rain is occurring outside.

Stop and think. How often during the day does the average or almost any person accept as true something that another says? Probably 90 percent of what people say, almost any part of a typical or atypical conversation, involves one person making a statement and the other accepting it as true. That is normal.

Someone has made an intriguing statement along these lines regarding metaphysics and truth. The expression is about the relation between positivism with implications about analytic thought. However, we can apply it to theories of truth. The statement is that positivists and many analytics always objectify or analyze and never start to live; while existentialists always live and almost never stop to analyze. Put in terms of inflation and deflation, inflation-only always inquires and seeks truth while never living a deflated life, whereas deflation-only always lives and accepts statement but never stops to seek truth.

For ethics, we are ethical when we use theories of truth as needed.

STUDY QUESTIONS

- Explain the difference between inflation and deflation, in terms of police investigating a crime, and someone coming into a building folding a wet umbrella and themselves being very wet.

- Explain the difference between a teacher telling a student he or she had lots of errors and shortcomings in an assignment, and you asking someone directions in a building or city and their giving you those directions.

INFLATION-DEFLATION DUALISM

Inflation-deflation dualism means that each term in the twofold theme occurs at a separate place and time. Times exist for each or both. However, we cannot and must not pin down the time or time and place for each. Individuals ought not to restrict inflation to one time of the day and deflation to another time of the day. They cannot and ought not to limit inflation to one day, two days, or any combination of days and deflation to the remaining days of the week.

Unfortunately, inflation-deflation dualism restricts each view of truth theories to specific times, days, and so on. This, of course, does not occur in reality. Philosophers do not behave like that. Typically, they use theories of truth if they are not deflationists. Most philosophers believe in theories of truth, and thus inflation, as an important field in philosophy. I am including inflation-deflation dualism only because I wish to show that this perspective is potentially a logical element in discussing inflation and deflation. This dualism, unrealistic as it may be, is simply an implication of what could happen.

A phenomenological approach to resolving inflation-deflation dualism is possible. It would mean reintroducing inflation, or objectivity, into deflation, or human interaction. That approach would signal a more humanizing view of truth. Truth is generally the acceptance of statements instead of ongoing or exclusively analytic methods to verify what people say.

STUDY QUESTION

- Predict how life would be if police investigations occurred only during a certain time and place, and normal communications requiring no need for truth theories or verifications occurred only during other times and places.

DEFLATION POSTMODERNISM

This option says inflation is only a function of deflation. The position of inflation as a function of deflation may also be deflation-only. The inflation-only thinker sees as valid the theories of truth in virtually all instances, and as the only way to deal with truth. On the other hand, the deflation-only philosopher sees theories of truth as useless during almost any time.

To the deflation-only thinker, a "theory of" truth is merely a function of deflation, of accepting a statement as true without inquiry. These thinkers do not see context. They do not distinguish between a criminal situation, requiring analysis to prove guilt, and someone entering a building and simply stating that it is raining.

Deflation-only or deflation-alone is dangerous and defied common sense. The serious deflationist seems to insist on accepting as valid nearly every statement. That can lead to danger. I cannot accept as true that midnight is the same as midday. A news item saying presidential candidate A is correct and qualified must be reconciled with another news item denouncing the same candidate as unqualified, indeed a menace to society. One of the two news reports is wrong. Perhaps both are true only in some partial sense.

If philosophy is inquiry into whether something is true and valid, whether something is real or unreal, deflation-only truth gets away from the love of wisdom. Yes, if I am in a room without windows and do not know the weather outside, I can believe as true someone entering the building and telling me it is raining. They may have entered the building immediately before the rain came. This would have ensured that they are dry.

However, if that same person tells me the president of the United States is visiting the city of Chicago in a week, I ought to check this out in case the individual misread or misunderstood something.

We are ethical when we never use theories of truth but believe only in deflation.

STUDY QUESTIONS

- Predict a world in which no statement required verification through a theory of truth.

- How would intelligence agencies and government policy makers do their work if they believed only in deflation theory?

- How would police departments and other law enforcement do their work if they practiced only deflation theory?

TRUTH: CHANGE AND STABILITY C.II

TRUTH CHANGE MONISM

Theories of truth change relations constantly. Their interpretations and levels of credibility change always. Do we need theories of truth? Or is deflation the only answer? Once deflation enters the picture, are we to jettison correspondence and coherence or determine some combination of theories and deflation?

The more complex a society, the greater the changes in the when and how of theories of truth and deflation of those theories. Theories of truth are needed in police work. But when laws regarding crime, criminality, mental illness, and freedom are constantly changing, then changes will keep occurring in what constitutes objective reality, for correspondence theory is required.

If police must decide whether a suspect's statements are consistent with those of what the officers believe or know, changing laws may impact on the nature and legitimacy of the officers' beliefs. A suspect may say she behaved in a certain way, and this is legal or ethical. The officer's beliefs that such behavior is ethical or legal may need to change as the law changes.

Similarly, the officers' views that some behavior is unethical or illegal may require change depending on what the changing laws demand. Coherence theory, then, may be more simplistic than the theory suggests. The theory needs to take account of cultural changes.

We are ethical if we change from one truth theory to another constantly or for the sake of change.

STUDY QUESTION

- Predict daily life if more and more statements occurred that require inflation theory.

TRUTH CHANGE PHENOMENOLOGY

Theories of truth change as needed. They do not change as an end in itself. Cultures change. But is this change taking stability into account? As Kant (1987) might say, truth change without stability is blind, and truth stability without change is empty.

Computer science sees change almost every day. But some people may complain that the changes are too quick and often irrelevant. They seek more stability. Someone can make a statement about a computer while learning the hardware or software. He then learns that a new system is developed. The truth of his statement is invalid because the objective reality to which it would correspond has changed. New computer software or hardware requires that our statements be changed. But many people object that those changes are unneeded.

Embodied computer software and hardware changes are those that occur as needed. A newer piece of software is not necessarily better.

Newer laws are not necessarily better. A statement about what is legal might need to change because a new law exists. But embodied legislation is lawmaking taking into account that the newer policy must be humane and of benefit to society or the local community.

We are ethical by changing ethical theories as needed. We find that the ethical theory we hold relative to truth theories is wrong.

STUDY QUESTION

- Predict daily life if we had an increasing number of situations that require inflation and deflation.

TRUTH STABILITY-CHANGE DUALISM

Theories of truth are stable at one point, then constantly change in another time and place. Imagine that theories of truth, and deflation, change frequently in one place or culture and remain static in another society. Individuals unprepared for the differences could experience culture shock going from stability to change, or the reverse.

TRUTH STABILITY POSTMODERNISM

Inflation and deflation never change. Monks and hermits speak only truth, and speak little. People in society generally never change their need for theories of truth, or they may start and always want deflation.

Never changing a truth theory or deflation is ethical. Changing from one theory to another is unethical.

STUDY QUESTIONS

- Explain the type of world where almost no new situations could occur that require either inflation or deflation.
- Rethinking the above point, how comfortable would you be in that kind of world? Explain possible types of society today exemplifying stability-only.

TRUTH: PROBLEM AND PERSON C.III

As people consider truth in terms of inflation, deflation, or a combination, problems will occur. When do we deal with these problems? Is it ethical to be alert and react to solve truth problems after they occur? Are we ethical as we prevent them before they occur? Does ethics mean ignoring and reacting to solve truth problems after they happen? Is it ethical to deny the truth problems?

TRUTH PROBLEM MONISM

We are alert and react to solve problems of inflation and deflation after they occur. People wait until a crisis in order to then solve a problem of which circumstances will demand verification and which will allow individuals to accept a truth devoid of validation theory.

We can have events at schools, churches, and other places. Only after attendees get confused as to where and how to register do those in power react. And they are prepared to react, posting signs and assigning monitors to help solve people's problems and answer questions.

TRUTH PROBLEM PHENOMENOLOGY

People try to prevent inflation and deflation problems before these occur. For events, along with positing signs with information, institutions can send out material notifying those who will attend of how to proceed when entering the event. These informational messages can be posted online. For Kant (1987), a truth problem without a person is blind, and a truth person without a problem is empty.

TRUTH PROBLEM DUALISM

Individuals ignore problems of inflation and deflation at one time and then react to solve them after they occur.

When do we demand validation of a statement, and when do we accept something as true? If I ask a stranger about the location of a street, and he or she answers with some confidence, I am not about to question the person or seek further verification. Deflation enters. No need exists for correspondence or consistency theories.

However, when police at the local, county, state, or federal level arrest someone, the person is a suspect until proven guilty through evidence. The arresting officers cannot simply take the person to court without evidence of guilt. Correspondence theory kicks in. Coherence theory can also be used. Is the suspect's statement consistent with what the police know as reality?

TRUTH PROBLEM POSTMODERNISM

People deny that problems exist with inflation and deflation. This can be a very dangerous attitude. Denied problems might mean not believing that a process can present a serious problem. Event parking at an institution holding a dinner can become a serious matter. If there are two or more driving lanes, one of which is a longer way to the event parking, officials can deny that a problem exists. If problems occur with driving toward the event parking area and officials deny these issues, some very angry attendees may express their feelings.

STUDY QUESTIONS

- How does alert-reactive problem solving in truth theories exemplify a world of unending statements requiring verification?
- Predict a society and communications where we can prevent problems in inflation and deflation.
- Explain possible problems in society with ignorance-reaction or truth problem dualism in inflation and deflation.
- Explain what could result if we deny problems in inflation and deflation.

CHAPTER FOUR

TRUTH THEORY REALITY:

CORRESPONDENCE AND CONSISTENCY

KEYWORD

theodicy: A part of theology in which we attempt to justify the ways of God to people.

Correspondence theory: Statements must correspond to an objective reality.

Consistency theory: Statements need only cohere with each other and one's beliefs.

Inside inflation, truth theory reality involves correspondence and consistency ideas. What I call truth theory reality involves theories of truth we find in traditional philosophy. A statement is not sufficient to be true when we hear or see it. Traditional theories of truth demand that the statement requires analysis justification or proof.

The major theories are those seeking an objective reality with which we compare the statement, and a view of consistency among statements.

CORRESPONDENCE AND COHERENCE D.I

TRUTH THEORY CORRESPONDENCE MONISM

Truth-validity reality, correspondence-only is truth-analysis monism. Truth-validity monism says this derivative reality is totally reducible to correspondence atoms. Correspondence theory-only is to see or hear a statement and then seek facts that correspond to that statement. We read that the White House is in the District of Columbia. The next and perhaps final step is to research that statement, looking in the dictionary, encyclopedia, or online to find the location of the White House. This is part of inflation theory. The statement about the White House is insufficient. This situation requires proof or evidence that corresponds to the statement.

Truth, according to correspondence theory, is that aspect of inflation theory in which a statement must correspond to an objective reality. Correspondence-only denotes the traditional correspondence theory of truth.

Aristotle (McKeown 1966), Aquinas (Clark 1972), Russell (2017), give us the correspondence theory of truth. These thinkers claim that statements are truth if they correspond to an objective reality, which is to say, facts independent of the thinker. This is an empirical approach. But empiricism has a flaw. Facts can deceive us. Stephen E. Ambrose (1998) writes how the Allies (England, United States, and European countries) deceived Adolph Hitler with "facts" before the Normandy Invasion. The Allied invaded Normandy to defeat Hitler, but fooled him by thinking we would attack through either Scandinavia or Calles, France.

The facts, while central to a correspondence theory, are to be carefully analyzed for their validity. Even if they "correspond" to truth, are they deceiving us? Hitler believed the United States would attack. And he asserted that we would do so through France. When he noticed the fact that the Allies dropped what appeared to be military equipment in Calles, Hitler took this "fact" to mean empirical justification or correspondence that an invasion would be through a place other than Normandy.

Or take police work. A criminal meets what he or she sees as a fact, a person wanting to help commit a crime. Unknown to the criminal is that the person is an undercover police officer, FBI, or other agent. Just as empirical evidence can be a setup, or any other form of deception, correspondence theories of truth have the major flaw that perception can be wrong. A problem in police work is the imposter. Someone can come to your home, in a police uniform, and show credentials. The facts are that you see a uniform and credentials. Unknown to you, the individual is impersonating a law officer.

TRUTH THEORY CORRESPONDENCE PHENOMENOLOGY

This theory argues that truth means seeking an objective reality corresponding with statements but that these statements also ought to be consistent with each other and our beliefs. Later in this chapter I will discuss theodicy consistency and theodicy inconsistency. An embodied correspondence theory could require that of five statements, one of them must correspond with objective reality and be coherent with what we already believe. Kant (1987) would argue that correspondence without coherence is blind, and coherence without correspondence is empty.

Correspondence phenomenology, or embodied, would involve the weather being what people term "drizzling." Someone tells me that it is drizzling or very spotty with raindrops here and there. I go outside and notice it is cloudy and apparently drizzling. I feel a raindrop or two, nothing really wet. But, clouds and apparent drizzling would also need to cohere with my idea of drizzling and raindrops falling. When people believe it is drizzling, some wear hats or open umbrellas, while others walk with their heads uncovered. Weather can be as subjective as objective, as cohering to our idea of rainy weather as much as corresponding to objective drizzling.

CORRESPONDENCE-CONSISTENCY DUALISM

This position in inflation theory means that correspondence and coherence theories are not necessarily either/or. Life or truth is not either the correspondence of statements with objective reality or the consistency of verbal expressions. For this dualism, truth can involve correspondence at one specific time and consistency at another time.

Ricoeur (1966) would say that we overcome the correspondence-consistency dualism by reintroducing correspondence objectivity into coherent subjectivity. Statements need to correspond to an objective reality. Yet they must be meaningful and coherent to the person with a broader view of reality than possible in a certain situation. A person can say it is raining, and I am inside a building and cannot see a cloud in the sky. Being inside a building prevents an individual from seeing a cloud immediately above the home, office, or other structure in which the person is standing.

CONSISTENCY POSTMODERNISM

Consistency theory-only involves some complex issues. Five statements need to be consistent or cohere with each other, without someone appealing to correspondence with objective reality. If the statements are consistent, however, they can continue to not correspond to objective reality.

An example of coherence theory-only is the following: (1) Chicago is a big city, (2) over 1 million people live there, (3) Chicago is by Lake Michigan, and (4) Chicago is a city in the state of Illinois. Each of those four statements is true and corresponds to an objective reality. Ironically, "coherence theory" is a misleading term. Because one of the statements must correspond to objective reality, coherence theory is only overwhelmingly dependent on consistency. It is not totally dependent just on coherence.

For example, the following statements are coherent, but at least one does not correspond to objective reality: (1) Chicago is a very small town, (2) Chicago is by Lake Michigan, (3) Chicago has railroads, and (4) Chicago is in the Midwest. The second, third, and fourth statements correspond to objective reality. The first one is wrong.

Consistency theory-only also can have theological or philosophical implications. People need consistency in life. We see evil and ask why it exists. People notice illness, crime, a bad day, and so on, and ask why do these negative things occur? Religious or theological individuals might debate why God allows bad things to happen, especially to good people. Rabbi Harold S. Kushner, for example, writes the book When Bad Things Happen to Good People (2004).

Brand Blanshard (2004) proposes coherence or consistence theory. For him, a statement is true when consistent with a set of beliefs we already have. However, the beliefs we have can be wrong or outdated. A person can believe most people in big cities are criminals, or that most neighborhoods are so safe you can walk down the street and trust everyone. A belief can be outdated. Bus drivers in 2018 do not necessarily know as much about travelling around different bus routes, as they did during the 1950s.

STUDY QUESTIONS

- Explain how correspondence theory might involve wrong facts.
- How would you discuss correspondence theory embodied?
- In what way is coherence theory a subset of correspondence theory?

CONSISTENCY THEORY COMPARES WITH THEODICY

Where coherence theory demands that statements fit together, theodicy holds an answer to whether we can accept what appears to us as incoherence. Theodicy is the attempt to justify the ways of God to human beings. The theodicy answers that what we see as negative is only our perception. God, according to theodicy and a consistency theory-only, acts in mysterious ways. Thus, if we witness illness, our reaction can clearly be one of disappointment. Illness is among the many things in life that are incoherent, inconsistent with what we wish. If our statements are "I am ill," "God has a plan for," and "I am not really ill," these are all consistent with each other. They may also be true, according to a theodicy-coherent theory. My illness is not so much an unfortunate state of health but a plan that God has, unknown to me at this time.

Theodicy responds that something good is ultimately going to happen. Our visit to the doctor will help heal us. In the healing process, we will become stronger and better persons. We want and seek coherence in life, not incoherence. Illness and many other problems are often a matter of perception. We witness what appears to us as something incoherent with our expectation in life. Yet in the end, things will turn out to be coherent as we become better persons.

Illness and other problems are generally events that we do not perceive as corresponding to an objective reality that we want. Negative statement such as "I am sick" or "I have been fired" may well correspond to objective reality but are inconsistent with what we may want in life. According to theodicy, we should not worry or panic when witnessing coherent statements that express negative things.

In view of theodicy's probable answer to negative things or statements in life, philosophers in what I call inflation theory may well one day develop a theodicy-incoherent, or theodicy-coherent theory of truth. Statements would be true whether coherent or not. Time is the factor. Statements may be incoherent now but become coherent in context at a much later time due to God's will. We would see in the future the benefits of current theological or philosophical life inconsistencies. The statements are short term or currently incoherent, do not make sense, or fail to satisfy our need for immediate joy. Theodicy coherence could mean that those statements will make sense in time.

The religious orientation makes coherence theory tricky. Two statements, "I am very ill" and "God has blessed and will continue to bless and heal me," may sound very much like incoherence. The individual says he or she is ill. That generally is negative. How can it be a blessing? But the individual claims that God has blessed him or her through illness. That attitude can denote that the sickness is a blessing. To most people, ill is never a blessing and is inconsistent with the love of a deity. According to the religious person, something more is occurring.

Jacques Maritain has suggested that atheism may be "religious illiteracy" (Munson 1968, vii). The individual denying God or God's blessings claims not to see God. But that attitude of not seeing God might be questioned by the religious thinker. The religious thinker looks at illness, or any shortcoming and negativity, and believes she is seeing the whole instead of the part.

Experience or training and experience play a role in any literacy. The rookie received training. This acquaints and prepares the new kid on the block for the job ahead. But experience brings about a literacy even more. Someone on the job after five, ten, or more years of experiences has developed an instinct to "see" what others lacking the experience fail to see.

A religious person "sees" divine, theodicy coherence in the long run. What the nonreligious individual perceives as a wrong or a misfortune may well be, according to the religious person, a short-term perception of the bad. The religious individual might compare the apparent incoherence with financial investments. Investing money is always an act of "giving away" the funds. Investors take their money and put it into an investment. In the short term, they are "losing," or no longer having, the money.

But perception is not always correct. The temporary loss is an apparent lessening of one's money. In the long term, investing money means that coherence comes into play. Invest the money now, "physically lose it," and in the long-term, down the road, the investor receives a profitable return.

As the investor talks with a banker or investment counselor, the later explains the money situation to the former. The investor goes from illiteracy to literacy. This means going from perceiving incoherence (money lost) to the perception of long-term coherence (money will return in greater amounts).

STUDY QUESTIONS

- How does theodicy of culture deal with incoherence in life?
- How do you feel about Jacques Maritain's notion of religious illiteracy?

COHERENCE THEORY MAY BE FLAWED

A problem with coherence-only theory is that one of its statements has to correspond to objective reality. At least one statement must correspond to objective reality in order for the others and it to be valid. The question might be the nature of the objective reality.

If a religious person appeals to God, someone familiar with correspondence theory validity for coherence theory might be skeptical. We generally wonder if an appeal to God in coherence theory involves a statement corresponding to an objective reality. An objective reality needs to be objectively and real. Many people will deny that God or spirituality are objective reality.

For a religious individual to say an illness is a blessing therefore presents a problem for the nonbeliever. God or any spirituality—anything not material, physical, or natural—does not seem to constitute objectivity. Theologians of culture might disagree.

Theology of culture is a scholarly pursuit. It is certainly not a topic that the general public regularly discusses. Most uneducated and even educated individuals are probably unaware of theology of culture, or the religious dimensions of the secular. Even the most religious individuals do not normally refer in conversation to theologians of culture.

Yet religious people are doing or believing approximately what the theologian of culture intends. The religious person is saying that culture has a spiritual basis. Any human activity regarding wholeness, health, or general theory can reveal God. Any human action or situation that does good or is "productive" can be a blessing from the divine. If something helps us become whole, it is potentially or actually holy. Thus, secularity, illness, and being fired from a job can reveal the whole in the long term.

Holidays may be secular, but as days of rest, as wholeness, reveal the holy. Days devoted to work reveal the holy when they produce wholeness in goods and services. Those of holidays reveal the holy as people pause to think about and put into holistic perspective the production of goods and services.

Coherence theory may have a flaw. It parallels human factors engineering's warning against the user-too-friendly design. For consistency theory, a statement is true if it coheres with beliefs we have. However, this tends to mean coherence for the sake of coherence. Coherence theory appears to suggest that our beliefs are valid. I believe that New York has less crime than Chicago, because my views of Chicago tell me that it is a relatively dangerous city. The idea of a safer New York coheres with my beliefs about Chicago. But what if my beliefs about Chicago are wrong? Then the coherence is wrong.

Coherence theory does not question our beliefs, only whether statements are consistent with what we entertain. What if our beliefs are wrong? What if the statements we hear or read are wrong? The consistency ought not to mean that statements simply cohere with our beliefs. Our beliefs must be just, moral, ethical, and humane. If they are just and moral, then statements that do not cohere with our beliefs may well be invalid. Coherence cannot mean mechanical coherence.

STUDY QUESTIONS

- How do you deal with coherence theory saying that statements are valid if they are in line with your beliefs?
- How do you explain a link between coherence theory, your beliefs, and ethics?

CHANGE AND STABILITY D.II

Is it ethical to change the relationship between correspondence and coherence theories for the sake of change, or is stability good? Does the ethical person change the relationship as needed, embodied in stability? Dualism says we are ethical in never changing the relationship and then constantly doing so in another time or location. Stability-only says it is ethical to never change the relationship.

TRUTH THEORY CHANGE MONISM

There are always new statements coming up to validate. Life is simply ongoing, endless statements for truth theory. This could occur with increasingly complex societies. Professionals are always telling us what to do. Doctors, lawyers, financial advisors, mass transit, and other customer services workers are giving us information. We find it necessary to always check out and validate new information about new situations.

One day some friends of mine were driving me to a Chicago suburb. They followed a road map. The map showed the on- and off-ramps of an expressway as being on the opposite sides of the expressway, but across from each other. We found the off-ramp only. Searching for the on-ramp for fifteen minutes, we gave up and had to drive miles to find the on-ramp. On the return trip we decided to stay on the highway to see the location of the off-ramp. It was at least a mile away from the on-ramp. The map was wrong. With constant change in either the maps or highway constructions, authorities can accidentally give out the wrong information.

TRUTH THEORY CHANGE PHENOMENOLOGY

There are needed statements, not just ongoing or endless statements for validation. The need for validation of truth is not something that occurs all the time. If this were true, people would need to pause and seek correspondence or coherence theories constantly. Imagine life if we needed validation each time someone spoke to us or we read something. Kant (1987) would say truth theory change without stability is empty, and truth theory stability without change is empty.

Integrating truth inflation (correspondence and coherence) with deflation parallels integration of positivism with existentialism, and analytic with idiomatic hermeneutics.

TRUTH VALIDITY DUALISM

There is a time for validation and a time for no validation. In its strictest form, truth-analysis dualism means that people divide time into two distinct, clear-cut ways. Certain days of the week, times of a given day, and so on are times when we expect to use theories of truth. Or we expect to use the theories when talking with certain people or dealing with certain events. Theories would not be necessary when dealing with other people or other circumstances.

TRUTH THEORY STABILITY POSTMODERNISM

No new statements exist for validation. Correspondence and consistency theories always have the same meaning. Their relationship continues the same throughout time and place.

STUDY QUESTIONS

- Explain your reaction if you heard statements that corresponded to an objective reality that were contrary to some of your beliefs.
- How would you react if statements did not cohere with your beliefs?
- How does theodicy strike you as an ethical system of truth?

TRUTH ANALYSIS: PROBLEM AND PERSON D.III

Four ethical options occur here. It is ethical to (1) be alert and react in solving truth analysis problems, (2) prevent problems of correspondence and coherence, (3) ignore and then react to solve truth analysis problems, and (4) deny such problems.

TRUTH THEORY PROBLEM MONISM

People are alert and react to problems of correspondence and coherence theories after these issues occur. We believe that both theories will be needed almost every time we hear or read something. Whether these theories are mutually exclusive or can occur in some combination is a matter for which we wait until it occurs.

TRUTH THEORY PROBLEM PHENOMENOLOGY

Individuals believe that problems regarding truth theories could be avoided. These problems are not inherent in life and can be prevented instead of merely solved. We study situations where the two theories can be used by themselves or in combination. If we might confront situations where we need correspondence or coherence theories, perhaps we can provide information to the individuals before they find themselves seeking the truth. Kant (1987) would say a truth analysis problem without a person is blind, and a truth analysis person without a problem is empty.

An institution of learning can make available information about its faculty, students, and other aspects. This data can be posted somewhere as officially verified. Thus, if someone seeks validity of a statement or answer to a question, the posted data is objective reality validating or corresponding to the answer to the question.

Our beliefs also ought to be realistic and consistent with social justice. This regards coherence theory where the statement is truth if consistent with our beliefs. What are our beliefs? An individual who is biased against certain individuals, groups, and so on has a set of unwarranted beliefs. To say that a statement is true if it coheres with our beliefs is inadequate if our beliefs are unjust. To prevent having to reject statements or situations inconsistent with unjust beliefs we have, perhaps we ought to change our worldview and the set of our wrong beliefs.

TRUTH THEORY PROBLEM DUALISM

This view means that two situations exist. We initially ignore problems we might have with correspondence and coherence theories. Then a crisis erupts, and we must react to solve the problem.

To avoid this time dualism, we ought to continually assess our beliefs as to be justified. This means being informed of our neighborhood and other neighborhoods. Information helps us prevent problems in neighborhoods later. Reacting from ignorance to sudden problem solving for truth is counterproductive.

TRUTH THEORY PROBLEM POSTMODERNISM

This situation in dealing with problem denial is very dangerous. People at the outset deny the existence of problems in truth finding. They claim problems of validity, of information, and of truth do not exist.

Everything they hear or read is true when these align with what they believe. Everything they hear or read is wrong and cannot be true if it differs from their mind-set. Nothing new can occur that would invalid or update what they know.

STUDY QUESTION

- Explain how problem prevention in the correspondence-coherence issue can be better than alert-reactive problem solving.

EXERCISE

The following exercise, when completed, is to become a small chapter.

1. Inside deflation is acceptance reality, involving social and biological deflation.

CHAPTER FIVE

PREDICTIVE REALITY:
DETERMINISM AND FREEDOM

KEYWORDS

predestination: The theological position that God has decided who goes to heaven and who does not.

Bayesian: The position in statistics that something will occur based on frequency and unknowns.

frequentist: The position in statistics that something will occur based on frequency.

Inside inflation and deflation is prediction reality meaning that determinism and freedom are two separate themes. Inside metaphysics, hermeneutics, and truth is the issue of whether we are free or determined. For that matter, freedom and determinism underlie previous and remaining chapters. At one pole, if we are free, our actions express our own will and voluntary intentions. At the other extreme, if someone or something determines everything we know and do, then our accountability is near zero. Determinism and freedom are complex (Kast and Rosenzweig 1970).

Prediction in philosophy is the philosophical version of the *p*-value in statistics. What is the probability that something will occur? On the basis of data, what is the probably of predicting an event? Philosophically, is that prediction free, or is it determined? People calculating statistics routinely try to predict based on data, and they do not think of this as philosophy. For them, such prediction is simply statistical instead of involving the notion of freedom or determinism. Yet philosophers can note that both statistics and mathematics of probability are perhaps two versions of the same topic. Are we predicting voluntarily or involuntarily? Philosophical determinism denotes that prediction will come true regardless of circumstances or data; mathematics/statistics says that prediction will come true given the level of statistical probability.

Individuals can also be a combination of determinism and freedom. This means people are generally determined or free. A dualism would denote that we are free during a specific time and place and determined at another time and place. Determinism disregards, is embodied in, is distinct from, and is a function of freedom.

PREDICTION AND FREEDOM E.I

Four ethical positions exist in deterministic reality. It is ethical to (1) predict without freedom or visible hand; (2) predict with freedom; (3) have total freedom, and then have no freedom; and (4) have total freedom, or the "invisible hand." In view of our use of "invisible hand," we can refer to Paul Samuelson and William Nordhaus (2009) alone, Samuelson embodied in Milton Friedman (2002), Samuelson-Friedman dualism, and Friedman only (invisible hand).

DETERMINISM MONISM

Prediction-reality monism is prediction-only. Prediction monism says deterministic reality is totally reducible to the sum of predictable parts or atoms. Freedom and people do not count. Determinism that stands alone typically means that people, events, and animate and inanimate realities have no freedom. Someone or something controls or determines their fate completely. If something or someone controls their actions or beliefs, individuals who are victims of this determinism do not act or believe voluntarily. In that case society or any law enforcement agency cannot hold people and animate things accountable for their behavior. Karl Marx (1983) says communism is inevitable.

Even when determinism stands alone, those attempting to control or predict behavior cannot do so with total accuracy. Individuals appear minimally free to act voluntarily. Once they exercise that freedom, perfect or even near complete control is impossible. Prediction is then not totally possible. A police state may well have one of its members become a spy for the enemy, or at least continue to be dedicated to the nation but turn against the leaders in power.

Bayesian and frequentist probability or stochastics occur here. The former tries to determine probability based on frequency and unknowns. Frequency couples with an unknown that impacts on regularity. Frequentist stochastics involves only frequency. If something occurs repeatedly over time, the frequentist then assumes only that repetition. The repetition or frequency is sufficient to determine if and when an event will recur.

Bayesian determinism-alone says we determine on the basis of the past frequency plus an unknown. Frequentist determinism-alone argues that determination is on the basis of the past. In either case determinism-alone may be impossible in the real world.

A good example of the unknown or Bayesian approach may be defectors, or double agents in a police state. Toward the end of Nazism, generals in Hitler's circle attempted to assassinate him with a bomb. They failed, but their actions showed that Hitler did not and could not run a totally deterministic police state.

Another example is the former Soviet Union. Coup d'états usually removed living and healthy heads of state. The heads of state, premiers, attempted to rule with an iron fist. Yet they were human beings who did not and could not know everything that occurred in the Kremlin. They could not know that a rival group was about to succeed in throwing them out of office. Kremlin leaders were also unaware of one of their own becoming a spy for the United States. In the former Soviet Union, Oleg Penkovsky (1965) became a spy for the United States.

Philosophical determinism that is alone is akin to theological or religious predestination. Predestination says that God or the gods have determined that individuals will go to heaven or hell, probably regardless of their behavior. In predestination, however, God's actions and determination are absolute and final. The bad person may go to heaven regardless of his or her evil deeds. A good person could go to hell regardless of good work.

Deterministic monism tells us that people are not free, and this leads to the issue of personal accountability. If environment, genetics, and any other factor have compelled someone to commit a crime, then can society punish the "criminal"? Is the individual really a criminal? This is the reason that we have the word "penitentiary," which derives from "penitence." If the individual was free and chose to do wrong, he or she needs to do penitence instead of being incarcerated. Only if the person was under determinism and therefore not free can we excuse the person for his or her actions.

This is where ergonomics enters. A human factors approach to criminal justice says check to see if the person's biological or environmental makeup forced them to commit a crime. If so, then change the environment, and if possible, the biological heritage. If a modified, redesigned gene or environment could prevent crime, then ergonomics is correct and can prevent or minimize future crime.

In deterministic monism, we can predict an outcome with virtually complete certainty. Human freedom does not exist. Very likely freedom within nature does not exist. All of nature and human beings behave in ways that are controlled by physical and chemical laws.

Deterministic monism or determinism-only means that natural phenomena will occur, and unless our intervention to prevent these is also determined, individuals cannot stop the occurrence. Occurrence of phenomena is independent of us. We have no control over events.

Determinism-only influences the nature-nurture debate. Both nature and nurture means that something determines the individual's behavior, future, and appearance. Nature means that individuals' genetic makeup determines what they will become, what they are. This is determination by nature, or natural determinism. Nurture, on the other hand, denotes environmental, social, interpersonal determinism. The person grew up in a good or bad family, and the parents and surroundings played the decisive role.

Deterministic monism provides grounds for the next chapter, regarding state origins reality. There, I discuss communitarianism and contract theory. Communitarians say that the state is natural and determines our identity. Freedom has little to nothing to do with our political or national identity. Communitarianism will be seen as communitarian monism. One reality exists, and it is the state.

STUDY QUESTIONS

- Explain situations in your life that justify Bayesian and frequentist theories.
- Why is a police state where no one becomes a traitor probably impossible?

- Predict how you would feel if you were destined to be an egoist, a utilitarian, a believer in God, duty bound, virtuous, or a believer in natural law ethics.

DETERMINISM PHENOMENOLOGY

Determinism phenomenology means predicting interacts with freedom. Prediction-only controls people, events, and animate and inanimate realities. Something or someone determines and predicts some of their behavior at times or every time. Vladimir Lenin (2013) tells us that individuals are responsible for revolutionary activities to bring about communism.

Politically, socially, and culturally, the police state has yet to occur where prediction is absolutely possible. As mentioned earlier, virtually every police state witnesses the defector, or member who turns against it as a spy for the enemy. Kant (1987) would say prediction without freedom is blind, and freedom without prediction is empty.

Theological predestination faces modification in determinism embodied. God does not predestine anyone to heaven or hell. If God and people are working together, God takes the person's deeds or lack thereof into account. From goodwill comes good. The evil will suffer. Of course, this does not occur in the real world. Evil men and women do well, and good people appear to suffer. Theologically, the feeling is that wrongdoers will eventually see punishment.

In criminal justice, deciding whether punishment or counseling is best can be tricky and complex. If a criminal's wrongdoing is a combination of nature (determinism), nurture (determinism), and freedom, then the criminal act is due to some things beyond the person's control and to other reasons within their freedom.

In social, political, and economic justice, two things occur. One is injustice, phenomenology, dualism, and only justice.

Inside phenomenology, justice can mean end-state alone (Rawls), end-state embodied, and process justice alone (Nozick, 1974). If phenomenology is correct, we must, as Riceour would say, reintroduce Rawls (1971) into Nozick (1974). That is, Nozick (1974) calls for rights and freedom, Rawls (1971) argues for state duty and equality. Rawls (1971) calls for end-state justice, where the goal is crucial. How we reach the goal is not critical. This seems like Kant's duty ethics, where we do our duty regardless of consequences to us. Nozick (1964) insists on historical or process justice, where how we achieve the goal is paramount. Phenomenologically, a systematic, Ricoeurian (1966) and ergonomic approach to freedom and determinism would involve rights or freedom friendly equality. Put another way, Ricoeur would want us to reintroduce end-state justice into process or historical justice. Rights and duties typically imply two mutually different items. But a state or individual impose duties on individuals too much or simply wrongly relative to rights, enough relative to rights, and too little relative to rights. Rights are the limits to which duties are imposed. In human factors language, the specialist designs duties by taking rights into account.

When we integrate freedom with determinism, the nature and nurture debate becomes more complex. Nature and nurture now must take into account more than the things over which the person has no control. Genes and nurturing social environment involve determinism, but free will can enter as embodiment. In determinism embodied, or embodied determinism, a person's behavior, future, problems, and all else depend on a complex interplay between things over which the individual cannot control and those he or she can and must regulate.

Regarding state origins, determinism embodied means embodied communitarianism. This integrates the state as somewhat natural but with acknowledgments for personal freedom and contract. In this sense, individuals are deterministically a member of the state but freely understand that they can abandon their citizenship and go elsewhere if they so choose.

DETERMINISTIC-EMBODIED ETHICS CAN MEAN THE FOLLOWING:

Determinism and freedom underlie egoism, utilitarianism, followers of God or of natural law, of duty, and of virtue.

STUDY QUESTIONS

- Compare predestination with a theological view that no one is destined for heaven or hell.
- Explain a criminal justice view that most or virtually all criminals are totally a product of their genes or environment.

DETERMINISM-FREEDOM DUALISM

Dualism in determinism and freedom means that people, events, and objects are free at some times and predictable at other times. These times are not random. It is not the same as saying people are free at some point and determined at another point. Dualism means that someone or something is able to totally control individuals during a specific, given time and place.

FREEDOM POSTMODERNISM

Total freedom may be almost as impossible as complete determinism. This is freedom-only. Rioters may succeed in destroying a city or organization that gives them the freedom to run through streets and hallways and to tear down buildings and other tangible aspects of authority. However, those same rioters will need to know how to swim if they fall into a river, the sea, a lake, or other body of water. The rioters might eventually determine a new authority for a group or city, but they will drown if unable to negotiate the water. Life is not totally free.

Anarchists seek the freedom to change governments, business, and national identities. They do not seek absolute freedom such as being able to violate nature, including flying by themselves by defying gravity. Determinism-alone seems parallel to the black hole, sucking in all things around it. Freedom-alone appears parallel to antigravity in the absolute sense if matter in the universe simply falls apart. Then planets, stars, galaxies, and solar systems are all in danger of dissolving.

If determinism-only, or deterministic monism, denotes that we are unaccountable for our acts, then freedom-only means the opposite. Freedom-only, determinism as a mere function of freedom, leads to nature and nurture meaning little. Freedom-only is a stance that nothing independent of us determines our life.

This has biological implications. Our genes, DNA, and other aspects of our biochemical, biophysical existence are under our control. We are free to do as we please despite our biological makeup.

Freedom-only also has major impacts socially. Bad or good parents, schools, and other social organizations have little if any influence on our future. Everything we think and do is our decision.

STUDY QUESTIONS

- Predict what happens in a society where determinism and freedom coexist.

- Explain what could happen if everyone was totally free.

DETERMINISM-FREEDOM CHANGE AND STABILITY E.II

PREDICTION CHANGE MONISM

The need to change predictions occurs daily with more and more things to predict. Monastery life has almost nothing to predict. At the other extreme, a highly technological society where scheduling conflicts occur daily, technology abounds, and human life is "on the go" will have prediction as almost a daily requirement.

No end exists as to things to predict. People need to predict the weather, whether their mobile and desktop computers will function, and if the car will start in the morning. At work, will the photocopier work? If I go grocery shopping, will there be long lines?

If determinism and change occur constantly, this impacts on the nature-nurture issue. Nature and nurture are aspects of things over which the individual affected by them has no control. If society changes for the sake of change whether nature or nurture is more important, we may be looking at the wrong cause of behavior. Greater freedom means that individuals can transform themselves and their environments, resulting in more accountability from them. Less freedom denotes decreased accountability for the individual.

PREDICTION CHANGE PHENOMENOLOGY

Predictions occur and change as needed. Technologically oriented society as above in change-only may not matter if the individual is not concerned about what will or will not work during the day or night. A simpler society predicts fewer things because life is much less complicated when there are fewer devices with which to deal.

If determinism-freedom changes are embodied in stability, then we can more easily predict the relationship of freedom to determinism. Embodiment makes changes less frequent and dramatic. Freedom and determinism, the nature and nurture dilemma, becomes less volatile. Whether a criminal has control over his or her life becomes easier to decide. Combining nature and nurture can increase the chances of deciding a young person's success in life. Neither nature nor nurture alone can make predictions easy.

Ways can then be found whereby institutions worry less about their future. Economic forecasting can make investments more successful and less stressful. Determinism-freedom change embodied can result in better strategies and tactics to prevent recessions and depressions in the production and consumption of goods and services. For Kant (1987), determinism change without stability is blind, and determinism stability without change is empty.

The revolving door notion involves institutions with high turnover rates for employees, especially executives. Predictive change embodied introduces ways of sensing and predicting, avoiding the departure of good executives. If institutions, employment policies, and top management decision practices are responsible for organizational instability and predictions, then changes toward stability will be welcome.

Anthropologists talk of species adapting to the environment. Adaptation is part of evolution. Human beings "are not programmed to behave in all the things or ways we do" (Park 2008). They are determined to the extent of being programmed, free or embodied to the point where individual decide their own fate and create culture.

DUALISTIC DETERMINISM-FREEDOM

Freedom and determinism are two distinct realities. Imagine living in the United States or perhaps London and then traveling to a developing country lacking 90 percent of the modern conveniences and technology. That is a dualistic experience. An infinite number of things exist to predict in America; almost nothing except the weather may exist for prediction in the simplistic country. This is especially true, and the dualism becomes more stark, if we compare Chicago or New York City with, say, a monastery even in America.

A Chicagoan is more likely to worry about losing his or her job than is a monk in a monastery.

PREDICTION STABILITY POSTMODERNISM

We deny that prediction-freedom change occurs. Nothing new occurs to predict. Few things change, if any. This may be the state of existence in a monastery. Walls of the monastic life involve the most basic foods, such as rice and vegetables, and the same kinds of clothing each day. Daily activity is simplistic and contemplative, and it rejects the lifestyle of either society or highly automated culture.

STUDY QUESTION

- Compare very simple and increasingly technological cultures requiring predictions.

PREDICTION PROBLEMS AND PERSON E.III

PREDICTION PROBLEM MONISM

When do people decide about determinism and freedom? At what point in time do they understand the meanings and positions of determinism and freedom? Alert-reactive prediction means that individuals are alert and react to understanding those positions after a problem occurs. They witness or experience and wish thereafter to solve the problem. Some citizens of a relatively free society might be alert and react to laws by a new leader who is creating a strong centralized state by eliminating most freedoms in the country.

People in a very highly technological society will be alert to solve problems after crises occur in crime, tornadoes, illness, and so on. However, a monk living in a monastery has little to predict. The more complex and technologically, scientifically advanced the society, the more the people tend toward alertness and reaction.

Employees worry about their pensions and are alert and react to having no money. Communities show concern regarding crime. Nations seek to predict a hostile nation's behavior toward them.

Prediction is crucial as society increases in complexity. People are alert and react after their predictions are right or wrong. If the predictions are correct, they may attempt to refine these. If the predictions are wrong, a crisis forces them to seek to understand why the prediction failed.

People will attempt to predict everything from the most serious to the most trivial. Indeed, the trivial may not be unimportant to them. A sports game outcome, who wins, who loses, could be as crucial to the gambler or betting person as a presidential election.

PREDICTION PROBLEM PHENOMENOLOGY

Determining behavior completely may be impossible, but prevention would help minimize unwanted actions. Educating children and youngsters in healthy lifestyles helps determine good health in their adulthood. Kant (1987) would assert determinism problems without a person are blind, and a determinism person without problems is empty.

People in complex, technological societies have much to predict. Among them is the weather, the chances of someone becoming a success in college and in life, who will win an election, when serious disease will strike.

The more complex the society, the more many individuals will try to control the outcome. With more and more variables occurring, individuals who have a stake in the outcome will try to control the variables as much as they can. Newer technology and better mathematics and physics become tools for people having an impact on events. The Bayesian-frequentist debate continues regarding statistics and prediction (Audi 1997).

These newer technologies and scientific advances also pose greater nontechnical issues of control. Knowing the human genome, knowing more about human behavior, force some people to wonder about how to control and predict that behavior. This, of course, brings ethics into play. Is controlling or genetically engineering human beings ethical?

PREDICTION PROBLEM DUALISM

This is also dualistic prediction. People ignore predicting something, then after a crisis, they attempt to predict that the event will occur. Individuals ignore the danger of muds until they deforest mountains. We ignore floodplains and build homes where flooding could occur, until heavy rains and thunderstorms bring floods.

PREDICTION PROBLEM POSTMODERNISM

Denial prediction involves ignoring a problem even after it strikes as a crisis. Individuals may continue to deny that the problem exists or involves them. If global warming is not occurring or not under our control such that we can stop it, those warning us are wrong. However, if the planet is warming and the heating up is under our control, some people will ignore and then continue to deny the problem, whatever the consequences are for them.

STUDY QUESTIONS

- Predict the results of laws where government tracks individuals' reading habits.
- Compare corporate profiling of buying habits and governmental profiling of people's reading habits.

CHAPTER SIX

SOCIAL ORIGINS REALITY:

COMMUNITARIAN AND CONTRACT

KEYWORDS

communitarian-only: The state alone is natural and prior to the individual's right.

Communitarian phenomenology: The state acknowledges the individual's rights.

communitarian-contract dualism: Some states are communitarian, others are only contract.

contract-only: Individual rights are natural and prior to a state. States are artificial.

Inside the determinism and freedom is social origins reality. This derived two-fold theme is of communitarian and contract. Communitarianism disregards, may be embodied in, distinct from, and a function of contract theory.

Social origins reality asks how society emerged. How did society originate? That is, is the state a natural phenomenon determining us, or are we independent persons free to choose our social context and identity? Communitarians believe the state is natural and determines our identities before we are born. We cannot change who we are. Contract theory argues that each of us is free to "determine" our identity, our social membership.

COMMUNITARIAN AND CONTRACT F.I

According to social origins' ethics, we are ethical if we are communitarian monists, communitarian embodied in contract, social origin dualists, or contract-subjectivity-only.

COMMUNITARIAN MONISM

This is communitarian-only theory. Communitarian-only is social origins reality monism. Social origin monism is communitarian structure rejecting contract reality. Social origins monism means communitarian-only is the social origin position that the state is a natural structure, independent of, purely objective, and external or prior to the members. The state is natural instead of artificial. It alone gives social, political, and cultural identity to members of the state. A society prior to the individual does not gain social meaning from the person. In communitarianism, we see the social philosophy where the state tells members they may not leave and continue to retain their identities.

Greek thinker Aristotle argued for communitarianism (McKeon 1966). Individuals cannot exist as private citizens, because each is fundamentally a social, political reality from which to derive one's individuality. Citizens have little to no input regarding their political identity. They contribute little to nothing to that state. The individual is made for the monistic Sabbath.

Ironically, sociology states that people are social beings. That would seem to make sociology an ipso facto communitarian discipline. If psychology maintains that we study people only as individuals, that appears to make the field contract theory.

COMMUNITARIAN PHENOMENOLOGY

A state that is communitarianism embodied is more than a natural society. The state tells members that they are generally members of the community, but they may contribute significantly to, and even emigrate to, another society. Members' identities are not tied to or held hostage in the state. The Sabbath and the person interrelate, and each can contribute to the other.

Contracting exists in the communitarian-embodied state. The embodied communitarian state allows individuals and groups to contract with each other for any number of reasons. They can contract to expand, diminish, or change the state's identity in some way. Citizens might change the process of naturalizing immigrants. For Kant (1987), communitarianism without contract is blind, and contract without communitarianism is empty.

Embodied communitarianism acknowledges individual rights and duties. Where communitarianism indoctrinates duty, embodied communitarianism teaches duties within the context of rights. I could refer to this situation as embodied duties. The communitarian state is a combination of natural and artificial, neither natural-alone nor artificial-alone.

Communitarianism embodied is akin to the phenomenological and Kantian perspectives. Like phenomenology, the contractor's values impact on the state. A Kantian approach (Kant 1987) means the contractor's ideas, categories, and any other logical or rational ability imposes on and organizes the objective state's identity. In both phenomenological and Kantian interpretations, the state is more than just an objective social group or nation. It is an objective social reality relatively oriented around subjective, citizenry limits and contributions.

This is akin to human factors engineering, or ergonomics. Human factors points out the reality and need for an environment: a system, airline cockpit, pencil, pen, any process, any idea that we share with people. Yet, human factors argues, the environment is more than just many different items and even people relating to each other. How we design that relationship is crucial. The environment is more than the sum of its parts. It is to be user-friendly. Thus, the communitarian embodied is a state that takes people's limits and individualities into account.

David Hume (1985) says that the state is neither communitarian nor contract. Instead, more often than we think, society originates through invasions and other violence. Readers may interpret Hume as seeing the origin of the state as relatively violent communitarianism, instead of neither communitarian nor contract. Whether as communitarianism alone, or embodied, nations attack or otherwise nonviolently take over another tribe, nation, or group of people, and the new state will have individuals see it as prior to them. Aristotle (McKeon, 1966), Charles Taylor (1985), and Hegel (2003), represent what I term nonviolent communitarianism, alone or embodied. Their view may well be simplistic. History is the history of globalization, change, and instability apparently mostly war or other violence.

STUDY QUESTIONS

- Compare how you would feel being a citizen in a communitarian-only and communitarian-embodied state.

- How is the communitarian-embodied state a more humane and complicated one?

HUMAN BEINGS AS INDIVIDUALS AND INTERRELATED

Hillel says, "If I am for myself, who am I? If I am not for myself, who will be for me?" (Hertz 1984, p. 15). These words suggest that we are both community and contract, or self. Hillel resonates with anthropologists Clyde Kluckhohn and Charles Murray (1967, p. 53), who say each person is "like all others, like some, and like no others." In other words, each person is social, semisocial, and individual. Charles Taylor argues that the self is relational; persons connect with each other (Taylor, 1985).

Within the state, the communitarian individual contributes personal ideas and views that influence policy, ethics, economics, and other areas of life. History books can show how the citizen accepts identity from the state, pledges allegiance, but also helps refine and clarify identity and allegiance.

In human factors terms, communitarianism is to be contract-friendly. A natural state is prior to the citizen but takes into account individuals' rights and abilities regarding obedience and doing their duties. This priority considers the extent to which a state may impose laws and duties on the citizen.

Micro ergonomics is relatively easy when listing human abilities and limits. Arms, legs, height, and other physical characteristics are measurable. But human factors or ergonomics implies macro perspective also (Chapanis 1960; Adams 1989). Ergonomics notes that human beings will always be part of the technology. This means humans have a need to relate to machines and any automation. This rejects monism. But in communitarianism, taking human rights including limits and abilities into account, we face a more nuanced, complex issue.

Macro ergonomics might have many lists or rights, abilities, and limits from social, political, and economics views, even if the human being ought to influence and be influenced by the state. What are our rights? What can we say of our social limits? When do we obey and question? These require philosophical debate and involve lists that cannot be reduced to numbers.

COMMUNITARIAN-CONTRACT DUALISM

This dualism means that the world is part communitarian, part contract nations. Some of the nations are natural, others are through contract theory. That would have to mean two kinds of human nature. Some human beings are part of natural societies, while others are members of artificial societies.

CONTRACT POSTMODERNISM

"Communitarianism as function of contract" theory is my phrase. Social, political, and economic theorists call this simply contract theory. I refer to the more complex phrase for a reason. If communitarian-contract dualism and communitarianism embodied can exist even as topics of intellectual inquiry, then "communitarian" and "contract" might well be incomplete sentences or statements. Thus, traditional communitarianism means the state is natural and never part of dualism, never embodied, never contract theory. Following this idea of the communitarian, contract theory needs to say it is contract without communitarian relations.

American thinker Robert Nozick (1973) is a popular contract philosopher. Other contract theorists include Thomas Hobbes (1982), Jean-Jacques Rousseau (1968), John Locke (1993), and John Rawls (1971). They argue that individuals are free to create and generally dissolve their states. The problem with communitarianism could be the extreme structure of a state, without (much) room for innovation, emigration, or immigration. However, a contract theory has another problem. An artificial state does not believe in natural continuity. Members may create and become part of the society. On the other hand, they may, perhaps at will, decide to dissolve their contract and move away. This movement could play havoc with continuity in government, business, and other state activities.

Such action of moving away would be less serious for the state's continuity than it is when communitarianism is embodied. Leaving the contractual community is even less serious than it is from the communitarian-alone state. The embodied state can indoctrinate in members that staying is much more beneficial than leaving the group. The contractual or artificial state teaches that people are inherently individuals with rights and abilities. These rights existed before they joined, during their membership, and after they leave.

In globalization, communitarianism-alone and contract-alone might well suffer. Natural community confronts unwanted movements. Artificial communities could become too shaky. Natural communities could perceive that globalization threatens their identities and sovereignty. Contract-alone state might find globalization hastening their dissolution and threatening to change their identities too quickly, if that is possible.

Contract denotes that each community originates through contract, and this is philosophically justified. However, a broader postmodern view leads to another conclusion. Who decides how to originate a state or community? Libertarians and anarchists argue that individuals decide. But two kinds of communities can be postmodern, each kind claiming it is right.

One kind might be postmodern individualism. Individuals contract to originate the state. However, another might be powerful individuals or leaders, perhaps revolutionaries, who originate dictatorships, democracies, caste systems. This second type might be postmodern leadership. Libertarianism usually means individuals come together and negotiate the community, leaving if they feel another community is better. Each libertarian, anarchic state is thus justified. But leadership postmodernism has leaders taking over a state, or developing a democracy or a caste system. Thus, a broad postmodernism for state origin suggests that democracy, dictatorship, caste systems, and libertarianism, are all justified and good. Two leaders can contract to make a dictatorship, or any type of political community.

STUDY QUESTIONS

- Compare Hillel and anthropologists Kluckhohn and Murray regarding their views of people as individual and social.
- Predict implications of globalization for communitarian-only and contract-only.

GLOCALIZATION

Glocalization could hold an answer to the global versus local question. It combines the global and local. This could be put under communitarianism embodied. The natural state is natural and prior to its own citizens. However, the natural state in a global political, economics, and social scheme now may or may not have the choice of joining, which is to say contracting, with other natural states in the world.

What we see may be meta-state origins reality. That is, what do we mean by communitarianism and contract? The citizen can be a contractor or communitarian relative to the state's origin. But is the state, in globalization, now a megacontractor? Is the world community now prior to the communitarian state?

I have mentioned Rawls and Nozick as contract theorists. But they differ significantly as to the result of the state. Rawls (1971) says the state is end-state justice, where we need to look at the end as justice now, disregarding the process of how we got there. Nozick (1973) objects to end-state justice, seeking what he calls process justice; justice and distribution of equality must consider the process whereby justice and equality occur.

Again we see a political monism in Rawls, where the individual is for the Sabbath, and a political existentialism in Nozick, where the other extreme occurs, and the Sabbath is simply a function of the individual. Embodied justice would mean, as Ricoeur might say, reintroducing Rawls's (1971) end-state into Nozick's process justice. Thus, we achieve equality through a humane process instead of Rawls's (1971) veil of ignorance. What we need is a Kantian empirical-rational, phenomenological object-subject approach to Rawls and Nozick. For Kant, rational categories color experience; in phenomenology the subject colors the object. Thus, a Kantian position could respond to Nozick and Rawls that process justice and rights color the end-state.

STUDY QUESTIONS

- How does glocalization impact on communitarians saying the state is natural, and contract theory saying the state is artificial?

- Predict the results if the world community decides that all states are less sovereign than they think because the global view of interrelated states is prior to a given state.

COMMUNITARIAN AND CONTRACT CHANGE AND STABILITY F.II

SOCIAL ORIGIN CHANGE MONISM

Society simply adds newer members to the populations in communitarian or contract society. Communitarian may mean the nation comes first, but this implies that the nation exists.

If nations emerge but then break up (Czechoslovakia from Czech Republic and Slovak Republic, and then back after breaking up), or a Soviet republic gained independence after the USSR dissolved, then of which country is the person a natural member? Which nation or sovereign was natural? These changes in national identity become crucial for the communitarian. If a "nation" has been a colony of a foreign, say England, the member is a colonist of the natural British Empire. But if and when the colony gains independence from England, is the member now a citizen of the newly independent nation? Someone could argue that England took over a natural community through military rule, but now the colony regains its own natural identity.

Contract theory seems more volatile as to identity (Nozick 1973). Individuals freely choose to create a nation. This is an artificial community. Change can come soon, over time, or over a very long time.

SOCIAL ORIGIN CHANGE PHENOMENOLOGY

Society adds to population as needed and planned. An embodied communitarian state, if militarily powerful, can change identity voluntarily, perhaps almost never. The contract state changes, if embodied, changes only when members deem it necessary. A Kantian (1987) view says social origins change without stability is blind, and stability without change is empty.

SOCIAL ORIGINS CHANGE-STABILITY DUALISM

The people are never added until at some point they are merely added without proper processes. Communitarian society never reflects on the meaning of citizenship or national identity and never thinks about a shrinking population. Similarly, contract theory might hold to the same views of what identity means in a given voluntary, contractual community.

Then crises or problems erupt at to the meaning of national identity. Should the communitarian become more liberal, become more conservative, or remain as it has been as to what is a citizen? A contract theory nation could face the same issue, but here a difference is possible. If a contract society has remained too conservative for some members, they find change easy. They have the right to leave the conservative community for a more liberal one.

SOCIAL ORIGIN STABILITY POSTMODERNISM

Society never adds new members. The society may eventually disappear. Communitarian and contract states, if seeing stability-alone, might remain stagnant for the foreseeable future. Change may be anathema. Continuity is the watchword. Contract theory states may have in their contractual agreement to change as little as possible, if at all.

The idea of national identity, of what is a citizen, never changes. Citizenship of either communitarian or contract perspectives remains constant from the past.

STUDY QUESTIONS

- What are the implications of communitarianism if empires force independent nations to join the empire, then the empire eventually breaks up back into independent nations?

- If contract theory is taken too seriously as to stability and members decide not to procreate, how would that impact on the state's survival?

SOCIAL ORIGINS PROBLEM AND PERSON F.III

How and when do we add people, understand communitarian and contract theories and the problem of statelessness? Communitarian and contract theories go on the assumption that people are not stateless. They are either current members of a natural community or individuals who are either in a contractual state or between such sovereigns. But suppose we have refugees or people who a state dismisses. They seem to have nowhere to go. They may not be aware of themselves as belonging to a communitarian or contract state. A sovereign nation must inform them. The refugees may be few or a million. They are flooding one or more countries. What happens to them? I will consider four possibilities.

SOCIAL ORIGIN PROBLEM MONISM

Some people in the world, including leaders, are only alert and reactive to refugees and others who are stateless. They understand that statelessness can occur during wars and other socially disruptive issues within nations. They wait and react by helping only after the people become refugees. Individuals may also alert and react when others cannot understand communitarianism or contract theory. Some students may have difficulty in understanding because of illiteracy, illness, and other issues.

The refugee problem is something to be solved after a crisis leads to disruption for states where the refugees wish to go for protection. Just as biological transplants have the problem of potential physiological rejection by the new body, so refugees could face social rejection in many countries to which they are heading.

SOCIAL ORIGIN PROBLEM PHENOMENOLOGY

Statelessness prevention is a very big problem to prevent. It is proactive. People can try to be proactive and prevent bad leaders from imposing social and other conditions forcing their citizens to leave the country. That is a problem that only major world organizations or a world power might can prevent. Communitarianism and contract theory are ways in which individuals gain social/political identity. They become members of a state. In a communitarian state, the family and school teach children about the priority of their membership in the state. A contract society teaches young and old that identity is voluntary and dependent on the person.

Yet a communitarian state can impose hardships, forcing members to escape. A contract state allows the citizen to leave, when the individual has little idea of what to do or where to go for membership in another state. Trying to prevent these situations becomes a monumental task. A Kantian approach (1987) would argue that social origins problems without a person are blind, and problems without a person are empty.

Preventing the problem of statelessness is the proactive approach to refugees. Here, nations and nongovernmental organizations are thinking ahead. They attempt to prevent unstable governments or societies where members may leave voluntarily or involuntarily. And the stable, proactive societies would have plans and preparations for refugees or other immigrants.

International relations theory plays a role in communitarian and contract problem prevention. Leaders in both kinds of societies can try to seek peace around the globe. Peace and better conditions in other countries minimize social disruption. Disruption is most probably the cause of refugees being forced to escape the foreign countries and seek new nationhood elsewhere.

International relations can pose a problem for communitarians regarding who qualifies for citizenship. Prevention of that problem might present a tricky situation for communitarian theory. If the state is natural, does it impose an involuntary citizenship on refugees, on immigrants? Does the communitarian country, devoid of contracts, allow refugees and immigrants? In other words, does the idea of the state as natural define as citizen only those born and raised within its borders?

A preventative communitarianism tries to develop citizenship policies to encourage world peace and discourage displaced people. But it develops citizenship policies to better integrate immigrants and refugees, defusing conflicts and anti-immigrant, antirefugee issues among current citizens.

Preventative contract theory probably is fewer problems to prevent. The contract is the new arrival's way of joining the current citizens. An artificial state is, by definition, proactive, preventing current citizens from the "us versus them" attitudes.

STUDY QUESTIONS

- How do alert-reactive and preventative statehood theories of dealing with problems impact on refugees?
- How effective does the United Nations seem to be in alert reaction, or in prevention, of refugee problems?

SOCIAL ORIGIN PROBLEM DUALISM

A nation can ignore and then, at another time, during a crisis, react finally to refugees. Where alertness, reaction, and prevention can involve a welcoming nation to have prepared for the stateless refugee, those who ignore and then react encounter a problem. They have not prepared to help the refugee.

Here, time dualism exists. There is an initial time when we ignore refugees, and a second time when a crisis occurs and nations react. For phenomenology, we overcome time dualism in statehood crises by reintroducing solving the problem into the idea of initial time of now acknowledging the issue and preventing it.

SOCIAL ORIGIN PROBLEM POSTMODERNISM

Ignoring and then reacting to statelessness as a problem eventually leads to solving the issue. The solution might not be pretty. Communities trying to help the refugees encounter disruption, perhaps crime and disease. Social services can be victims of ill planning. Denial of the problem, however, can be even more severe for nations rejecting the problem as real and for the refugee.

The nation that denies a problem from the start might well never acknowledge it. The refugees become victims not just of expulsion or escape from the homeland, but of a denying nation's attitude of "not in my backyard." One serious problem for the denying nation is the potential of the refugee for that country. A blanket rejection of the refugee issue as a problem could result in losing a refugee who can be of major help to the denying nation.

A brilliant scientist, engineer, or other intellectual in the hard sciences would benefit a country's scientific and technological needs. An artist, poet, playwright, or other humanistic professional might not find a cure for illness or contribute to a significant scientific or technological problem. But the humanist might well contribute to the nation's citizens interested in soft culture. Of course, humanitarians will argue that a refugee needs help on humanitarian grounds. Nations need not wait for the stateless person to be Einstein or a brilliant engineer. Helping a humble human being escape poverty and death are part of reality and life.

STUDY QUESTIONS

- Predict the implications of ignoring a refugee problem.
- Predict the implications of denying that refugee problems exist.

Below are dual themes, each of which the reader ought to try to articulate into a brief chapter.

EXERCISES

The following exercises, when completed, are to become small chapters.

1. Inside communitarian and contract, community reality is expression (Claude Shannon) and silence.

2. Inside expression is body reality, as verbal and nonverbal.

3. Inside verbal is conveyance reality as digital and oral.

4. Inside communitarian and contract is the sovereign reality means church and state.

5. Inside state is patriotic reality of nationalism and individualism.

6. Inside church is ritual and congregationalism.

7. Inside ritual and congregationalism.

8. God and world is God and culture/secular. This book theologically interpreted.

9. Inside theology, there is theology of culture which religious dimensions of the secular. There are also theological themes as below, from scriptural to architecture of houses of worship.

10. Church and priesthood of believer, of all believers of churches, all workers, all people, all nature

11. Written, oral

12. Literature reality: scripture, person

13. Legal reality: law, story

14. Mythological reality: myth, person

15. Eschatology reality: end and person

16. Meaning reality: literal, figurative

17. Belief reality: fundamentalist, liberal

18. Theological validity reality: argument, faith

19. Ritual and congregational

20. Works and faith

21. Culture or book reality: applications, metaphysics

22. Ecclesiastical reality: people, church

23. Calendars reality: days and holidays

24. Calendar reality: days and birthdays

25. Calendar reality: days and anniversaries

26. Workers' reality: workers

27. Four walls and ornate

CHAPTER SEVEN

UNIFIED GENERAL THEORY OF ETHICAL REALITY:

DOING AND BEING

KEYWORDS

institution: A social system or structure, such as transportation, wherein people "do" or produce and consume goods and services.

doing: Human institutional activity.

world-rejecting ascetic: Someone who withdraws from institutions and thus society.

inner-worldly ascetic: Someone who engages in society and its institutions, trying to humanize it.

ORIENTING THIS CHAPTER

Inside church and state, ethical reality means the institutional object (doing) and ascetic subject (being) twofold theme. By institution I mean the social system, structure, and framework within which individuals "do." Generally, "institution" here means a social context whereby individuals do right or wrong. The individual may choose to leave society and thus its institutions. In the extreme form, this is world-rejecting asceticism. Remaining in society leads to people doing enough that a large, complex ethic results. The less individuals do, such as leaving society for a monastery and a very simple life, brings on as simplified an ethic as possible. An observer might call this transition an Ockham's razor (Audi 1993) approach to right and wrong, to ethics. Society multiplies what to do and the ethical questions.

A social institution is "outside" or "external" to the person. "Institutional object" means a social structure we derive from objectivity. An institution involves the social or cultural activity of human beings doing or being in motion with others: Transportation is the institution requiring physical movement; education is the institution involving teaching and learning. Anthropologists might call the institution a social system or structure. For Weber (1968), an ascetic is the person, derived subjectivity, usually disciplined to behave in some manner toward humanizing or making ethical the institution and not merely "doing" or being anonymously institutional. The ascetic subject is a person we derive from subjectivity.

The present chapter is unique. I shall explain this uniqueness by comparing this chapter with chapter 1. Indeed, I will note that it can be compared with the previous and remaining chapters. This chapter is a unified general theory of ethics.

The first chapter shows a general theory or conceptual framework for all chapters. What is real? My second chapter applies or derives hermeneutics from metaphysics. The third chapter is about truth reality. My fourth chapter is inflation. The fifth concerns prediction reality. My sixth is about social origins reality. Now, the seventh chapter deals with ethics reality. This is a special applied one, which applies reality to ethics but also reverses and applies ethics to the two previous chapters. For chapter 1, metaphysical positions would debate what "ought to be," what we ought to believe of reality. Four metaphysical options exist, but which one ought to be? And which one ought we to believe for remaining chapters? Those are ethical/metaphysical questions. Chapter 2, social origins positions, derives from metaphysics and debate which social position is ethical in how society originated. We "are" metaphysically, and "are in a state or social institutions."

Each institution is derivative ethical reality, but also applies to metaphysics and social origins. We do the real, but do this ethically (as atoms or robots, as neighborhood members or individual person, as one and the other, or as world-rejecting individuals we do little or nothing). We accept some position on the origin of society, but each position sees itself as ethical.

I refer to this chapter as a unified general theory of ethical reality: doing and being. But doing and being are life itself. As derivative or applied metaphysics, theoretical ethics follows theoretical metaphysical positions. We derive meta-physics as it is in "concrete" social science/humanities fields. This becomes economics (Gottheil 2009). Doing means, in part, choosing, deciding on using scare resources in producing, distributing, consuming goods and services (Samuelson 1979; McEachern 2015; Mankiw 2015). If so, then theoretical ethics is theoretical economics. Theoretical and applied economics as ethics, as choice and decision-making, is a steering from something not wanted, ethical, or available, toward the wanted, ethical, or available. The Greek term for steer-ing is cybernetic. Thus, ethics or economics is cyberethics or cybereconomics. Again, cybercrime, cyberwar, and cyberweapons are misnomers, distorting the Greek meaning. Cyber can have one meaning, as steering, or two meanings, one as steering and the second more-current one of *digital*.

STUDY QUESTION

- How does this chapter fit in with the other chapters?

ORIENTING THIS CHAPTER: RETHINKING ETHICS

Where the general theory tells us what "is" in all chapters, and social origins indicates how the state originated, ethics applies to applications and theory as to what we ought to believe about what "is," what we ought to do in light of what "is," and what we ought to believe about state origins. Doing is a subset of what "is" objective-subjective. Positivists say positivism ought to be. This is an ethical, not exclusively metaphysical, position. Ethics is applied or derived as ethical reality. As a "general theory" of ethical, all other chapters, including the first one on metaphysics, are derived ethics. But ethics speaks primarily the language of what ought to be, not just what is. We are accustomed to a general theory applied. We are not accustomed to a general theory applied, and then one of the applications, even the first, as a secondary general theory applying in reverse and then to others.

Any general theory applies forward. We proceed from general theory to its applications, but no application applies back to a general theory of reality and of how human society started. Application of a general theory is typically unidirectional. A bilateral or bidirectional application does not appear to exist. Ethics may be the only one back to the theory, and forward to remaining applications. It tells us of right and wrong in all applications, including metaphysics. But metaphysics also has an ethical dimension. Atomism, phenomenology, dualism, and existentialism are four metaphysical positions. For present purposes I omit pragmatism, postmodernism, and solipsism. Holders of each of each of these four positions would consider others unethical. Existentialists are taking an ethical stance in criticizing atomism (analytic and positivism) as wrong. Hence, ethics is application of metaphysics, general theory of ethics applied to metaphysics and applications.

Ethics usually starts with or underlies applications through traditional ethical theories: Consequential thinking includes egoism and utilitarianism; nonconsequentialism means divine command, virtue, natural law, and duty. But the conceptual framework in ethics should be based on or derived from (metaphysical positions of) atomism to existentialism, and not on or from ethical theories.

I find ethical theories (Boss 2014) insufficiently general. Consequentialism says results are central. But nonconsequentialism must also have results. We do not just follow authority for following and then ignoring results. Nonconsequentialism says authority is the ultimate standard, but consequentialism is also relates to authority: What is an authority? Different kinds of authority exist. Jeremy Bentham is an authority on utilitarianism. Nonconsequentialism says regardless of consequences, but many do rely on consequences and hope bad results do not occur. We may emphasize results in consequentialism but acknowledge that bad results can occur. Utilitarians weigh good and bad, but the differences may be philosophical. If bad results occur, utilitarians might not stop what they believe to be good intentions and actions. We may emphasize authority in nonconsequentialism regardless of results, but divine command, virtue, duty, and natural law do expect that good results will occur. We do not expect authority to demand young and old to become ill, die, fail, and the like as people follow a nonconsequential theory.

Traditional ethics implies that divine command, duty, virtue, and natural law are different, perhaps mutually exclusive. Yet take divine command. This appears different from natural law, virtue, and duty. But God can command that we do our duty, or follow natural law, be egoistic, lessen pain, or be virtuous. Divine command, then, is not necessarily inherently different from duty (deontology), natural law, egoism, or utilitarianism.

We can lessen pain due to natural law, virtue, God, duty, egoism. Egoism involves selfishness or self-centeredness instead of altruism and doing good for others. However, egoism can mean utilitarianism. The two theories are not mutually exclusive. Ethicists or anyone need not be either egoistic or utilitarian. Utilitarian who wish to do their utmost in helping people may well do so for personal, egoistic purposes. Their actions can be the most helpful of any human. They could be model utilitarians. However, they have a certain agenda. Their aim is to help the underprivileged or anyone needing assistance, only because utilitarians find an opportunity for self-enrichment.

Showing that the traditional ethical theories are synonymous, I give the following sentences. Divine command can tell us our duty is, in part, to follow natural law, being egoistic utilitarians and thus virtuous. Put another way, natural law says our duty is to follow divine command, to be egoistic utilitarians and thus virtuous. Speaking of egoism brings in the topic of sacrifice. American thinker and ethicist Peter Singer (2015) says we need not sacrifice to do good. If sacrifice means giving up something we need, then that is not necessary. We can do good by doing what interests us and is socially desirable. But I return to the egoistic utilitarian.

One good example of the egoistic utilitarian may be the politician. The politician seeking office will campaign. The activity might involve language promising to help the poor and needy. It could also include photo ops of the politician appearing with the poor and needy. Those needing help, and even others who are well off with financial resources, might vote the politician into office. The politician has expressed concern for others, has demonstrated or given lip services to utilitarianism, for personal gain. Once in office, the politician's selfish agenda continues to an extent. Indeed, the politician, now in power, can act as a utilitarian, spending huge amounts of tax money on the needy.

The problem here is that the help is not genuine outreach. Help is not real help. Egoistic utilitarianism, if selfish, is not true humanitarianism. Tax money can go to the needy on an ongoing basis, putting the poor in a situation for continued and increased dependency on public funding. The politician's utilitarianism is egoistic. Political power is going to help the poor survive, but depend always on the government. Dependence on the government is the politician's way of staying in power. Thus, egoism and utilitarianism are not mutually exclusive.

Any given traditional theory can include or say what other traditional theories say. Any given traditional theory seems semantically, not substantially different. However, atomism cannot be interchangeable with phenomenology, dualism, or existentialism. Thus, the traditional theories must be seen in the context of atomism, phenomenology, and so on.

STUDY QUESTIONS

- Explain how a general theory is also derived from one of the derived chapters.
- Looking at traditional ethical theories, how can an egoist be a utilitarian?
- Looking at traditional ethical theories, how can any two of those theories be synonymous?

ORIENTING THIS CHAPTER: ETHICS AND METAPHYICS

Ethics is applied metaphysics. But ethics also applies to metaphysics. The existentialist implies that the positivist is unethical. This shows the ethical impact on metaphysics. Ethics suggest ethical behavior in metaphysics and social institutions. I am showing that we can go from unilateral to multilateral idea of general theory. Metaphysics is about what "is." It is conceptual framework for ethics and so on. But human beings do, including selecting and implementing metaphysical options. Thus, we are doing isness: atomistically, phenomenologically, dualistically, and existentially. We speak of reality, and then speak of prediction reality, social origins reality, ethical reality, and other forms of reality. Ethics, based on a metaphysical conceptual framework, is derived reality and ethical framework for metaphysics and so on.

In ethics, I deal with theories regarding institutions in relation to persons. Institutions involve or are the structures and cultural contexts in which we are "doing" or "acting." Persons "do" or "act." Ethics involves doing, although the Jains said that to be ethical, refrain from doing. In doing, ethics becomes interdisciplinary. My ethical theories are as follows: doing as an end in itself disregarding people (user unfriendly), doing as an end in terms of or friendly to the human means, dualism as not doing and then doing, and doing almost nothing.

Doing is the consumption, and in some cases production, of goods and services. This is economics. Economics is social behavior. Economics thus seamlessly links with sociology; sociology and economics and ethics deal with the individual and group: sociology studies the group, psychology the individual. Production and consumption involve disposing or recycling, and thus ecology after production and consumption. The individual in or rejecting society as production, consumption, and ecology is at least two forms of asceticism. Ethics becomes religion. The unifying study of society appears to be anthropology. Thus, ethics is economics-sociology-ecology-religion-psychology-anthropology. Ethics is perhaps the most interdisciplinary field; certainly it is the social sciences, arts, and humanities (Kuhn 1970; Boulding 1968; von Bertalanffy 1968; Frodeman, Klein, and Mitchem 2010).

STUDY QUESTIONS

- Explain how ethics is interdisciplinary, as economics-sociology-ecology and other fields.
- How can ethics and metaphysics be so related?

INSTITUTIONS AND ASCETICISM G.I

People are ethical if they allow mere automation or institutional production and consumption of goods and services; embodied institutions; dualistic institutions; or rejection of institutions. Within society, they debate ethics of self-defense instead of murder, lying only when for someone's good, playing by the rules and not cheating, and so on.

"Institution" and "ascetic" denote doing and discipline, respectively. This includes objectivity (doing) only, phenomenology, pragmatism, dualism, and monastic existentialism (being) only. For my purposes, I omit pragmatism, skepticism, nihilism, and solipsism. Do we only do, do embodied as in doing disciplined, disciplined and doing, or disciplined only? "Ascetic," "yoga," and "discipline" mean an intentional, focused method of exercise relating to the world.

The typical definition of an ascetic is a person who exercises severe discipline to refrain from material pleasure and activity. Most images of asceticism portray the religious individual who withdraws from social or cultural institutions. That definition is inadequate. An ascetic is a self-disciplined person. But such an idea requires clarification. Self-discipline does not mean withdrawing from the world and society. Instead, ascetic self-discipline, or simply discipline, denotes two things.

Weber (1968) is saying that the inner-worldly ascetic disciplines himself or herself by monitoring what, when, how, and why they act. This ascetic sees matter, time, and space as good. For this ascetic, society, people, individuals, and the body are good. Institutions are therefore good. Being an inner-worldly ascetic denotes what acts to do, when to do them, how to act, and why.

Niebuhr's classic *Christ and Culture* (1958), talks of Christ the Transformer of Culture, and Christ against Culture. Christ as transformer is akin to the innerworldly ascetic, and Christ against culture is like an outerworldly or world rejecting ascetic.

For example, the inner-worldly ascetic decides what, when, how, and why to produce and consume goods and services, engage in sex, work, change, remain the same, analyze, and wonder. That ascetic acts in a manner thinking about the options and consequences of ethics: how institution relates to the person. This ascetic, according to Weber (1968), is disciplined to remain in and improve society and not to see discipline as a negative. Negative discipline would mean to negation of matter and society.

By thinking of the options of that relationship, the inner-worldly ascetic decides to be in, instead of withdrawing from, society. Weber's (1968) inner-worldly ascetic decides that withdrawal from social institutions is not the way to salvation, personal enrichment, or the social good. In other words, withdrawing from society and matter is unethical. By rejecting or withdrawing from matter implies seeing sex, the body, and possibly marriage as evil.

Ethics inquires as to whether individuals merely "do," do as people, are those not doing and others who merely do, or never engage in society. Is culture mere motion, human motion, dualism, or no activity? By an ascetic I mean a disciplined person. The individual may be disciplined to the extreme by rejecting society and becoming what Weber (1968) calls the world-rejecting ascetic, withdrawing from society. Asceticism can also mean moderate, socially involved discipline, meaning Weber's inner-worldly ascetic. That ascetic engages in and opposes dehumanization instead of withdraws from society.

Opposition means attempting to change it by making culture more humane, more like an object-lifeworld. The person without discipline is no ascetic, no individual with discipline. They become anonymous cogs in the machine. These are institutional, ethical derivatives of metaphysical statics.

Let's look at institution or structure-alone (individuals do not oppose institutions or dehumanization); institution embodied (defining structures, interacting with the family or inner-worldly ascetics who transform institutions, and the family itself); dualism; and "family" of world-rejecting ascetics.

STUDY QUESTIONS

- How can asceticism be inner-worldly and world-rejecting?
- Predict the interdisciplinary studies of discerning that yoga, asceticism, discipline, as exercise relating to the world.

DISCIPLINE AS BEHAVIOR AND STUDIES

Discipline, then, can mean two opposite things. Persons can discipline themselves to produce and consume in a pure technical society such that they will not humanize or withdraw from society. They can also define discipline as a spiritual method transforming or withdrawing from society. An inner-worldly ascetic disciplines himself or herself to transform, not withdraw from, society. The world-rejecting and inner-worldly ascetic disciplines himself to humanize or reject technology. For the purpose of this book, I will define "discipline" as the effort to humanize, instead of either accepting dehumanization (doing-only) or rejecting society.

Toward that, three areas in ethics deserve reference. Metaethics is that area of ethics that asks people to clarify the meanings of terms in ethical issues. If someone is for or against the death penalty, metaethics asks the definition of death penalty and what we are doing when we ask questions of ethics.

There is also the is/ought or descriptive and normative problem. Description describes ethical theories, normative prescribes them.

Finally, ethical relativism says no one standard is possible, while ethical absolutes argue that ethical standards are needed and possible. Relativism is postmodern, where multiple realities exist and can lead to chaos; absolute-only to monism and an ethical disregarding of human beings.

Ethics asks what is right and wrong as to human behavior. But people behave or "do" in a civic context, not a vacuum. In doing so, ethics is the following:

- Broadly speaking, city planning and behavior. People do most often in a "social" context, even in a monastery. They "do" sometimes alone, sometimes with one or more other people. As such city or civic planning, ethics as the inquiry into right and wrong, would denote the following aspects of civic life, whether individuals accept or reject society.

- Society or institutions is a people behaving in groups. Academia calls this study "sociology." This can be sociological ethics.

- People in groups in all parts of the world, and their artifacts. Academia refers to this study as "anthropology." This would mean anthropological ethics, though I have the problem of separating anthropology from sociology. Biological and similar aspects of anthropology probably belong to biology and chemistry.

- Human groups as right when they seek the real. For Mircea Eliade, this is called "religion" (Munson 1968) or "theology of culture." Theological or religious ethics can involve the "doing" in relation to a divine command. However, God or divine command can relate to our duty, virtue, ego, lessening pain, and obeying natural law.

- Groups of people in all parts of the globe produce and consume goods and services. For academia, this is "economics." We see here economics as ethics, and how and why "doing" is the production and consumption of goods and services.

- Human groups protecting the environment as they produce and consume goods and services. "Environment" here is meant in the broad sense of nature and animals. We need to protect nature and similarly respect all living things other than human beings. All have the right to exist instead of being exploited. Academics call this "ecology." I would term it ecological ethics, a very close cousin of economics. How are we producing and consuming while protecting the environment?

- The groups of people everywhere produce and consume goods and services by understanding and influencing each other. For academia, this is called "psychology." Psychological ethics brings in the notion that in relating to people and ecology, we are influenced by and influencing people.

- Human groups everywhere behaving in a hierarchy where policy makers lead the followers of policy. For academia, this is called "political science." Political ethics is more than how leaders behave. It is the ethics of the social group dealing as a policy-making hierarchy.

- People taking each other into account, and in specific instances, design technology to take people into account. Academic call that "human factors engineering." Ergonomics is all but synonymous with philosophy. I call philosophy a qualitative and nonqualitative ergonomics.

- Human groups understanding their past and present and heading toward the future. Academia refers to this as "history." Historical ergonomics means that reality as society and nature have a past, present, and future through all cultural artifacts, as follows in the next section.

- Human groups appreciate history through their cultural artifacts, and academia calls these "literature," "physical objects," "processes," "music," and "art." Cultural ethics looks as the expressions of culture.

- Thus, ethics is sociological, anthropological, ergonomic, religious, psychological, or economic. Put another way, we can have ethics as city planning. This can mean total automation, embodied machines and cities, dualism, or the monastery.

STUDY QUESTION

- Explain the implications of ethics as foundations of interdisciplinarity metaphysics, wisdom, and city planning.

ERGONOMICS AND ETHICAL THEORY

Below are four general ethical theories: ethical monism, phenomenology, dualism, and subjectivity. They involve kinds of society or culture. More accurately, they involve whether we are ethical in accepting a thoroughly automated society, a somewhat automated society, dualistic societies (some very primitive, some very automated), or the rejection of society. The kinds of societies here are a philosophical/ethical, and ergonomic issue. Chapanis (1960) and Adams (1989) from ergonomics already implied that the user's presence in technology is a philosophical and ethical issue. Ergonomic orientation is ethical orientation, broader than traditional ethics theories.

Traditional ethical theories are insufficiently general. They start by saying we are ethical when being virtuous, following God, lessening pain, and so on. But the ethicists ignore that first, they are in a society or reject it. They are in an ethical or unethical society before they are lessening pain or doing their duty. Before being egoist or following natural law, they are in a totally, humanly automated, dualistic, or monastic society. Ethics occurs in a social setting, not vacuum. Descartes (1999) made the same mistake, isolating thinking from the body. We do not first think and conclude that we therefore exist. Descartes ignored that he was in France, and a white male, as the context in which he was thinking.

Traditional ethical theories such as egoism, utilitarianism, and so on assume simplistically that people do things outside a social, cultural setting. But people do things either in social institutions of production and consumption of goods and services or very minimally in monasteries rejecting society.

ETHICAL INSTITUTIONAL MONISM

This is institution-only or doing-only: Ethical monism is ethical reality totally reducible to sum of behavioral parts or atoms. It is ethical to be institution-only or doing-only. Mere production and consumption of goods and services is ethical, according to institutional monism. "Institutions alone" is the ethical position that persons do not count in deciding morals or ethics. Matter is the only reality and people are almost completely reducible to atoms. Generally, we look at society as the institutions where technology predominates, and is virtually the sole good. People engage with devices more than with each other. The person is for the Sabbath. Our humanity is sacrificed for mere production and consumption. Monism is interdisciplinary, as are phenomenology, dualism, and subjectivity or world-rejecting asceticism. But in ethical monism, automation exceeds all.

Institutional monism is almost without humanity. Mere doing is the answer to everything.

Matter, power, and speed are keywords. Workers are anonymous if they exist at all. Automation predominates. "Production and consumption" are automated, nonhuman motion. People need and use devices for long and short distances. Long distance communication and transportation are routine. Mircea Eliade (1966) speaks of the modern person as doing-only mechanically. Sex, nutrition, and all other activities have no ceremony or sacrality but are only physical, physiological, motions.

However, if society is the institution alone, then people are ethical in believing production, distribution, consumption, and discarding of waste are reducible to merely physical motion. Automation and outsourcing replace people. If persons move, their motions are simply mechanical: getting from here to there. If an object is to move, its motions are similarly only mechanical: physically moving the thing from here to there. Matter and society are real, and good, but only physical realities. The human dimension does not exist. The social person participates in the institutions, the production, distribution, and consumption of goods and services. However, society disregarding Weber's inner-worldly ascetic demands societal activities and belongingness solely on society's terms.

Social identity, broadly speaking, involves material gain, marriage, families, and use of the environment, with or without ecological concern, primarily or only as physical activity. The individual must daily engage in societal, cultural affairs, and the production, distribution, and consumption of goods and services exclusively as mechanical actions. Individuals must accept technology and its advances as societal norms, practices, ideas, affairs without question. Little or no dialogue exists between the inner-worldly ascetic and society.

Where a society reduces all human activity to physical motion, the human being is in danger. For example, work, as motion, becomes mobility alone. Society, and specifically the workplace, can replace any worker with a machine. Automation becomes the norm. Efficiency in the workplace replaces improved human activity. The efficient workplace is now merely an institution without a face, dignity, or smile. Work is anonymous, and society can replace workers with technology that simply "does work" of "production and consumption."

The society where institutions are alone, disregarding the person, makes paramount paramount. In doing so, speed and power are crucial. People need to get things "done now," instead of fulfilling humane goals and moving individuals and objects at a reasonable pace. Society finds itself seeking speedier computers, automation, communications, transportation, and all else. Devices are needed for long and short distances, and long distance travel is routine. When institutions are alone, disregarding people, a separation is occurring between institutions. Home is in a totally residential area, separated from work miles away. Entertainment, medical facilities, and most other needs do not have to be within walking distance. They are miles apart. Getting from one place to another, from home to work, from home to doctor, requires speed and power.

For instance, transportation becomes an intriguing situation. Society seeks speed to get from the downtown area to city limits. We once had two-ways streets. The number of vehicles and level of traffic forced cities to change many avenues to one-way streets. But cities also created highways and expressways to help speed up traffic as mere motion. Some expressways have the ultimate in motion devices. In Chicago an express lane exists in the Kennedy Expressway for getting from the Loop to O'Hare Airport. These are express lanes within expressways, where drivers wishing to move speedily directly to the airport may have an open lane dedicated to the airport.

"Institution-alone" is my term for Weber's notion of the person who is active in but never opposed to cultures institutions. The individual merely "does" or is in motion, without humanizing, thinking of justice, or otherwise improving society. Institution-alone is the idea of institutions disregarding the person.

Husserl and Schutz speak of what I call the 'approach live world.' They appear to reject the mathematization, reflection or analysis of our surroundings. Readers can interpret *surrounding* to mean where we live, the geographical locations as cities, towns, or monasteries. Reflection is how someone studies that geographical place. Institution-only monism, then, might mean urban sprawl. Husserl and Schutz appear to object to reflecting on the big city, but not to its existence (Schutz 1970). Hence, Schutz seems to accept someone simply believing that a subway will work, and thus would not share our concern to stem "the tide of sprawl" (Greene 1999).

This is institution-only egoism, utilitarianism, divine command, virtue, duty, and natural law. A central problem with the traditional consequential and non-consequential theories is that they are not in a social context. Ethicists feel that their six theories are in a vacuum, that people are ethical in a nonsocial context. For example, people do God's command, but we do not see whether they do so in a massively automated, somewhat automated, dualistic, or monastic community. People need to be in some group, at least a monastery rejecting society, in order to be ethical or unethical. Thus, the type of society—whether thoroughly automated, people friendly, dualistic, or monastic—is the basic ethical context. The six theories are wrong. People must be in a society, even monastic one, in order to be ethical or unethical. Thus, the basic, most general ethical or unethical social milieu is the kind of social group in which we live.

People in institution-alone have not disciplined themselves to work or behave as human beings for reasonable health. They are not disciples, ascetics, or yogas, but mere machines. Ritual comes first (Giles, 1969). The disciple starts occurring in the next section, institutions embodied, disciplining themselves to follow a human leader instead of "do" motion. Society can and does replace people with automation, or put any person in a job or activity, because human activity is only motion.

Communication and transportation are for long and short distances. Speed, power, and motion, all hallmarks of technology, are fundamental. People require and almost totally depend on devices for communications and movement. Handhelds, texting, automobiles, and mass transit are critical to daily, routine needs. Pedestrian traffic and interpersonal social skills are either unimportant or minimal.

STUDY QUESTIONS

- Predict what kinds of jobs are available for people in a society that is totally automated.
- How do the traditional six ethical theories show that people do things out of the social context?

ETHICAL INSTITUTION PHENOMENOLOGY

This is ethical phenomenology or doing embodied. In ergonomic language, philosophy designs institutions or human structures to be person friendly. Social groups must take into account (embody) human behavior. Weber's (1964) inner-worldly ascetic, Confucianism (Waley, 1938) exemplify embodiment. It is ethical to do-embodied. Doing is in human constraint. Matter, power, and speed are within human context, and society is irreducible to these physical ideas. Production and consumption are embodied in family activities. Family business predominates. If we study people in groups, our research involves sociology, anthropology, family, and production and consumption of goods and services, and thus economics. Phenomenological economics does not involve just applying, hiring, and firing. We study social science, and groups of people are in a political hierarchy. The real is the family business; thus, social science connects with religion.

Human business is irreducible to mere production and consumption of goods and services. If the institution is embodied, it is in dialogue with the person. The individual may contribute input, even if this input is against accepted social norms. Society allows open interaction with individuals. Weber's inner-worldly ascetic colors institutions through input. Work, marriage, family, matter, and all institutions are good, but must take in the human factor and not be mere motion. Children are seen and heard. Motion is generally, but not completely or overwhelmingly reducible to physical movement. People do not just get "from here to there." Kant (1987) would say institutions without asceticism are blind, and asceticism without institutions are empty.

Weber's (1968) inner-worldly ascetic works within institutions, but opposes them by always trying to humanize motion and objects. People do things, and are not constantly at the mercy of powered objects. The Sabbath is for the person. As I noted above, the disciple practices discipline, following a human leader. Further, the disciple is the inner-worldly ascetic who disciplines himself to eat, procreate, walk or move, produce goods and service and consume, heal, talk, and so forth as a reasonable human being with technology and other people.

The inner-worldly ascetic is roughly the civil engineer. I call this macro ergonomics or macro human factors. It involves city planning (chapter 12), including what we have in all chapters (and exercises) of this book. The civil engineer builds roads, bridges, parks, waterways, and all other civilian objects, processes, and environments. But civil engineering does more than just add a road here, a bridge there. City planning is ethics, and comprehensive instead of just a la carte. I rename civil engineering as macro ergonomics, and all other engineering (chemical, electrical, mechanical, etc.) as micro ergonomics or micro human factors.

The phenomenological view in ethics and city planning would take into account, and share the concern of Greene (1999). That view maintains that urban sprawl is bad and that a smaller, humane city, is ethical.

In doing reasonably, the disciple as an inner-worldly ascetic is as Weber implies, opposing institutions. The disciple opposes being or being dependent on a machine. In that opposition, the disciples oppose being institutionalized. Our image of being institutionalized is much stricter than Weber's view might be. We think of the physically, emotionally, or otherwise disabled who we commit to an institution because the individual cannot be self-sufficient. However, institutionalization can mean something broader.

To be institutionalized can mean perfectly healthy people totally dependent on, but working and living like a machine. A person in 2017—totally dependent on computers, handhelds, and almost completely dedicated as a workaholic—may well be an "institutionalized" individual. That individual is not disciplined, not a disciple, but existing in institutions-alone. The inner-worldly ascetic opposes institutions in that he or she humanizes society and institutions. The Sabbath (institution) is for the person, not the person for the Sabbath. Society is the biological family, nuclear and extended, engaged in family business.

As a theory of ethics, this is institution-embodied egoism, utilitarianism, natural law, virtue, divine command, and duty.

- Institution-embodied egoism means being in and humanizing institutions is in our self-interest.

- Institution-embodied utilitarianism says lessen pain within the social context.

- Institution-embodied divine command means follow God through humane institutions.

- Institution-embodied virtue says moderation is good within humane institutions.

- Institution-embodied natural law means our nature is that of being in humane institutions.

- Institution-embodied duty denotes our obligation to engage in humane institutions.

INSTITUTION-ASCETIC DUALISM

Two kinds of places exist in the world, according to institution-ascetic dualism. One is society as institutional monism with mere production and consumption of goods and services, the other is the monastery or any world-rejecting ascetic. To paraphrase Abraham Lincoln's famous "a nation cannot survive half slave, half free" (Foner 2010, p. 54). I might argue that the world ought not live half technology-only and half monastic.

Disciplinary and interdisciplinary implications become clear. To talk of society and the society-rejecting ascetic, this world-rejecting ascetic is withdrawing from all cultural institutions and social activity. Such dualism of culture and withdrawal from culture involves our disciplines of sociology, anthropology, ethics, political science, religion, economics, art, ecology, and virtually all social science and humanities. Sociology studies societies, not necessarily just the monastic "society" that the world-rejecting ascetic enters. Anthropology may study both.

Ethics may study both institutions and world-rejecting ascetics. The study of institutions means that ethics concerns what we find in the typical book on ethical behavioral. That book analyzes what is right and wrong activity. On the other hand, that same book might generally not tell of behavior of world-rejecting ascetics. Their "activities" consist of very minimal motion, eating, walking, talking, and interacting with people. The world-rejecting ascetic would not engage in sex, family, or procreation.

Political science emphasizes political engagement and thus society. We would not find much on world-rejecting asceticism in political science.

Religion is very broad, concerning society and its rejection. This discipline speaks of society and world-rejecting ascetics. The latter is rejecting the world on religious or spiritual grounds. Matter and society are evil, and thus salvation comes through withdrawal the social realm.

Economics studies the production, distribution, and consumption of goods and services: a societal activity. If the world-rejecting ascetic is turning away from matter, he is withdrawing from the world wherein people are active in the production, distribution, and typical consumption of goods and services. I doubt that too many economics books spend significant time and effort discussing the world-rejecting ascetic.

Art is societal activity. The artist, whether musician, painter, sculpture, or other type, acknowledges matter and manipulates it for exhibiting emotion, style, and other aspects or meanings of art.

Ecology is a societal concern, not that of the world-rejecting ascetic, unless we take into account the Jain, who refuses to harm insects.

To overcome institution-ascetic dualism, Ricoeur might argue that the phenomenological approach involves reintroducing institutions or "objectivity as doing" into the person. This recovers or restores the institution as an embodied entity.

Institutional-ascetic dualism as ethical reality reminds us of the double standard. Indeed, any dualism as we see through this book represented the double standard. Two realities exist. In dynamics with time-dualism, a double standard exists regarding time. Two "times" exist or occur. Dualistic behavior argues that one kind of behavior is legitimate during one time and place, another is acceptable during other times and places.

In that sense, the phrase and meaning of double standard gain legitimacy and losing stigma. Dualism generally bestows legality, morality, and ethics on two forms of behavior. It means that "doing" and "not doing" (as in the world-rejecting ascetic) are ethical, legitimate, and not to cause concern. Dualism may well be a subset of postmodernism. The postmodern suggests that many realities exist. That is, an infinite number of realities can exist. Dualism can be the subset arguing that at least two realities, two ethics can exist.

I should immediately point out that I am using "standard" in two different meanings. "Double standard," as I now use it, has the usual definition: Some people do one thing one way, while other individuals do them a different way. The meaning of "standard" in the exercise below is different. The term "standard" in the exercise means uniformity or sameness in different times or places. That is, a double standard can exist in a society, city, or other specific location. If that double standard also exists in another society, city, and so on, then we can say the double standard is standard.

That statement appears redundant. Yet it may be legitimate. We can inquire as to whether a double standard between the rich and poor exists in an American state or city, or in America as a nation. Then we may ask whether that double standard also exists among the rich and poor in Canada, Mexico, Germany, or other nation. To be precise and avoid confusion, perhaps we can say that two definitions of "standard" can exist. One is socioeconomic or cultural: double standards for rich and poor, or any two non-national groups of people. The other may be geographical, sovereign, or national: Is the double standard the same in two different countries or other geographical locations?

Another distinction between the forms of standard could be cultural and spatiotemporal. A double standard can exist between rich and poor. This is cultural; it can be racial, religious, or whatever. That double standard can then be the same or standard in another space and time.

STUDY QUESTIONS

- Compare institution-embodied and institution-ascetic dualism as to how individuals seek to enhance their humanity.
- Compare institution-embodied and institution-ascetic dualism as to how people seek to enhance spirituality.

ETHICAL ASCETIC POSTMODERNISM

This option is twofold. Both kinds involve lack production and consumption of goods and services in the second sense of society, institution embodied. However, one kind in subjectivity-alone is the primitive or ancient, where, involuntarily, historically tribes produced and consumed only as needed, and as ancient, preindustrial groups. Machu Picchu in South America, societies before the 1700s, or any developing country qualifies. They might be what we call Stone Age or later groups. None involves the person or member "rejecting" society. Members marry, raise families, travel as capable, and "do" the very minimal.

The other is the monastery of any age. The institution exists as a mere function of the world-rejecting ascetic. Ergonomics calls it ascetic-too-friendly, and institutions are rejected. This is the opposite of institutional monism, or institutions disregarding persons. When person disregards the institution, we see Weber's world-rejecting ascetic. There is almost no motion, power, machinery, and so on. The people do everything, but there is little to do. In the mild form, we may have some Amish.

Then there are Shakers, Taoists, Jains, Theravada Buddhists, as the world-rejecting ascetic. To be fair, Taoism is subjectivity-alone in the widest sense, and not strictly the traditional understanding of world-rejection. Taoism seeks an anarchic, small town or other anti-ritualist environment; one can easily see it as anti-institutional in the broadest sense. This is ethical or institutional subjectivity disregarding institutional objectivity. In a sense, culture or society is human, social activity in the broadest sense: People are doing whether merely or humanly active. A culture-, society-, or world-rejecting ascetic refrains from social activity whether it is mere or humane. Adults leave society because society and matter are evil.

I should point out the relation here between ascetic subjectivism and ethical standards. Ethicists ask whether ethical standards exist, or are ethics relative. Do people in different cultures share universal rules, or do cultures and then individuals generate their own ethics? Those questions apply basically to institutions embodied, for only the social being accepts institutions and thereby ethical codes. The world-rejecting ascetic rejects institutions, and thereby would care only in a restricted sense about whether morality is universal or relative. A monastery belongs to or represents a religion, a kind of social group. Technically, it is Theravada Buddhist, Jain, Mahayana, or a form of Christianity, and so on. A monastery follows its faith's prescriptive ethics. To that extent, the monks abide by a standard that is "universal" to members of the same division within a religion. Rejecting institutions does not mean escaping the cloistered life. Standards and relativism exist in some form among "social" groups. Even a monastery is a social group.

A study of ethics, perhaps ascetic-only, can well qualify this book to be at least supplementary to world religion courses.

STUDY QUESTIONS

- Predict the kind of cities and world if everyone became a world-rejecting ascetic.

- Predict scientific and technological progress if ascetic subjectivity became our only way of life.

ETHICAL CHANGE AND STABILITY G.II

ETHICAL CHANGE MONISM

Institutions (doing) and discipline change for the sake of changing. Their meanings and values change for its own sake. This view is most likely that of a technologically oriented society. Theologian John Cobb Jr. and economist Herman Daly (1969) join forces in their Whiteheadian warning against commodification of air, land, and water. They admonish against a society that atomizes natural resources and changes constantly for the sake of profit.

A society changing systems of mobile devices for the sake of change forces people to learn such newer ideas for the sake of learning new things. This becomes learning overload.

ETHICAL CHANGE EMBODIED

Doing and discipline change as needed. For human factors and phenomenology, institutional and ascetic changes ought to take stability into account. Change ought not to be an end itself. Continuity is important. And such stability ought to be human orientation. A society asking people to learn about new mobile devices as needed, takes into account that people do not need to learn new communication systems more frequently than they ought. For Kant (1987), ethical change without stability is blind, and ethical stability without change is empty.

The social group ought to be the biological family. Within that sociobiological framework, production, consumption, and ecological factors ought to include the human being.

ETHICAL CHANGE DUALISM

Only discipline as a humanizing force exists during one time. Then only "doing" or institutions emerge in powerful technological times. This is akin to the emergence of the Industrial Revolution, perhaps the computer revolution.

ETHICAL STABILITY POSTMODERNISM

No change exists in ideas of ethics and persons. This may be the hallmark of primitive tribes or small towns that refuse to change. Developing telephones does not mean a home requires a phone in every room or each family member with his or her own phone. Each home having one phone may be insufficient, but two phones may be sufficient. A person who refuses to have a phone, a television, or a computer may well be sacrificing technological need for the life of the cave.

STUDY QUESTIONS

- Explain the implications of any social group where change is an end in itself.
- Predict how people would live if one community changed for its own sake and another only a mile away believed in stability-only.
- Compare the economic implications of a society of constantly changing systems in mobile or handheld devices with one of mobile or handheld devices that change as needed.

ETHICAL PROBLEM AND PERSON G.III

ETHICAL PROBLEM MONISM

People decide to believe in institutional, ethical atomism, interaction, dualism, and rejecting institutions after alertness and reaction to a problem. This is ethical alert-reactive problem solving, the solving of ethical problems after they occur.

This would be alert-reactive ethical problem egoism, utilitarianism, divine command, virtue, natural law, and duty.

ETHICAL PROBLEM PHENOMENOLOGY

Ethical problem phenomenology argues that people ought to pursue an ethic of preventing a potential ethical problem from becoming an actual one. People change only as needed. This is ethical problem phenomenology. Stability colors change. Technological changes and advances need not outpace social, moral, or human constraints. Harry Howe Ransom (1958), in his *Central Intelligence and National Security*, admonishes that social, ethical, and human factors ought to be the ongoing framework for scientific approaches in intelligence gathering and decision making. Society can easily generalize and translate that CIA and national security orientation to the necessary ethical foundations for institutions and human behavior. A Kantian (1987) view would be that ethical problems without ascetic are blind, and ethical ascetic without problems is empty.

This view is ethical problem alert-reactive egoism, utilitarianism, natural law, divine command, virtue, and duty.

Michael Anft (2017), presents a powerful look at how urban scientists are trying to develop 'human cities' which can prevent urban decay. Researchers are attempting to maintain cities as "vibrant and sustainable" (Anft 2017, B9). Cities need be more than the juxtaposition of neighborhoods, some of which are very good, while others show poverty (Sharkey, 2017). All neighborhoods ought to be those where children can grow up and achieve economic and other forms of well-being, and adults can take pride in where they live. Anft and Sharkey are reporting on academicians and others working on preventing what a phenomenologist and I would call the atomistic-only geography, or atomistic-only G.

ETHICAL PROBLEM DUALISM

People initially ignore, and then believe in their ethical position after a problem occurs. Our ethics is wrong, but we ignore unethical until problems arises. Then we suddenly react to solve the ethical problem.

ETHICAL PROBLEM POSTMODERNISM

People deny there is a problem when an institutional or problem occurs. Nothing is unethical. Perhaps most of the things which society says are unethical depend on the individual and not on society's views.

STUDY QUESTIONS

- What would be the consequences of living in an alert-reactive problem-solving society?
- What kind of society would exist if people denied the existence of ethical problems?

SUMMARY

To summarize ethics, the ethical individual does things mechanically, humanly, both minimally and mechanically, or is in a monastery. Within each context, that act is ethical as it relates to varying institutions in society, which I enumerate as chapters and exercises. In each case, the four ethical options derive from and apply to those of metaphysics: atomic or structural ritualism as the human-unfriendly, human-friendly ritual, dualism, and a-ritualistic.

Four ethical theories exist, at least in my present volume, of object and subject. People ought to be replaced by machines or merely do. People ought to do, and do the right things. People ought to refrain from doing, and another time and place they ought to merely do or be replaced by machines. People ought not to do. Four ethical theories of problems are: do the right thing after a problem is solved, do the right thing to prevent problems, ignore and then react with the right thing after a problem occurs, and deny that problems occur.

Economics ought to be retermed "ethics." Four general scenarios exist. One is total automation, where we see mere, anonymous "production and consumption of goods and services." Second is *persons, human beings as family members in a neighborhood* producing and consuming goods and services, and producing and consuming the services of thinking about production and consumption. Third is dualism, where an ancient people involuntarily and monastics voluntarily produce and consume virtually nothing, and then an automated society exists where only technology and produces and technology and people consume. Finally, ancient people produce and consume minimally, and monastics do so even less.

CHAPTER EIGHT

SOCIETAL REALITY:
WORKER AND FAMILY

KEYWORDS

gesellschaft: A society based on people as worker roles.

gemeinschaft: A society based on people as family members and the I-thou relation.

I-thou: The relationship between two or more people in which each acknowledges the other as a human being with dignity instead of only producer and consumer.

Inside institution-ascetic twofold theme, societal reality involves gesellschaft and gemeinschaft twofold theme (Tonnies 1957). The former sees people primarily in specific job roles, the latter as members of a community. Within the idea of the inner-worldly ascetic accepting matter and society, and transforming institutions, the gemeinschaft-gesellschaft twofold theme means persons can transform roles and needed technology in terms of the neighborhood or family. Where the ascetic alone will reject matter and people, technology and institutions, gemeinschaft-alone means the person accepts social activity, reasonable technology and institutions, rejecting dehumanizing roles and technology within institutions.

Let us explore the gesellschaft-alone (defining institutions and change as mere human motions and jobs, bureaucracy); gesellschaft embodied (defining specific job roles in terms of the family business, as gemeinschaft neighborhood residents of parents and children); dualism; and family as isolated tribe.

GESELLSCHAFT AND GEMEINSCHAFT H.I

WORKER MONISM

Gesellschaft-only denotes a society where anonymous work acts constitute roles disregarding the family and person. Societal monism says society is totally reducible to atomistic view of work roles and technology within society. Communication, transportation, education, worship, medicine, sanitation, electrical power, recreation, government, shopping, and housing occur through people using devices primarily, are the watchword of gesellschaft or work rejecting the person. Gesellschaft-only or work-only society is consistent with ethical (role) atomism. In this kind of society, people merely do, with their physical bodies, according to Mircea Eliade (1966). Gesellschaft disregarding the person, like gesellschaft society for Tonnies (1957), are consistent with institutions which Max Weber (1964) implies have no humanizing opposition. Martin Buber's (1970) I-thou relation does not exist. Weber speaks of the inner-worldly ascetic as in but opposing institutions. If gesellschaft regards the person as only role player, then the person is not opposing institutions with a human, existential, or spiritual stance.

If we describe gesellschaft society as one reducing the person to mere worker, Dunkelman's (2014) *Vanishing Neighborhood* holds that gemeinschaft is quickly disappearing, or reduced to, the gesellschaft.

Gesellschaft-alone sees human use of technology as not just good, but crucial for nearly all human activity, for almost all times and places. Technological advances for the sake of advances, upgrades for their own sake, "progress" of material kind are all ends in themselves. Desktops, laptops, and handhelds are in use the great majority of time.

Young men and young women go on dates or friendly meetings with a third party. The third party is the electronic handheld device. If the two people, friends or lovers, are technology oriented, they spend a few minutes out of three hours talking, and the rest of the time are looking at their handhelds. If the two people are not tech oriented, they spend much of their time enjoying each other. The immediately previous sentence probably belongs to gesellschaft embodied.

Where institution-only ethics replaces persons and workers with automation, or at least with machines, gesellschaft-alone ethics is slightly gentler. It replaces the person with another worker. That other worker is probably less expensive, and accept less, perhaps far less, pay. Automation and outsourcing can occur in institution-alone, outsourcing most likely occurs in gesellschaft-alone.

Motion, speed, and power are paramount in modern society, even with people, without automation as in the previous chapter. The neighborhood also disappears (Dunkelman 2014). In gesellschaft society, buses, trains, and cars emphasize motion, speed, and power to physically get from here to there. Vehicles simply move people for short and long distances routinely. Bicycles can do the same but are under rider control and are moving the body at the body's pace, not just under motorized ability. People are working, but only as economic roles instead of human beings.

People routinely travel long distances with vehicles. This robs them of their neighborhood's economic and social matrices. They routinely use vehicles for short distance. This discourages local residents from walking in the neighborhood. Motorized vehicles for short and long distances routinely reduce transportation to math and physics.

Husserl (1970) and Schutz (1970) talk of a mathematical world that is not their lifeworld. But lifeworld, we said, is object and approach. This section talks of institution as object, as Tonnies' gesellschaft or nonlived world. But gesellschaft, institution can be "approached" through lifeworld as prereflective and the reflective or atomistic. Approach-lifeworld is our prereflective way of acting in gesellschaft as object-lifeworld (atomism of cities), as in Husserl (1970) and Schutz (1970). Reflective or mathematical approach is to do things in gesellschaft with analysis and calculation. The mathematical approach means, in Weber's view, to do things in institutions by not opposing institutional activity, by not taking a stance for the human or interactive perspective. Weber says that seeing institutions or doing as mere, physical activity, means that people are reducing themselves to atoms, machines, and otherwise dehumanized motion.

Human resources offices in corporations as dehumanizing institutions merely read applications (lately online, with possible Skype interviews), hire, and fire. Workers are only the anonymous "employee." Only minimal community exists in an anonymous corporate world. Politeness, courtesy, and respect for the applicant can be minimal community in the anonymous institution. Fred Davis (Davis, 1972) notes that a community, or what I call approach-lifeworld, gemeinschaft exists even in what we call gesellschaft or nonlifeworld society. Institutions disregarding people can be a "highly secularized society" where rendering of services can be relatively "crass," anonymous, or mechanical.

Davis (1972) talks of the secularized society, whereas Eliade (1966) speaks of modern society where individuals treat sex, nutrition, and other activities on a purely physical instead of sacramental level. Both thinkers, one a sociologist, the other a religious historian, use different words (community, sacrament) to denote the same thing. The sacramental may be synonymous with the gemeinschaft, prereflective.

Physical or secularized society means empty ritualism (sacred and secular) in all institutions. Ritualism, atomism, mere doing, occurs in church, state (ultranationalism), education, procreation, criminal justice, sex, national security and the defeat of the enemy, transportation, housing, eating, and so on. As ritualism means motion, a society practicing pure motion can replace people with machines: automation.

Institutions are the object-lifeworld: education, fire, police, rulers, church, procreation, food, military, medicine, transit, communication, and play. In gesellschaft, they are separated in time and space separate. They are isolated from each other. Institutions become windowless monads. Society, even the small town, becomes one of physical entities, anonymous motions. People fulfill goals atomically, online activity becomes the primarily or only option. Examples are suburbs without sidewalks, homes without porches, and towns we call bedroom communities. These communities may be large or small, but have only homes. Stores, houses of worship, recreation, and other aspects of life or work are miles away, requiring auto or bus transportation.

STUDY QUESTIONS

- Predict the consequences in a society where gesellschaft-only may have problems or contradictions such as shopping only online and totally automated retail stores and transportation.

- How does a gesellschaft-only suburb affect one's health if sidewalks and any outside walking are discouraged?

WORKER PHENOMENOLOGY

"People" in an I-thou relation ought to perform economic roles and therefore work in the neighborhood. People, not automation, run economics. Sociology and anthropology become the humanistic study of the economy. Machines ought not to produce goods and services as their primary function. Indeed, people should not just play economic roles of anonymous producers and consumers of goods and services. They ought to play economic roles as persons located in the neighborhood. Neighborhoods exist where family businesses are such that members live, work and play together routinely. A Kantian (1987) view is that gesellschaft without gemeinschaft is blind, and gemeinschaft without gesellschaft is empty.

Gesellschaft is a society which anthropology (Podolefsky et al. 2009) calls one of *faceless anonymity*. Personal relationships are one-dimensional, worker to worker. This contrasts with what anthropology (Podolefsky et al. 2009) refers to as *multidimensional*, or the worker-person, relation. Here, in a "small-scale social system" (Podolefsky et al. 2009), we see the gesellschaft-embodied, gesellschaft-gemeinschaft notion. Workers are family members.

Embodied gesellschaft morally or ethically constrains technology. It is not as restricted as it is in gemeinschaft-alone such as a monastery. Embodiment rejects less technology and advances than does gemeinschaft-alone. Rejection, according to embodiment, is exemplified by mere advances in manual typewriters and blanket use of desktops. YouTube is fine but ought to be in context. It is perhaps acceptable in certain situations, more so than in gemeinschaft-alone. The social event as theater is more important than a home movie. Attending concerts is better than attaching earphones to hear "music." This is the difference between "sound" and "music." Music is sound, but sound is not music.

In all the talk about automation and how it is throwing workers from jobs, we also hear equivalent cries regarding outsourcing. I hear of talks and warnings about automation and outsourcing. Yes, people work. But which people work or ought to work? If individuals are in jobs, and the companies suddenly see the chance to outsource for lower wages, then the issue of people as producers becomes an ethical one. The idea of persons needing work does not mean just any person. Individuals in the United States who are qualified for a job ought to be those to hire.

All too often, a company's priority is simply saving money. This is akin to a person who seeks to save expenses the easy way. They will cut back on food, clothing, and shelter. Cutting back for them would not be a matter of financial strain, but simply because they want to spend less.

Employers might do the same. They see the chance to save money. The company is not suffering from financial woes. It merely wants to save on paying people. The employer either seeks outsourcing, or someone comes to them from the outside and offers outsourcing opportunities. Many employers jump at the idea. Neighborhood residents may lose their jobs. But with gesellschaft embodied, the neighborhood receives respect.

Neighborhoods become central. People as workers ought to be worker atoms in the neighborhood context. Production might be for the world. A neighborhood store or factory might produce to any buyer, but the priority is for the neighborhood common good. A neighborhood household ought to distribute goods and services to other families in the same area. Economics is more than producer, seller, and consumer. The economic process might be people producing for anyone. But selling ought to primarily be by one household to another in the same neighborhood. This is ethical or institutional phenomenology. Families own businesses and sell mainly to neighbors. People know and help each other. Sidewalks exist between homes, shopping centers, schools, houses of worship, recreation, and other institutions. Gesellschaft embodied means the neighborhood respects and ergonomically considers the pedestrian. Vehicles are basically for long-distance travel and ought not to be for routine use.

Shoppers use paper currency instead of credit and debit cards. Credit and debit cards reduce the person and money to atoms, science, and technology. I find it intriguing that coin and paper currency is federally produced and protected. The US Secret Service pursues counterfeiting of money. But the private sector, not the federal government, produces and monitors credit and debit cards.

Gemeinschaft society (Tonnies 1957) exists as object and approach. Atomistic, reflective or nonlifeworld approach to gemeinschaft atomizes everything in a humane town. Lifeworld approach in lifeworld or gemeinschaft is prereflective approach to family business. The prereflective approach means activity involves doing as persons, moving as person instead of through machines. Movements among people are irreducible to physical motions (Eliade 1966). Transportation involves routinely personal acts for local distance of space and time. Vehicles are good for distances, but such travel and community is non-routine, never a daily need. Vehicular transit, telecommunications ought to be rare if ever for local needs. This is the gemeinschaft approach. It differs from the reflective approach to small, humane society.

The Power of Clan (Wolf and Bruhn 1993) is a classic, well-known analysis of sociology of medicine. It demonstrates work within the context of a tightly knit community. More specifically, the volume emphasizes the medical benefits, preventing heart disease, of a powerful clannish group: family, neighborhood.

Gemeinschaft is probably homologous to Max Weber's inner-worldly asceticism, people accept institutions and work therein as ascetics or the disciplined, but oppose dehumanization. Opposition to institutions denotes opposing mere institutionalism, which is dehumanization, and demands institutions as human roles. Institution is good, institution-only is dehumanizing. People are more than physical bodies, motions, power, and rituals. However, the inner-worldly ascetic can also engage in gesellschaft, attempting to always humanize or spiritualize that culture.

STUDY QUESTIONS

- How can a gesellschaft-embodied society be beneficial for health?
- Explain how a gesellschaft-embodied society reduces our demands on energy resources.

WORKER-PERSON DUALISM

Two versions of human social life exist in a society or culture. One is the gesellschaft society, the other the gemeinschaft. This can be consistent with a Cartesian sociology with one place being an object-lifeworld, the other a purely scientific world. That dualism is not unlike a nation half slave, half free. However, I must interpret gesellschaft and gemeinschaft in the dualistic framework. In dualism, one group is a neighborhood, the other group is a huge mall or a "neighborhood" where people are mostly workers.

The dualistic idea of the two kinds mean a gesellschaft society with more and more automation and technology, and another as gemeinschaft with people doing things, generally without technology. This dualistic notion appears present in the world. Developing countries contrast with highly industrialized nations. Indeed they are opposite the world powers. People in the developing countries lack utilities, education, transportation, health care, money, and all other opportunities and amenities we see in industrialized nations.

Citizens of the world powers visiting developing nations could well experience culture shock, just as developing citizens probably undergo surprise visiting an industrialized nation. We may find citizens of developing nations living in community, where families are together. But there the comfort ends. Poverty and lack of opportunity exist in a world power and in industrialized nations, but the poor and disenfranchised may be a significant part of the population of a developing nation. A nation, warned Lincoln, cannot live half slave, half free. However, the world of 2017 seems to allow a globe where a few nations are overwhelmingly gesellschaft, and most developing countries gemeinschaft but without opportunities.

A phenomenological approach to resolve gesellschaft-gemeinschaft dualism involves reintroducing producing, distributing, and consuming of goods and services into community. This revitalizes the neighborhood and restores people's identities. It minimizes or eliminates anonymity.

PERSON POSTMODERNISM

Inside institutions persons, where gesellschaft disregarding gemeinschaft means the anonymous economy, roles, society, and the like, gemeinschaft rejecting the gesellschaft suggests that matter and society are good, but that persons resent technology as an end in itself. Gemeinschaft-alone is the neighborhood family business, where people rarely, if ever, communicate with other neighborhoods.

Gemeinschaft-alone, or disregarding gesellschaft, is not as extreme as is institution-as-function of the world-rejecting ascetic. The world-rejecting ascetic rejects and leaves society (even gemeinschaft-alone), believing matter and society as evils. However, gemeinschaft-alone individuals reject only the gesellschaft and roles ideas. They do not reject society, technology, or innovation as such. Many of the Amish and others have telephones. Forty or more years ago, I exchanged typewritten letters with a professor from Temple University who was Amish.

Put another way, world-rejecting ascetics leave society and reject sex, the body, and typical social and sexual activities of the body. Matter is evil. On the other hand, once we are inside institutions or culture, gesellschaft-rejecting people are in gemeinschaft-alone. This situation involves perhaps the inner-worldly ascetic accepting matter and society, but rejecting technology for technology's sake. Technology and science are good, but within a very limited context.

Gemeinschaft-alone persons might reject the computer, handhelds, and other electronic devices. These individuals could, in time, learn to use them in the most basic ways, but attempt to minimize the use. However, they could well enjoy and use at length the manual typewriter if these continue to exist.

If gemeinschaft-only individuals learn to use the computer, they may restrict using it to typing or word processing. They do not use the computer for every possible reason that the manufacturer intended. The average desktop computer may have hundreds of uses. Gemeinschaft-alone questions and rejects most of them.

Gemeinschaft-only questions prolonged and perhaps any use of YouTube, movies, and the like. While watching them occasionally for relaxation or distraction, the gemeinschaft-alone could prefer way away from the computer and resting on a sofa, going for a walk, and so on. The issue of YouTube presents a problem for gemeinschaft-alone. This view does not like most of technology. YouTube might have a limited place in Gesellschaft embodied, but little or no place with gemeinschaft-alone. In gemeinschaft-alone, movies, plays, and concerts ought to always be social events, not something to be merely viewed on a home desktop or home and traveling laptop. The media will not occur. Any entertainment or instruction ought to occur on-site, at a theater, school, or other appropriate social gathering. Media at home or traveling will have little or no place.

Technology is good but very limited. Gemeinschaft-only does not reject the manual typewriter. But even here, technology has limits. Gemeinschaft-alone wishes to hand write on a greeting card, or send a hand-written letter to friends and relatives. Not every recipient requires or ought to have a typed document. Gemeinschaft-alone seriously limits the use of the manual typewriter. Gesellschaft embodied uses the manual typewriter more liberally, but seriously limits, perhaps prohibits the modern desktop computer. This embodiment might reject or seriously limit the laptop and the handheld devices.

STUDY QUESTIONS

- Explain how gesellschaft-gemeinschaft dualism can impact on neighborhood business.

- How comfortable would you be in a gemeinschaft-only neighborhood, though it would be in a typical city?

SOCIETAL CHANGE AND STABILITY H.II

SOCIETAL CHANGE MONISM

Society consists of more and more interpersonal acts where we try to be gemeinschaft amid gesellschaft. In one day, the individual goes to the pharmacy, hair stylist, bank, grocery store, and mass transit station. More things to humanize. Persons as merely workers and as I-thou change as ends in themselves. In transportation, change-only would mean bus stops and routes are never stable: They change constantly, confusing people as to where to catch the bus and which streets are part of its route.

Once change in the identity of the individual as person and worker takes hold, society may attempt to reestablish stability and human dignity in the face of changing job market. A worker could become a "pencil pusher," sitting behind a desk in a bureaucracy.

Paperwork and red tape become keywords in a fast changing society.

SOCIETAL CHANGE PHENOMENOLOGY

Gemeinschaft-gesellschaft change embodied. Work changes as needed. No change occurs for its own sake. Reflection helps people and leaders to decide if new kinds of jobs, complexity, and change are needed. Politicians calling for jobs is simplistic. Jobs ought to be humane, performed by people, and respectable instead of meaningless work. Kant (1987) would say societal reality change without stability is blind, and societal stability without change is empty.

Once embodied change, over a period of generations, has been from blue collar (manufacturing or industrial) to white collar (information or knowledge worker), society progresses, according to people like Daniel Bell. However, slow as that has been, Bell (1976) claims it is good, where Andrew Dubrin (1974) questions sharp demarcation between knowledge and manual work. He points out that zero intellectual and zero manual work do not exist. Physicists continue using their hands; custodians their thinking. We will always need blue and white collar workers. Embodied neighborhood change in the workforce warns us to transition carefully and never jettison manual labor, industrial work, or manufacturing.

SOCIETAL CHANGE-STABILITY DUALISM

One neighborhood is pure community without complex roles, while another is only anonymity, industry, and change.

SOCIETAL STABILITY POSTMODERNISM

A neighborhood is only the family farm in rural areas. Minimal if any technology exists.

STUDY QUESTIONS

- Explain the impact of constant change in gesellschaft-gemeinschaft change-only regarding bus routes and bus stops.
- Predict a gemeinschaft-gesellschaft stability-only community's future in a big city.

SOCIETAL PROBLEM AND PERSON H.III

SOCIETAL PROBLEM MONISM

We are alert and react to solve problems of gesellschaft and gemeinschaft. Blue collar unions usually emerge as the workplace is alert and reacts to solve the problem of reducing the I-thou relation to mere worker and even further reduction.

People may be workers, but when they need be alert and react to endless reduction as mere worker, problem solving becomes routine, and prevention is forgotten. Union leaders wait and watch for companies where working conditions deteriorate. The leaders then move in, or try doing so, after deterioration of the worker's dignity.

SOCIETAL PROBLEM PHENOMENOLOGY

People prevent problems of gesellschaft and gemeinschaft. If good company executives prevail, government regulations may not be needed. Ethics codes within companies, or more accurately, ethical attitudes on company executives' parts, could help prevent workplace deterioration. For Kant (1987), a societal problem without a person is blind, and a societal person without a problem is empty.

Unions would not need to exist if corporations, including nonprofit and not-for-profit institutions, have good executives and policies. Those policies see the worker as a human being, a "thou," instead of a mere producer.

SOCIETAL PROBLEM DUALISM

We ignore the problems of gesellschaft and gemeinschaft, then we react with the goal of understanding and solving the problems after a crisis occurs.

As a result, national regulations either come to be or increase. Unions emerge or expand. This is time dualism. An initial time occurs as we ignore the worker. But when crises, unrest ensues and the government or unions decide to react on behalf humiliated workers.

SOCIETAL PROBLEM POSTMODERNISM

People deny from the start the existence of problems of gesellschaft and gemeinschaft. This is a broad social or cultural version of political isolationism. A corporation might deny that it is reducible people to anonymous producer and consumer. Sufficient unrest by workers, unions, or the governments can result in the company shutting down.

STUDY QUESTIONS

- Predict the consequences of alert-reactive problem solving in gesellschaft-gemeinschaft.
- How would problem denial impact on the gesellschaft-only neighborhood?
- How would problem denial impact on the gemeinschaft-only community?

CHAPTER NINE

PROPERTY REALITY:
PUBLIC AND PRIVATE

KEYWORDS

theocracy: The church is the state.

homology, isomorphy: Derivations of a reality are variations of a basic shape.

Inside societal reality is property reality as a public and private twofold theme. In any state, perhaps in a church, property can belong to any of at least four owners: the entire membership, membership as individual-friendly, membership-individual dualism, and individual-only property.

John Rawls (1971) and Robert Nozick (1973) give the egalitarian and liberatarian/anarchic social/political/economic philosophies, respectively. One aspect of their divergent thinking goes into the public-private dual theme. If, as anthropologists Kluckhohn and Murray (1967) posit, human beings are in some ways the same, somewhat different, or totally unique, then in simplified terms, any organization or society itself is partially public and partially private.

The relation of public and private can mean at least four views. Taxes from the people and/or exports are the only support; income which the state or church receives by producing and selling goods or services pay for public property and events. Second, people pay taxes for public property but can own and sell something for profit on such property. Third, no connection might exist between public and private property (the government or taxpayers might be unable to send police, firefighters, and so on to a private area). Finally, a land might have only or primarily private ownership with no tax support or basis.

PUBLIC AND PRIVATE I.I

PROPERTY PUBLIC MONISM

Any social organization can be public-only. This is property monism, where one property reality, public areas, exists. The government, the public, is property structuralism and owns all things. Individuals own little or nothing. Revenue for "public-only" activity and artifacts usually comes from taxing the public or from income that the public government receives through sales of state-owned production of goods and services.

Taxation may or may not exist. The revenue usually depends on government selling to other governments or to its own people. Another source of money is from tourism. When people from a police state or a democracy, anarchy, or caste system visit a centralized, public-only state, their spending fuels that government.

When people think of public-alone, the state owning everything, they usually have an image that is common. That image suggests a secular dictatorship, probably rejecting God. In fact, a theocracy can have centralization, and can be public-alone. All property might belong to the nation. In a theocracy, a government exists, but goes by what the leaders feel is the rule by God. The leaders are (most likely) clergy.

In a theocratic public-alone nation, the church is the state. Its revenue may come from a good it produces. This could be oil or any critical export. Most if not all services are free to the citizens. Schools, health care, and communications, which can have private ownership in democracies, are government run or public-alone in the theocracy.

PUBLIC PHENOMENOLOGY

A state can be a combination of public and private property. Democracy is usually such a government, in that it allows or encourages private enterprise. Where the totally public government produces and sells goods and services for income, and must therefore have major exporting, a democracy relies on taxes. A democracy, relying on private corporations and individuals for taxes, has little to nothing to sell which the state produces. Kant (1987) would say public without private is blind, and private without public is empty.

Public embodied allows for private enterprise and private property. However, virtually every community where private property exists, the private owner can and does call public police and fire departments. In public-embodied areas, the public and private mesh together.

Among the state-owned items that a democratic state uses are military uniforms and weapons, federal law enforcement badges and weapons, military and civilian schools and buildings, and other things we call "federal property." The government in a democracy contracts with private companies to produce these goods and services. It uses tax money to pay the private and public employees. If the federal government in a democracy builds federal roads, it awards a contract and pays with tax money the employees of a private firm to produce the transportation needs.

Tensions can occur in public embodied economies. Politics, economics, social problems, and the like, could erupt when some suggest nationalizing the private corporations. Some people believe that nationalizing private firms could be a way of preventing corruption. That reaction to corruption in private companies raises the question of whether evil or incompetency cannot occur in state owned or nationalized organizations. A public enterprise has the supposed advantage of minimal to no competition or chaos among competing groups offering the same good or service.

This nationalization can look similar, however, to something in a free enterprise system that provokes government antitrust regulation. The government usually opposes private sector monopolies. But a state-own property as the organization of production of goods or services can mean a monopoly. A monopoly in private enterprise is supposedly bad, because prices can be fixed. But we can see chaos in the public sector where monopoly does not exist.

Nationalization does not necessarily end chaos. In providing services, the public organization in a state can be equally chaotic. Take law enforcement. Evolution of police organizations on the federal level in the United States now includes the US Secret Service, Federal Bureau of Investigation (FBI), Drug Enforcement Administration (DEA), US Marshals Service, Bureau of Alcohol, Tobacco, Firearms and Explosives (ATF), and others. Jurisdictional disputes, blurring of jurisdictions, interagency task forces, and the like can result from the belief that integrating federal law enforcement automatically means smooth functioning. The agencies we note above are public instead of private police. Yet reflection and not just nationalization can prevent chaos, disputes, and uncertainty. For the sake of efficiency, the US Secret Service ought to be under the White House, while the FBI also ought to be under the White House, instead of the US Department of Justice, and include the DEA and ATF.

In the public or government sector, a similar situation exists with intelligence agencies. Sixteen agencies gather intelligence. That is clearly no monopoly. But the CIA came into being after Pearl Harbor because the government felt centralizing in the public domain can result in better intelligence. Wrong. After September 11 the president established the Director of National Intelligence to whom the CIA would now report. Before September 11, the CIA reported to the National Security Advisor, and a Director of National Intelligence under the Advisor did not exist.

The military is a good example of the central/public. The army, navy, marines, and air force are different. Our government built the Pentagon building to bring these public institutions together.

Private companies produce the uniforms, weapons, badges, and most other equipment which the Defense Department and intelligence agencies use. Private companies produce fire arms training facilities for federal law enforcement.

Private organizations such as colleges and other educational institutions know the game. Seeking and accepting tax money in a democracy means the government, the taxpaying public can criticize and stop state funding for a private institution. If the private institution violates what a lobby or pressure group perceives is a federal protecting a minority, lobbying members can protest the private organization. The private institution must either change and conform to federal standards or lose funding.

STUDY QUESTIONS

- Predict your life if you lived in a state that acknowledged little or no private property.
- How would private firms relate to public/government agencies in such a scenario?
- Explain the controversy if taxes support private institutions.
- Predict the problems of a public-only theory of ethics.

CHURCH AND STATE

Among the most delicate problems in public embodiment is state funding of activities in a house of worship. Should the taxpayer pay for even a secular program which a church, synagogue, or other religious group runs? Many taxpayers might resent that their hard-earned taxes are supporting a religious institution in a country acknowledging separation of church and state, regardless of the secular activities involved.

The issue of separations is complex. Separation can be of church and state, of public and private secular organizations, and the like. Should a religious group meet and otherwise be active in a public school or other tax-funded location? Taxpaying members of religions whose youngsters do not meet in the public building will argue that their taxes are paying for a location where another religious group meets. How much should the state intervene, regulate, or oversee a private bank, club, or corporation? Private bankers could well object to such state activity on the grounds that government is intruding instead of helping the free enterprise system. An issue that confronts the public is the display of religious symbols on city property. Should a religious organization display a spiritual theme on city property during that religion's holiday? Citizens belonging to another religion, of that or any city, could protest that such display violates church-state separation. Atheists would join the objections, arguing that tax-funded public area seems to be supporting a religious symbol, forcing them to visually acknowledge a belief system to which atheism opposes. And to complicate the matter, should the city allow a religious group other than the initial one to display a symbol representing its faith?

Speaking of religion and public property, the debate over prayer in public schools is legendary. Taxes from citizens belonging to different religious groups, pay for public schools. Should the state allow students or anyone to pray with words representing one group? A Jewish group could argue that the school is forcing their children to pray a Christian prayer. If it is possible to make this more complicated, another question arises. People claiming to be atheists pay taxes. These taxes go to support public education. Should the state allow prayer in a school when the money from atheists is supporting a public school, especially where their children attend? This is akin to the atheist's opposition to religious symbols on public property. Atheists will argue that their taxes should not fund a public institution which forces atheist children to pray at all.

One aspect of the separation of church and public state has had a good track record. Few have complained. Public schools cannot teach a religion class where the aim is indoctrination. However, many tax-funded, public schools, especially in higher education, have courses on world religions. Here, the state, the taxpayer atheist or agnostic, is simply funding a public program where all students can critically examine world religions. Public and private property discussion can include the church.

A house of worship generally depends on voluntary donations from members. In any case, revenue from those who belong to the church become funds for operating the institution, which belongs to everyone. Church property belongs to all members. The property is private relative to the state unless the sovereign country is a theocracy. In a democracy with some separation of church and state, church buildings, land, playgrounds, and other facilities are private, belonging only to the church.

As property that is private relative to the secular state, the church's physical facilities are "public" or held in common for all members of that institution. The public nature of the church facilities is embodied during specific times. For example, when members or visitors wear coats and hats as they enter, they generally seek to hang these on coat hangers inside the building. Their coats are private relative to the church building. The house of worship must acknowledge a particular individual's privacy in that sense. A member's coat or other wearing apparel belongs only to that individual, not to the church. It does not become part of the church's property. One member's wearing apparel is never public within the church.

Wearing apparel even of the clergy is private and does not belong to the church. Clergy members purchase their outerwear, which they have during worship services. Their gowns and any religious symbols they wear are never "public property" belonging to other clergy.

The church can also have a public-private relationship with free enterprise unrelated to the religion. If a church owns land, it builds a building and may lease it out to businesses, schools, any nonreligious organization.

Secular properties can include integrative policies. Public buildings facilities frequently have newspaper stands and even food and drink stores. Private facilities can contract with the local, state, or federal government to have public offices, probably serving the community. Public embodied includes a systems approach to property. This is a true human factors perspective. Public property, tax-supported, ought to match the limits and abilities of private ownerships and citizens.

Philosophically, a dualistic approach to property, in the following section, makes no sense. Public and private properties cannot and ought not to exclude each other.

If by public we mean shared private activities and ideas, the educational system has an interesting thought on integrating the public and private. Private educational institutions must have accredited courses, which students can transfer to other private schools, and to public ones. Private physics, private history, and the like, do not exist. Knowledge is public.

Private citizens and public officials contribute to knowledge. But public and private schools have to work together in terms of teaching transferrable courses. A school at any level can introduce a new course. However, that course or discipline must eventually accord with established knowledge. If discrepancies and anomalies emerge, they eventually need to be acceptable aspects of public knowledge.

STUDY QUESTIONS

- Predict the controversy if taxes support a secular activity in a house of worship.
- Why must a private school be careful to offer courses that can transfer to public school?

PUBLIC-PRIVATE DUALISM

Most residential or commercial/industrial areas of a city are combinations of public and private property. A private home, company, club, or house of worship is still situated ultimately on public land, or within a public city. Yet private citizens, company owners, club leaders, or religious institutions can and must call city police or fire departments in emergencies. Imagine dualism in these cases. Imagine that a home, company, club, residential area, or "city within a city," is totally distinct from the public, thus the government.

That dualistic scenario almost occurs within the state in a democracy. A top-secret military base or building may be all but self-contained. It becomes a city within a city. The Pentagon may be such a place. However, this is not total dualism. A dualistic system occurs in two ways. One is when the people may well belong to either one, but not both places. The people would have to exist totally in only one of two locations. They live, work, play, and do everything in only one public or one private place. The other is when individuals live in a bedroom community and travel routinely to shopping in a mall five miles or more away in another suburb or distant part of town.

Pure dualism does not necessarily exist even in the Pentagon or in any self-contained city-within-a-city. People working in the Pentagon buy newspapers, wear civilian clothing, and use computers and handhelds that they bought from private companies.

PROPERTY PRIVATE POSTMODERNISM

This relation of the public and private may be libertarian, perhaps anarchy. The private individual is the only or primary power. Such individuals ought not to simply pay whatever level of taxation the public or state demands. Indeed, Nozick (1973) argues that a contract theory would mean that the public is a function of the private, and the individual together with other persons determine the public's power of taxation. Public as a function of the private is the private-only or private-alone.

A major problem with private-alone is chaos. If private-alone or almost alone is the rule, what of currency? What of language? If each individual has their own currency, a federal government might well consider that counterfeiting. If each person developed their own language, this could well become cultural and linguistic dissolution lacking national identity. The example of the Tower of Babel may be too strong here, but it could be appropriate as a reference to results from private-alone.

As noted earlier, the public-alone and central-alone does not prevent or end chaos. The federal government can have many agencies in law enforcement, all tax-funded. With overlapping jurisdictions, chaos can occur even with public agencies. The problem of chaos seems to depend not on what is private or public, but the number of organizations serving the same purposes in the public or in the private sector. A nation, state, or city ought not to have too many law enforcement, medical, or educational agencies. The country ought to limit or monitor the number of agencies in each category.

Huston C. Smith (1966) speaks of the existential and analytic polarities. The former dislikes systems and object reason, the latter do see existential language as substantial or cognitively meaningful. Smith (1966), like Hartshorne, wants something between the two extremes. In the public-private debate, the private-alone dislikes government, the public-alone finds private-alone as seriously curtailing, perhaps stopping the system from functioning. I need to clarify a point in philosophy and thereby in the public and private issues.

Subjectivity in philosophy ranges from existentialism, to postmodernism, to nihilism, solipsism, and skepticism. This range tells us that subjectivity is not monolithic. Similarly, perhaps homologically or isomorphically, the private sector or public-alone might well not be monolithic. The two major ideas in private enterprise and private government are libertarianism and anarchy. Libertarians want very little government. Anarchy, by etymology, means "an-archy," or no government.

Private-only property is homologous with idiomatic-only, contract-only, or existentialism and subjectivity-only. Yet technically, a private home or other property owner has the right to call police or fire departments when need be. No town can insist that private citizens require private safety facilities or resources. Private-only property means that a community may have no public property, but that could lead to anarchy.

STUDY QUESTIONS

- Explain the notion that total dualism does not exist at a public place like the Pentagon.
- How is the private-only issue a variation of the metaphysical subjectivity-only principle?
- Explain how private homes and business are ultimately public embodied.

PROPERTY CHANGE AND STABILITY I.II

PROPERTY CHANGE MONISM

Properties public and private change constantly. Their meaning, limits, and opportunities change always.

In the past twenty or thirty years, controversy has hit religious expression on public property. Religious groups have argued that Christianity is among other religions, and courts ought to allow display of symbols from various faiths on public areas. Exasperating the problem are antireligious groups. Atheistic organizations argue in court that religion has no place on public or tax-funded property.

PROPERTY CHANGE PHENOMENOLOGY

Public and private change only as needed. Taxation is part of ongoing debates regarding religion, schools, and tax money. Parents sending their children to church-related school argue that they should not be forced to pay taxes. Their children do not attend public schools. For Kant (1987), property change without stability is blind, and property stability without change is empty.

On the other hand, others complain that houses of worship often seen tax money for charitable work done for the entire community. A church, synagogue, or mosque might not inquire of the poor seeking the institution's help about their religious beliefs or lack thereof.

PROPERTY CHANGE/STABILITY DUALISM

Property change/stability dualism means that property is private one day and public the next day. Or one is totally private, and the other is totally public. Private enterprise and other nonpublic activity may not occur on public property. Similarly, public events cannot take place on private property. Taken too seriously, private citizens at home cannot call public police or fire departments. Police and fire departments serve only public officials and property.

PROPERTY STABILITY POSTMODERNISM

Property as public or private never changes. A city or town usually has both kinds of property. If neither changes, a city-owned building or tract of land will always remain a tax-supported property. Private homes and business will continue indefinitely as owned by a citizen.

STUDY QUESTIONS

- Explain the issue if public and private property never change.
- Would you feel comfortable in a small town or large city regarding the speed of change in public and private property?

PROPERTY PROBLEMS I.III

PROPERTY PROBLEM MONISM

We are alert and react to solve property problems after they occur. Adherents of this view know that religious and atheist organizations exist and will attempt to display or go to court to stop religious displays on public property. Kant (1987) would argue a property problem without a person is blind, and a property person without a problem is empty.

PROPERTY PROBLEM PHENOMENOLOGY

Problems in property are prevented before they occur. According to this preventative approach, religious, legal, antireligious, and other civic groups can meet to discuss differences regarding theological symbols on public property.

PROPERTY PERSON-PROBLEM DUALISM

Property problems are ignored, then solved after reaction. Communities ignore possible controversies and antagonists relative to the use of public property for private purposes. Religious, political, and other civic organization simply act in the belief that their displays on public areas will provoke little, irrelevant, or no outcry. But once the protests and complaints start, the problem erupts and the displaying organizations now react after ignoring the issue.

PROPERTY PERSON POSTMODERNISM

No problems of public or private property exist.

This situation is an extremely naive and idealistic position. Its presumption is almost impossible. Society presupposes that all issues of public and private property are solved or prevented. That state will not insist on taking whatever private property exists. Individuals will not have disputes regarding private organizations displaying symbols on public property. The state will not initiate any privatization, and individuals or groups will refrain from expand any existing public property.

Realistically, property person postmodernism means every situation of public and private property is valid and need not change. A tribe is correct, a completely socialist state is fine, a totally libertarian or anarchic political system is valid, as is public-private dualism. No situation, no relation between public and private is unjustified.

This postmodernism might well be the global version of anarchy. No world standard of the relation of public and private exists. Nations may do as they please, tribes and other political sovereigns can engage in their own notions of state and property.

STUDY QUESTIONS

- When problems occur regarding public and private property, explain the importance of a Supreme Court decision to set a law in place.
- Explain how easy or difficult it is for a small town of homogeneous religion or political views to avoid problems or controversy regarding placing symbols on public land.

Below are exercises for this chapter. They are intended to be like chapters when readers fully articulate them. I have stated that each earlier exercise consists of a reality that, in turn, consists of new twofold themes. Readers are to write in some detail how each exercise ought to be a chapter.

EXERCISES

The following exercises, when completed, are to become small chapters.

1. Inside public and private is authority reality of central and local.

2. Inside central and local is career reality as town work and gown work. Town is the production and consumption of goods and services. Gown is the production and consumption of thinking about production and consumption of goods and services. Town involves earning money through production and consumption of goods and services. Defense work is not inside the idea of money; law is not from inside international relations.

3. Money reality: chemistry and money irreducible to currency

4. Banking: physics (digital) and irreducible to technology

5. Defense reality: conventional and unconventional forces

6. International relations reality: enemy and friend

7. Intelligence reality: techint and humint

8. Inside humint, spy and academic

9. Police reality: criminal and innocent

10. Firefighting reality: chemical and beauty

11. Food reality: nutrition and humanity

12. Clothing reality: threads and culture

13. Shelter reality: physical and humanity

14. Transportation reality: motion and humanity

15. Recreation reality: money and fun

16.   Medicine reality: illness and health

17.   Procreation: babies as chemistry and as beauty

18.   Sales/shopping reality: purchasing and socializing

19.   Water reality: chemistry and humanity

20.   Utilities reality: chemistry and humanity

CHAPTER TEN

THEOLOGICAL REALITY:
GOD AND PERSON

KEYWORDS

pantheism: God is the world.

theism: God is one, manifest in history.

deism: God is distinct from the world.

atheism: God does not exist.

agnosticism: God may or may not exist.

theology of culture: The religious dimensions of the secular.

Chapter 9 concluded with exercises, one of which was the church, inside which is the twofold theme of God and person. Chapter 10 now articulates that theme.

Although I use the word "God," my intention is more than explanation of the personal deity of Zoroastrians, Jews, Christians, and Muslims. My discussion in this chapter touches broadly on the spiritual as in Buddhism and Taoism, which is beyond quantification or verbalism.

Is God everything (pantheism)? Is God historical (panentheism, theism)? Can we say God is distinct from the world (deism), and along this line, are there many gods distinct from each other (polytheism)? Finally, some many object to my putting together two different issues: do we know if God exists (agnosticism), and the position that God does not exist (atheism).

Chapter 6 concluded with exercises including the relation between arguing for and faith in God. The present chapter, dealing with God, considers the major arguments for the existence of God. These are the ontological, cosmological, and teleological arguments.

ONTOLOGICAL ARGUMENT

The ontological argument (Deane 1962), for God's existence is more philosophy than theology. It says that God exists because I have the idea of God. I have an idea of that, than which nothing higher exists, according to Descartes. The problem here is that I can have an idea of anything, such as little green men from Mars. That idea does not mean that little green men from Mars exist.

Benedictine monk St. Anselm (1033–1109) first proposed the ontological argument for the existence of God. Descartes and others continued the argument. For St. Anselm, God is "that than which we can conceive of nothing greater" (Davis 1997). God, according to St. Anselm, is someone other than the West's notion of the historical God. The creator is also something more than traditional polytheism, pantheism, or nontheism as in Taoism. St. Anselm's God is a strictly philosophical idea, about whom or which people think.

COSMOLOGICAL ARGUMENT

St. Thomas Aquinas gives us five ways of the cosmological argument (Clark 1972). I restrict myself to three of the ways. First, God is the unmoved mover. Motion exists in the universe, but God is the primary or unmoved mover. A critique will ask how why does motion require an unmoving mover? Second, God is the uncaused cause. All effects have a cause, but God is the uncaused or First Cause. Third, God is a necessary instead of contingent being. To be necessary means God is everywhere during all times. This is an ideal which resonates with many groups of people. Civil rights and human rights advocates will demand that all people have dignity.

The cosmological argument (Clark 1972) is associated with and receives intellectual, scientific support from the big bang theory in physics. According to this argument, every effect has a cause, and every cause is thereby itself an effect of a previous cause. This can and will lead to the infinite regress, unless we have an unmoved mover, or uncaused cause. God, according to the cosmological argument, is the first cause.

The idea of creation comes into play with the cosmological argument. This argument has tended to conflict with steady-state theory of the universe. What matter created, or is it eternal? But if the universe is many, perhaps infinite big bangs, then God might well be able to continually create and de-create the universe. Matter and God being coeternal may not delude the cosmological argument, or power of God. God and the world, God and matter, are partners, with God as the center.

However, if we design God as the authority to take our fallibility into account, what does that mean? For an ergonomic theology, it could mean that God is central and creator, but this divinity is one that takes us into account.

TELEOLOGICAL ARGUMENT

The teleological argument (Paley and Knight 2008), points out that every design reflects a design. For this argument, the universe is a design. Therefore, the design, orderliness, system, structure, reveals a designer: God.

This argument assumes that the universe is a designed, orderly reality. While Newtonian and relativity theories consider the universe as orderly, quantum physics sees something else. Disorder, or at least something that physicists have detected as lack of regularity and counter-intuitive reality, seems to underlie subatomic physics.

But disorder could well be part of a larger picture. We may not understand in 2017 what could appear intelligible in the future. If by order we mean a reductionist perspective where all this is predictable, our chapter on prediction suggests as one option the reintroduce of determinism into probability. Purpose, goal, or telos must be embodied in the human. Could this mean that goal or telos ought to be seen as probability-friendly?

William Paley (2010) gives a good account of the teleological or design argument for God. If we see a watch and how it is designed, the conclusion is that a watchmaker designed it. According to Paley, the world is a harmonious, well-designed place. It must therefore have a designer. This designer is God. If people see hate, the Holocaust, wars, disease, how do we account for design? Theodicy says God has a plan or design of which we are unaware. But a flaw in that point is what could be the purpose of the Holocaust? Some might argue that it shows human failure. God has a plan, but has given us freedom to violate divine laws. It is human responsibility to co-work God's plans.

GOD AND PERSON J.I

GOD MONISM

Pantheism is a combination of "pan" (all) and "theism" (God). This combination says that God is everything. In that sense, God-only as pantheism exemplifies theological monism. Theological monism means theological reality is a deity structuralism where individuals and the world have no identity. No difference exists between the world and God. Deity is the world, the entire universe. In this case, God is not the creator, but instead, is the world itself. If God is the world, then deity is not acting through the world, for the universe is the deity. History as we know does not exist. What is occurring is deity. Just as God does not act through the world, the deity is not acting in history. The world and history, if there is a distinction, are the deity.

GOD PHENOMENOLOGY

Theism is the theological position that God is acting through human beings, the world, or history. Scholars call this the historical God. If you wish to "see" God, look at history. History reveals the powerful, awesome nature of God. Scholars call theism as monotheism, because the historical God is one instead of many Gods. A Kantian view (1987) would be that God without a person is blind, and a person without God is empty.

If the one God is awesome, powerful, and is everywhere at all times in a sense, then theologians and others have a problem, or at least a question. Pantheism means God is literally everywhere at all times. If the historical God is omnipresent but not pantheistic, then scholars coin another term: panentheism. This word denotes a God or deity who or that is all-in-a-sense. This God is not pan-theistic but is theistic, which appears in derived, mysterious, holistic ways, all times and places. What we see is not God, but "parts," aspects, images, or messages of deity. Thus, this is pan-en-theism. Panentheism becomes a compromise, as it were, between pantheism and theism.

The compromise denotes a modifying of omnipresent. God is everywhere at all times in terms of aspects, or limited revelations of deity. A rock, a person, or an event are not God. Each is a specific, limited expression of deity.

Theism or panentheism involve the idea of "theology of culture," or "the religious dimensions of the secular." A connection exists between God and history, between deity and time-space-matter. Where theology and religion speak of God, and perhaps of the human condition, theologians and religious leaders open themselves up to a possibly very productive implication of spirituality and the secular, material, and historical.

A discussion of theology of culture, or the religious dimensions of the secular, can start with pantheism. If God is everything, then the secular all but does not exist. In deism, God is distinct from the world. Polytheism may be more connected with the secular, worldly, historical. In theism and panentheism, to say God acts through time, space, and matter, in short, history, then God is thereby revealing a holiness in the world. A spiritual, holy, Godly dimension exists in human and nonhuman activities.

Culture, according to theology of culture, is never merely secular (Kazanjian 1971). Culture, secularity, is more than human. Human activity is more than a material, mortal, human action. Specifically, theology of culture might spell out religious or theological dimensions in terms of the holy.

The words "holy," "holistic," "whole," "health," and "wholesome" relate to each other. They derive from the Latin *hale*, according to getwellstaywellamerica.com. This roughly means whole. The holy describes God or spirituality as being whole, instead of capable of being reduced to parts. The whole of each chapter is the whole we see in the right hand word of each dual or twofold theme. In object and subject, the first chapter, subjectivity may be the whole: this is the irreducible human being.

Theologians of culture might say that seeing the whole person, means seeing something of the holy God. Any word on the left side of a twofold theme in each chapter, is the atomistic, structural, changing, or systematic topic we must then put into the context of the person. They ought to represent or reflect and be in dialogue with the person.

According to theology of culture or the religious dimensions of the secular, the spiritual or theological is the power reflecting secular, human effort. A book on theology of culture differs somewhat from this present work. This book starts with the metaphysical and applied the idea of reality to all chapters. Among the ideas is theology, as in the present chapter. My book is a secular work. Its primary, some might argue, exclusive, aim, is for a general audience including the religious and nonreligious. If my book were a theology of culture, the first chapter would most likely be this one, or a variation. I would indicate the notions of God, or spirituality as foundations for all derivations. The derivations or different chapter would then show how secular thought is essentially sacred.

A theology of culture may not be possible for pantheism, deism, agnosticism, or atheism. It might be possible for polytheism. For some thinkers, religious dimensions of the secular could include deism. Deists could argue that God created the world, instilled the holistic as the derivative holy, and moved away. The religious dimensions of the secular reveal a God or spirituality which is not now connected with the world.

Harvey Cox's (2013) brilliant *Secular City*, Teilhard's (1967) *Divine Milieu*, and *Paul Tillich's Philosophy of Culture, Science & Religion* by James Luther Adams (1973) exemplify a few efforts in theology of culture. The secular is not just secular, the sacred is relates to and can be found in the secular.

Nontheism could also involve religious dimensions of the secular. Mircea Eliade (Munson 1968) informs us that non-Judeo-Christian religions exhibit spirituality. These religions involve members who act in certain ways instead of moving merely physically. They do as the gods did in primordial time, a time before history. Because the individuals behave in certain ways, their actions are sacraments instead of reducible to physical motion. Moving about, eating, sleeping, sex, playing, and so on in certain ways, as sacraments, shows the people are being spiritual and real. They reveal a religious, sacred, more-than-secular dimension. Their behavior manifests the sacred dimensions of the secular. If Buddhism, Hinduism, Taoism, Shinto, Jainism, Sikhism, do not believe in the personal God, they are polytheistic or nontheistic.

The whole person orients the word on the left hand side. If the left hand word is God or spirituality, theology of culture says the human being has a spiritual or religious dimension. That means that the person would act in certain ways, even perhaps believe certain things, thereby becoming holy or whole. Ancients and people of nontheistic religious, according to Eliade (1966), saw reality as the holy because they would act in certain physical ways to become holy or real.

Members of those societies sit, eat, engage in sex, walk, go to war, plant food, hunt, or do other routine things in the ways that primordial gods did them. Today human factors engineering, or ergonomics, tells us to do things in ways compatible with our anatomic makeup. Diversify and use care in handling of heavy objects, type for a reasonable time, walk in ways reflecting skeletal and muscular ease. Do not just do something. That is not wholesome. Do something where the physical gestures take into account physical, mental, and psychological limits and abilities.

Human beings are not totally reducible to arms, legs, heads, and fingers. We are holistic and must take care of the body, acknowledging its limits and abilities. That would mean the approach of theology of culture. Could not we behave in healthy manners, avoid mentioning God, and still be good? Could people not do things in a healthy way and be atheists? Theology of culture suggests that we may be religiously illiterate if we think we are not acknowledging God or spirituality when behaving in a healthy manner.

STUDY QUESTIONS

- If the world is God, how legitimate do history and science become?
- Explain how God acting in history enables us to understand the nature of deity.
- What implications for the presence of God in time and space does theology of culture offer?

GOD-PERSON DUALISM

Pantheism and theism help us put deism in context and definition. Pantheism means God is the world. Actually, it denotes one God as being the world. Theism (and panentheism) denotes that one God expresses through the world or history. With theism, God is differentiated from the world, where pantheism tells us that God is identified with and not differentiated from time, space, and matter. Deism says that God is totally distinct from the world. Deity created the world, then moved apart. The world moves by itself, independently of the creator. Where deism implies there is one God distinct from the world, we can associate polytheism with deism by suggesting another distinction.

Polytheism means that two or more gods are distinct from each other, whether or not they are relating to history. "Poly" means "many," and "theism" is God.

Phenomenologically, a theology would reintroduce the deistic God into the world, restoring the embodiment of the deity. Philosophical or mind-body dualism appears more strongly and seriously as a problem than does deism.

Calling someone a deist does not seem to have the same issue as dualism. Critics might not ask how it is that the deistic God relates to the world; that God simply does not, and that is that. Of course, Sian Beilock (2015) notes that mind-body dualism does not appear to be the stigma or problem which the phenomenologist sees in Cartesian dualism. Some (Beilock 2015) suggest that thinking does not affect the body. Thus, deism may be a legitimate theological stance for many. God is not acting in history. But to do so, we would then, in Ricoeurian fashion, reintroduce God into the world, and recover deity's spatiotemporal historicity.

Nontheism means a spirituality exists such as Nirvana, which is not monotheism, polytheism, or henotheism.

THEOLOGICAL PERSON POSTMODERNISM

With nontheism, agnosticism and atheism, we come full circle on the nature or existence of God. Pantheism is certain that God exists to the point of identifying deity as the world. Theism, panentheism, deism, and polytheism express certainty that God exists. Nontheism, agnosticism, and atheism, appear to fit into another class. Some may argue the nontheism does not mean the person is alone. One interpretation could mean, however, that the person does not have a personal God.

Nontheism believes in a spirituality which is not a personal God. Buddhism and Taoism may be nontheistic. Agnosticism expresses uncertainty as to God's existence or reality. Atheism clearly says that God does not exist. These three theological positions range from the view that only a nonpersonal spirituality is real, to skepticism about spirituality and God, to clear denial of spirituality or God.

STUDY QUESTIONS

- Explain the implications of deism and atheism for human factors engineering, which insists on the technology-person interface.
- Compare theology of culture's emphasis on God doing good in the world and atheism saying we ought to do good in the world but there is no God.

THEOLOGY CHANGE AND STABILITY J.II

THEOLOGY CHANGE MONISM

Theology changes always, even if not needed. This change can involve a religion's encounter with cultures different from those of members who are accustomed to or part of an initial society. Cultures clash. Technologies and times change. Newer ideas infiltrate. Suddenly, a theology finds itself perhaps having to change, or thinking that it must adapt to a newer worldview. A view of God and the world may change for the sake of change.

These changes as ends in themselves may occur as theology meets secular views. Secular society seeks a more worldly, less religious stance. A Hindu man told me that each time an astronaut went into space, some of his friends in India and here rethought the existence of a Hindu god.

Changes as ends in themselves can also occur when different theologies converge and perhaps do battle. Islam and Hinduism did battle, and the Sikhs emerged.

Theological change can occur due to illness or tragedy. Mary Baker Eddy (Stafford 2017) discovered and founded the Church of Christ, Scientist after reporting miraculous recovery from a serious fall. She claimed that good thoughts helped her. Health, she proclaimed, depends on how we think, instead of medical assistance. According to Eddy (1934), God created everything good; therefore, illness cannot and does not exist. Illness is in our minds. Eliminate the thought of illness, crisis, any problem or obstacle, and the concern goes away.

Theological changes in the ideas of God and person are the basis of splinter groups in religion. The Protestant Reformation was not the way Martin Luther (Roper 2017) called for refreshing the Roman Catholic Church. He sought reform within the church. Luther demanded the priesthood of all believers. He came centuries after Buddha tried to reform ritualistic Hinduism. However, various Protestant groups splintered and emerged thereafter as Lutherans, Presbyterians, Episcopalians, and Methods, many mistrusting each other. And splinter groups abounded in America, including Mormons, Seventh-Day Adventists, Christian Scientists, New Thought, Plymouth Bretheran, and others.

Theological change-only could mean religious notions of creation adapting to evolution without regard to interpretations of the divine.

THEOLOGY CHANGE PHENOMENOLOGY

Theology changes as needed. The Protestant Reformation, noted above, was basically trying to reform the Roman Catholic Church. "Protestant" meant that Catholics "protested" or put forth their faith. Observers can understand the Reformation as an attempt to reform, not replace, Catholicism. A Kantian (1987) view would be that theological change without stability is blind, and theological stability without change is empty.

Change for its own sake can mean creating a new theology or church. But embodied change acknowledges stability. In that sense, change is the effort by current members of an existing theology to modify, reform, and otherwise humanize an existing church.

Jesuit thinker Pierre Teilhard de Chardin (1965) believed that creation and evolution could be reconciled. For him, the change of evolution occurs within the stability of God's love. God is in process but does continue from the start as God. Christ is from the beginning as well. For many, Teilhard might have been the starter of a new view within either the Catholic or Protestant religions.

A new religion is not totally new. It is the cleaning of existing religions, a going back to basics or stability of religion. Early Christians did not intend necessarily to replace Judaism. Buddhists did attempt a religion different from Hinduism. Martin Luther wanted to reform the Catholic Church, not establish the Lutheran Church. Mary Baker Eddy believed that the Church of Christ, Scientist was simply revitalizing early Christianity.

THEOLOGICAL STABILITY-CHANGE DUALISM

Theology is stable at one point and then merely changes. A person can grow up in one religion and for various reasons change to another or others.

Very likely in this position is the scenario of going from belief in God to agnosticism or to atheism. Persons can initially be religious. Then any number of reasons can persuade them to change to no belief. Those reasons can include sudden tragedy, illness, living conditions, the world situation, or academic and intellectual development.

THEOLOGY STABILITY POSTMODERNISM

Theology never changes. A theology that never changes might eventually become irrelevant and disappear. For example, a religion whose members reject society, technology, and most aspects of modern civilization could soon die out. On the personal level, a person might be born and raised in a religion and never change throughout his or her life.

The controversy over evolutionary theory is one area in which stability-only appears. A person might have been born and raised into a creationist theology. That individual may wish to never change. He or she will always be antievolution.

Theological stability-only can also be interpreted as a church or religion completely devoid of missionary interest. By this, I do not mean sending missionaries to other countries, but doing good in our urban areas. Gibson Winter's (1961) *The Suburban Captivity of the Churches* criticizes Christian congregations for moving to or having started in the suburbs, neglecting helping the unprivileged in the cities. They are in captivity in the suburbs, homologous or isomorphic to the "Babylonian captivity" in France of the pope.

STUDY QUESTIONS

- What are the implications of changes in theology as an end in itself for religion adapting to new times and places?
- How comfortable can you be if theology never changes?

THEOLOGY PROBLEM AND PERSON J.III

When do individuals or groups decide on theological options and problems? Do they do so after alertness and reaction to a theological problem? Is the decision based on preventing problems? Do people ignore and then react to theological problems? Is their decision based on denying such problems exist?

THEOLOGY PROBLEM MONISM

Alert-reactive theology is attempting to solve or try to solve theological problems after they occur. Such theology is not proactive. Persons holding a theological or philosophical position regarding God or spirituality will be alert and react to solve what they perceive is the issue. This could mean that the holder of a position meets someone who believes in another theological view. The holder has been attentive to such incidences and perhaps has a plan to implement when meeting the individual who has a different idea about God.

If the individual holding one position meets someone with another view and thinks that other belief is wrong, the first person can convert or engage in dialogue. In a world of diversity, dialogue can involve an intellectual discussion with both sides understanding and analyzing differences. Dialogue might well include one individual attempting to solve the problem of the other person not understanding the first person's theological orientation.

People holding and understanding religious or theological knowledge may also be alert and react to those who lack understanding of this knowledge. Many people today have misunderstood, or never heard of, Buddhism, Islam, Taoism, and other religions. These individuals lacking such knowledge are typically Americans who have not encountered a diverse population or have not studied different people and religions while in school.

THEOLOGY PROBLEM PHENOMENOLOGY

In preventative theology the basic idea is to help teach children a theological position before they grow up. Family, schools, and houses of worship, if there are any, reach the children regarding a particular position about God. A good education for theology centers on teaching children about the family's view but also how these relate to other theological or religious perspectives. Kant (1987) would say a theological problem without a person is blind, and a theological person without problems is empty.

Such outreach is proactive. It prevents children from growing into adulthood with misunderstandings regarding religious perspectives.

I find it disappointing that adults I have met do not know the difference between Catholic, Christian, Presbyterian, and Eastern Orthodox within Christianity. The number of adults who do not understand Hinduism, Buddhism, and Shinto is astounding. People have told me that Jews, Christians, and Muslims share the belief that God exists. These individuals do not further articulate that Jews who are other than Secular believe in the coming of the Messiah, that Christians believe Christ has come in Jesus, and that Muhammad founded Islam. Preventative theology would prevent such religious illiteracy.

THEOLOGY PROBLEM DUALISM

Where alert-reactive theology denotes individuals who are alert and react to religious illiteracy, or other theological issues, ignorance-reaction dualism may be more serious. Here, adults ignore religious thought. They have not studied or argued pantheism, theism, deism, polytheism, nontheism, agnosticism, or atheism.

A rude awakening occurs to those ignoring religion. Suddenly, they meet people who discuss religion, or daily headlines regarding suicide bombings, regional conflicts as in the Middle East, or see a new neighbor wearing non-European clothing and speaking a foreign language. The awakening can also occur for military members finding themselves in a foreign country. US military members accustomed to separation of church and state, may be uneasy or perhaps overwhelmed when assigned in another country where. That other nation takes religion seriously and fundamental to their daily life. And the member, at worst, can encounter what to do when amid people whose religious orientation is nothing as the military person has seen in America.

Adults exist lacking early exposure to different religions. These individuals may have attended religiously affiliated schools of the most strict kind. They could have studied in secular educational institutions. In their late teens and early twenties, they do not know the difference between Catholic and Protestant, or types of Protestantism.

Only a crisis in life jolts them out of their comfort zone and they need to react. A former student of mine told me of a family problem. The parents and children were raised Roman Catholic. One of their children was a son. He decided to marry a woman who, it turns out, was Protestant. My former student told me she was curious about the whole situation and not very upset. The parents were upset and confused. They talked with their son, little with the future daughter-in-law.

The son had heard that his girlfriend and eventual wife was not Roman Catholic. With a serious desire to understand religion, he had inquired into the girl's religion and inferred she was Christian. She mentioned that her family did believe in Christ but was not Roman Catholic or Eastern Orthodox. With the least amount of knowledge about her religion, the son concluded that she was a Christian, but not Catholic. His family upbringing had made him believe the world is either Roman Catholic or not. But since his future wife believed in church and Christ, this led him and his parents to conclude that Roman Catholics and Christians exist, each believing in Christ, and then other religions are also real.

I noted to her, in a world religion class, that Christianity is a major religion with at least three divisions. These are Roman Catholic, Eastern Orthodox, and Protestant. The former student was adjusting to culture shock, as were probably her parents. They went from ignorance to trying solving a problem of understanding religions, especially Christianity and Roman Catholicism.

THEOLOGY PROBLEM POSTMODERNISM

Where ignorance-reaction theology will initially ignore, then react to an encounter with religion or religious illiteracy, the denial theological stance refuses to acknowledge that a religion or religious illiteracy are a problem.

For denial theology, other nations and other people within this country can believe what they wish about God or spirituality. That is not a problem for individuals in denial theology. They do not ignore and then react to a religious problem; these individuals deny that the problem is real and needs attention.

Problem denial theology frequently involves people trained and fixated on one religion as the truth, unwilling to see what other Faiths offer. Confrontation with other religions is not an opportunity to react and solve a theological problem. Encountering another religious or theological position is simply a chance to insist on the validity of one's own religion, and the others' error.

Jessica Stern's (2003) powerful *Terror in the Name of God* could well serve as an insightful primer into theology problem of denial. The suicide bomber, even the terrorist who plans to live in heaven after terrorizing, believes his or her religious position is absolutely valid. Other religions either do not exist, are not religion, or are infidel.

STUDY QUESTIONS

- Explain alert-reaction, ignorance-reaction, preventative theology, and denial theology dealing with theological problems in a very diverse, quickly changing world.

- What are a few implications of dealing with theological problems during times when suicide bombers commit their acts in the name of a God?

EXERCISES

The following exercises, when completed, are to become small chapters.

1. Inside gown (student) is academic reality as intern and campus.

2. Inside campus is university reality as buildings and people (Ryle).

3. Inside buildings is infrastructure reality as facilities and persons (facilities alone, prison; facilities via persons; facilities and people; chaos of facilities).

4. Inside facilities is a room reality of lab and class.

5. Inside lab and classroom is teaching reality, meaning teacher and student.

CHAPTER ELEVEN

KNOWLEDGE SOURCE REALITY:
EMPIRICAL AND RATIONAL

KEYWORDS

empiricism: Senses are the source of knowledge.

rationalism: Reason as innate ideas and tendencies is the source of knowledge.

Kantianism: Senses and reason work together for knowledge.

Within the teacher and student twofold theme exercise in chapter 9, epistemological or knowledge source reality means the two themes of empirical and innate ideas. Is knowledge sensory experiential? Do we know through inborn ideas or tendencies? Or is knowledge some combination? Put in other words, are teacher or student learning from sensory experience, innate ability, dualism, or a combination of sense perception and innateness?

Epistemology is derived, epistemological reality. That is, it is the epistemological application of metaphysical atomism and structuralism, interaction, dualism, and existentialism. How I place epistemology demands a summary or comprehensive outline of philosophy. Philosophy underlies all knowledge and human activity. Philosophical unity comprises metaphysics and all applied topics. This book is about perhaps the thirteen most prominent "branches." While metaphysics is loftiest, ethics is near the top as general.

The traditional position of epistemology has been high in philosophy. Philosophers speak generally of branches, including the main ones of metaphysics, epistemology, and ethics. Philosophers see epistemology as equal in stature to the studies of reality and ethics. Unfortunately, philosophy isolates epistemology, the source of knowing, from all academia or the educational and psychological fields.

This isolation is ironic inasmuch as education and psychology are the disciplines dealing with knowledge. In isolating epistemology from academia, as the study of the origins of knowledge, philosophy restricts this field to the debate involving empiricism, rationalism, and Kant (1987). In other words, philosophy has limited its vocabulary to knowledge as sensory experience, innate ideas, or a combination. But we know today that knowledge is in our nature, or to be nurtured by teachers, or is a combination of nature and nurture.

Today nature and nurture probably best explains epistemology's two themes of the innate and the experiential. We are aware and speak of the child prodigy, very slow child and adult learner, and the average student (Bukatko and Daeler 2004; Rathus 2003). Human beings need teaching and mentoring even if they are gifted. Some will argue that I have demoted epistemology by separating it so far from ethics and metaphysics. Others will disagree that I put epistemology with education and of traditional philosophy. This is wrong. I only put source of knowing where it seems to belong, in the teacher-student relation instead of just behind or even before metaphysics and ethics. The teacher-student relation includes analysis of sources of knowledge in broad, holistic, interdisciplinary terms: biological, neurological, psychological bases of cognition, emotion, and related dimensions of knowing. As to whether I have taken epistemology from philosophy and put it with education, I argue that philosophy, broadly speaking, includes all human knowledge, and thus education.

EMPIRICAL AND RATIONAL K.I

Is epistemology atomic (empirical disregarding the rational), Kantian, dualistic, or rational disregarding the empirical? Philosophy books usually treat epistemology by appealing primarily or only to traditional philosophers who have written about knowledge. That practice is fine, except that it may express only debates and speculation instead of references to modern scientific advances in knowing. This chapter will not detail such advances, but it will attempt to clarify four traditional options.

In this chapter on epistemology, we learn about four options to knowledge: empirically alone, through empirical-rational interaction (perceive data within a rational context such as Kant's categories), sensation and reason as distinct, and reason alone. Empiricism disregarding reason derives from metaphysical objectivity disregarding subjectivity. Kantian epistemology (Kant 1987) of empirical-rational interaction derives from metaphysical objectivity-subjectivity interaction (phenomenology). Epistemological dualism derives from metaphysical dualism, and reason disregarding empiricism derives from metaphysical subjectivity disregarding objectivity.

In epistemology, scholars learn about the traditional philosophical positions of empiricism, Kant, rationalism, and romanticism as sources of knowledge. Do people gain knowledge through experience (learning), experience and innate ability with which we are born, or cultural context with possible innate sources? Traditional philosophy does not discuss parallel questions about the causes of crime. Yet, criminology (Gaines and Miller 2012, 43–52; Conklin 1995) routinely discusses whether criminals are born, learn, or a combination of the two. Association of criminal justice and the typical area of epistemology seems obvious, inasmuch as crime is knowledge.

STUDY QUESTIONS

- What are the implications of isolating epistemology from psychology and education regarding the sources of knowledge?
- How is epistemological dualism derived from metaphysical dualism?

EMPIRICAL MONISM

This is empiricism-only. Empiricist epistemology usually calls it simply empiricism. I call it "empiricism disregarding rationalism" to make it more precise, or epistemological atomism. My reason follows. Kant (1987) says that the empirical and rational work together. Descartes argues that they are dual realities (Haldane 1968). If this is the case, then we need more linguistic precision for empiricism: what I call empiricism disregards reason. I could also call it "empiricism alone," or "only empiricism." "Empiricism" by itself means only that it is sense experiential. Given Kant (1987) saying empiricism and reason are together, and Descartes (1999) that they are two realities, I argue for "empiricism alone" and "rationalism alone." The empirical is disregarding, interacting with, distinct from, or being disregarded by rationalism.

Put another way, given Kant and Descartes noting a relationship between empiricism and rationalism, "empiricism" and "rationalism" standing by themselves are incomplete sentences. In Kant (1987) and Descartes (1999), sensation either explicitly interacts with or can deceive relative to reason. The word "empiricism" is an incomplete phrase or sentence. We need empiricism-disregards-reason, in order to see that emphasizing sensation as the source of knowing means empiricism disregards the rational.

John Locke (2010), George Berkeley (1897), and David Hume (Millican, 2008) are empiricists. Among Arabs and Muslims (Morgan 2007) Ibn al-Haytham, Ibn Sina or Avecina, and Ibn Rushd or Averoes are empiricists. For empiricism in India, there are the Nyaya (Audi 1993) and the Charvaka (Audi 1996) schools of philosophy. They argue that most fundamental knowledge comes to us through experience. Tasting a lemon gives us the idea of sourness, and sugar the notion of sweetness.

From Hindu thought, Charvaka philosophy (Charvaka 2017) is the position of empiricism and materialism. The senses give us knowledge. Many Hindu thinkers embraced the notion that this material world was all there is. Sensory experiences of sight, sound, and touch, provide fundamental knowledge of reality.

EMPIRICAL PHENOMENOLOGY

Kant is a major leader here. This is epistemological phenomenology before phenomenological thought emerged, though Kant is not associated with the phenomenological movement. In *National Geographic* (Edmonds 2017), talks about genius. The article tells us two points about knowledge. For embodied or phenomenology, knowing originates through innate ability and external nurture, with luck and opportunity added in. Knowing is more than empiricism. It is also rationalism or innateness. But this also points out the limits of empiricism. The rational or innate also plays a major role. The genius is born with something more in the innate than typical people. But the genius is a good example of, and makes a good case for, innateness and rationalism.

While philosophers do not publicize it to a great degree, the romantics' disagreement with Kant deserves notice. Kant argues that categories are rational, logical, and universal (Velasquez 2011). Romantics disagreed (Blanning 2012; Velasquez 2011). Categories, if they exist, are more than rational, or perhaps not reason at all. They are also not universal. According to the romantics (Applebaum 1996; von Humboldt 1993), knowledge is not just rational and global, but particular and nonrational. Sociologists (Berger 1967), argue for a sociology of knowledge, where knowing is a social enterprise as people construct reality. This is akin to Gadamer and the later Wittgenstein saying knowledge is interpretation.

Categories and whatever might color our perception, reflect culture. This means particular cultures or societies. Knowledge in Germany reflects German culture, perhaps even parts of Germany. Meanwhile, people in the Philippines know reality in terms of their island nation, and indeed in light of different parts of their country.

Michael Polanyi introduces his famous *Personal Knowledge* with the words that there is "personal participation of the knower in all acts of understanding" (Polanyi 1962, vii), individuals participate in what they experience. Knowledge is not simply "out there." This Kantian and phenomenological view very generally correlate with Jerome S. Bruner's idea that our mental (and noncognitive?) structures influence perception. Jeremy M. Anglin (1973, 397) compares Bruner's pedagogy with the perspective that "cognitive structure, theory, generic coding system, internal model, and system of representation, gives meaning and organization to regularities in experience." That organizing "goes beyond the information given" (Anglin 1971, 397) but does mean as it does for Hume that organization, cause and effect, are only in our minds. Inferring that the mind organizes and colors perception of the disciplines does not mean an objective reality does not exist. Anglin (1971) say the mind contributes to and does not, as in solipsism, invent objectivity.

Noam Chomski (1998) argues for language structures, and Kenneth Boulding speaks of the image (1968) with which people are born. *Hidden Persuaders* (Packard 1957) says advertisers and product makers know we are innately prone to be attracted by certain colors when buying. Medicine knows very well the placebo acts on the patient's inherent willingness to believe medical authority and the ability of medicine to cure an illness. From the field of criminology, psychological profiling (Osterburg and Ward 1997) exemplifies cybernetics and Kantian epistemology. Profiling steers away from mere investigation or gathering of facts, and toward a general idea of the suspect or perpetrator. More accurately, profiling ought to steer between (away from) mere positivism or gathering of facts, and negative bias devoid of facts. Around 1970, related to criminology, sociology, psychology, indeed all social sciences and humanities, someone suggested what we might call positive psychology: what are the causes of good behavior, or the person who is not a criminal? Kant's categories provide us with "phenomenon," or the "thing-for-me," which is what we can know, while his idea of "noumenon" or "thing-in-itself" (Kant, 1987) is what we cannot know. I would argue for thing-in-itself as objectivity alone, thing-for-us, and thing-for-me as subjectivity or rationalism alone. Technically, Kant ought to have said there are three things in epistemology: thing-in-itself, thing-for-us (knowledge which all know), and thing-for-me (almost solipsism).

STUDY QUESTIONS

- Compare empiricism and rationalism as to the source of knowing.
- What is Kant's contribution to epistemology?

COLORING PERCEPTION AND ACTION

A church dinner held a surprise for me. I learned something along this line of empiricism embodied. The season was fall. People were raking and bagging leaves on their lawns. During conversation with a friend, a church leader at the dinner was discussing what he saw was a relatively unusual event. A friend of his is an engineer and works with mathematical precision. According to the church official, the engineer did more than just rake and bag the leaves, and close the bag. He made sure the bags were full with as equal as possible content of leaves. The bags then appeared to be the same size, with the same volume of leaves. The engineer then taped the bags shut in a precise cross shape.

This may not mean that every engineer does the same thing. It does reflect something which the church leader noted. "The man," he said, "is an engineer. And so, he filled each bag with as precisely the same as possible a volume of leaves, taping the bags in exactly the same way." The implication was clear. The leader felt that nonengineers simply fill the bags with leaves, and tie the draw strings, not worrying about the volume. If draw strings are not involved, than any other reasonable means will shut the bag.

The engineer's background played a decisive role in the bags. Of course, the engineer reflected a profession, not a culture as we know it. But it did reflect something underlying the act of raking and tying up the bags. If nonengineers rake and tie bags in different manners, it seems to mean that the romantics see something that Kant did not. Kant might have argued that every individual rakes and bags leaves the same way globally. Romantics would argue that different cultures, professions, and other contexts rake and bag according to their own contexts.

I mentioned above the phenomenological movement. Thinkers, especially phenomenologists, tend to identify phenomenology with metaphysics or a study of reality. In that sense, phenomenologist will contrast the subject-object interaction with positivism, even linguistic analysis where the emphasis is on objectivity.

Phenomenology has implications for epistemology. Knowing, according to phenomenology, would be as much context and subjectivity as it is objectivity. The chapter on interpretation gave us strong implications about this. Simple-only language means that people know only what is an objective meaning. No interpretation is necessary. However, simple-language-embodied involves idioms and thus rejects total objectivity. In epistemology, empiricism embodied becomes a phenomenological position, where values, social context, interpersonal interactions, in short, subjectivity, plays a major role in what and how we know.

Kantian epistemology argues that innate categories organize our perceptions (Kant 1987). That is a rational, logical approach. It is a continuum of sense-reason. Phenomenology is another continuum, this of sense-values. Phenomenological is more than a logical approach looking at the rational dimensions imposed on sense perception. The phenomenological view involves emotion, feeling, value, and other nonrational, nonlogical resources. Yet Kant and Husserl, indeed the former and most phenomenologists, share the idea that perception is in the context of something within ourselves. We do not just perceive, says Georg Gadamer (2013). Culture and even biology color our perceptions and actions. Kant's (1987) view is that perception without concepts is blind, and concepts without perception are empty.

A modern, biological interpretation concerns the eyes. The color blind individual cannot distinguish between certain colors. The empiricist might have argued that all persons perceive green, blue, red, and other colors as these appear outside us.

A major reason that epistemological thinkers generally do not associate themselves with Kant is their values' perspective. Kant is strictly thinking of the rational, logical context of perception. He argues for the "subject-object" interaction for epistemology, but certainly is not defining subjectivity in the phenomenological, values sense. For Kant, subjectivity is a rational foundation for perception. Phenomenologists see subjectivity as nonrational existence and conditions for rationality.

It seems to follow that a new perspective is necessary for empiricism embodied. This might mean redefining or broadening of embodiment, of subjectivity, or of the subject-object interaction. Subjectivity implies the person. However, the person is rational and nonrational, as well as irrational. John Searle may be in the analytic tradition, but his refutation that "knowing" Chinese is its understanding, with the Chinese room experiment, suggests phenomenological lines. If we translate one language into another with help, this is empirical knowledge, not a lived experience understanding the language and its idioms.

STUDY QUESTIONS

- How does our background color our actions?
- Compare phenomenology and Kant as to knowledge.

METHOD AND SPONTANEITY

Empiricism embodied puts empirical method into subjective context. But method does exist, and Karl Popper (2002) believes in hypothetical method governing knowledge. We proceed methodologically but take subjectivity into account. Pure empiricism or induction is wrong, according to phenomenology, Kant (1987), and Popper (2002). But method there is, and here, Paul Feyerabend (2010) objects in his *Against Method*. Feyerabend, perhaps more appropriate for the epistemological subjectivity, innateness, and spontaneity section in this chapter, says knowing, science, and human progress depend individual initiative, lack of authority, and the antimethodological approach. Lakatos (2000) attempts to reconcile Popper (2002) and Feyerabend (2010) and appears to therefore take on a more balanced, phenomenological/Kantian view.

Stephen Pinker's (2003) *Blank Slate* is a well-documented treatise rejecting the empiricist-only argument that the mind has no innate capabilities for knowing. As I have argued to my students, a piece of paper cannot be taught. The slowest student in history can be tutored for relatively modern knowledge.

EMPIRICISM-RATIONALISM DUALISM

Plato and Descartes are the big names here. Plato (Hamilton, Edith, and Huntington Cairns, 1964) speaks from a cosmological view, while Descartes (1968) explores the noncosmological perspective.

That is, Plato sees two worlds, the ideal involving or known through mathematics and the forms, and the material (our present) world of change. For him, the ideal world is one of reality and truth, where knowledge is valid. Knowledge in this material world is sensory and illusory. What we know and understand through recollection involving thinking, is real knowledge. Sensory knowledge and material experience are invalid.

Descartes says something similar. He speaks of two realities but as mind and body, not about this and another world (Haldane 1968). The body and its senses give us imperfect, wrong, invalid knowledge. Our minds, however, contain innate, certain knowledge.

Surprisingly, phenomenology spends much time attempting to overcome Cartesian metaphysical dualism of two realities but little time publicizing epistemological dualism. Maurice Merleau-Ponty (1995) may be an exception, speaking of the body's role in perception. Paul Ricoeur (1966), writing about restoring the embodied mind, could well have said much about reintroducing the empirical into the innate. He could have extolled and praised the virtues of Kant's (1987) bringing together sense perception and reason.

Where phenomenology talks of phenomena as "anything that appears to consciousness" (Husserl 1982, p. 110; Stewart and Mickunas 1990), adherents to the movement might well write about knowledge phenomena as any knowing that appears to consciousness. Phenomenology can refer to epistemology as well and metaphysics. Empiricism-alone sees cognition as resulting from sense perception. Rationalism-alone says cognition results from innate ideas. But cannot cognition be any cognitive capacity appearing to us innately? Of course it can. Positivism uses the term cognition to say that existential and emotional statements have no cognitive meaning. So they associate cognition with a metaphysical movement.

Ironically, even a cursory analysis reveals an intriguing point in both men. Mathematics is true knowledge in Plato (Hamilton, Edith, and Huntington Cairns, 1964) and René Descartes (Haldane 1968). That view bothers me. The history of any discipline shows change, evolution, and development. Plato and Pythagoras (Cornford 1966) believed mathematics has an unchanging, eternal quality to it. Today we know that mathematics changes and develops almost every day.

STUDY QUESTIONS

- How does empiricism embodied differ from empiricism-reason dualism?
- How does our background color our perception and actions?
- Explain the implications of Feyerabend, Popper, and Lakatos on whether method is important in developing knowledge.

RATIONAL POSTMODERNISM

Godfried Wilhelm Leibniz (Leibniz, 1951) and Descartes are the big names here from the West. For the Arabs and Muslims (Morgan 2007), Omar Khayyam, and Abu Jafar Abdullah al-Mamun are rationalists. In India, Mohandas K. Gandhi was a member of the Jain religion whose adherents were rationalism, and the Vedas also involved innate knowledge. This position is epistemological subjectivity almost disregarding objectivity. Some knowledge is a priori. Descartes, a dualist, admits that sensation gives knowledge which can deceive (Haldane 1968). But he also insists that we have innate ideas, which are certain (Haldane 1968). Leibniz (1951) and Descartes (1984) differ on their notions of what is innate. Leibniz (1951) says we have innate tendencies, while Descartes argues that we have complete ideas (John Cottingham, Robert Stothoff, and Dugald Murdoch, 1999).

If empiricism is the epistemological view that knowledge originates from sense perception, outside the observer, innateness includes rationalism as the position that we know in terms of innate ideas. Look in almost any philosophy or epistemology work, and you find the term "innate ideas." Philosophers repeatedly state that knowledge is either sense perception or innate ideas. Thinkers seem to identify innateness with ideas.

Descartes believes in innate ideas (John Cottingham, Robert Stothoff, and Dugald Murdoch, 1999). Perhaps Plato agrees (Hamilton and Cairns 1964). As noted, Leibniz (1951) disagrees. According to Leibniz (1951), human beings have innate tendencies and potentialities, not fixed, clear, distinct ideas. The child prodigy and the brilliant adult exhibit unusual intellect or physical ability. However, geniuses at any age normally do not and cannot achieve their goals alone. They often need tutors and good instructors to help them develop their inherent levels of knowledge (Kessen 1966).

Probably the most advanced or gifted adult or child requires a sympathetic mentor, coach, or guide. The mathematics whiz needs a mathematician, the physics prodigy must have a physicist. A child or adult with a major talent in history, psychology, or social science will be frustrated without an historian, psychologist, or social scientist. Similarly, the usually talented child or adult athlete requires coaching.

Also part of innateness are the romantics. They argue that knowing originates from within, but that a given culture colors our perceptions. Where Kant says innate categories are rational, logical, and universal, the romantics maintain that particular cultural contexts influence sensory experience.

SUMMARY

Let's upgrade or update philosophy through epistemology. Reason as the source for knowledge can be innate ideas, or innate tendency. However, let's add wonder (romantics versus Kant's rationalism). Still, these leave philosophy with sources of knowing which omit or ignore examples likes the slow learner, average student, and child prodigy. The slow learner learns primarily through sensory experience, tutoring, life experience, and other external motivations. Average learners learn in what the school calls reasonable time. The child prodigy plays the piano, learns calculus, draws outstanding art, and performs athletics perhaps starting at age four or younger.

STUDY QUESTIONS

- What does a child prodigy seem to prove about innate knowledge?
- Explain the difference between Leibniz saying we have innate tendencies and Descartes saying that we have innate ideas.
- Predict an implication of humans having innate tendencies.

KNOWLEDGE ORIGIN CHANGE AND STABILITY K.II

KNOWLEDGE ORIGIN CHANGE MONISM

This position means philosophers change our ideas of the source of knowledge as an end in itself. Speculation may well occur without empirical research.

KNOWLEDGE ORIGIN CHANGE PHENOMENOLOGY

Philosophers change epistemological positions as needed, regarding the source of knowing. A Kantian view (1987) might be that a source of knowing change without stability is blind, and stability without change is empty.

EPISTMOLOGICAL CHANGE-STABILITY DUALISM

Philosophers change ideas on the source of knowledge in some area, and never change on other ideas regarding the source.

EPISTEMOLOGICAL STABILITY POSTMODERNISM

People deny that an epistemological problem exists even after one occurs. This may be epistemological dynamic subjectivity disregarding objectivity. A new idea occurs, but society denies that it is important.

People deny that understanding empiricism, reason, Kantian thought, are important. Individuals may refuse to see the significance of studying the sources of knowledge. This could be particularly dangerous when traditional philosophy declines to acknowledge advances in psychology, chemistry, biology, ethics, education, and pedagogy for philosophy and epistemology.

Too often, the typical philosophy course in epistemology persists in teaching about Locke, Berkeley, Hume, Descartes, Plato, Aristotle, and Kant. While the history of philosophy and epistemology is good, so is modern science contributing to epistemology. We cannot overlook references to Daniel Kahneman with thinking fast and slow. Let us not overlook allusions to Steven Pinker in whether our minds are blank slates.

Since college, when I first learned of Kant, I have continued to wonder if the categories are real and where they might exist in the brain. Philosophers seem to take for granted that Kant's categories exist. But these same thinkers apparently fail to bring into the classroom and collaborate with experimental and social psychologists, biologists, and neurological experts.

STUDY QUESTIONS

- What could be an economic impact of change-only in knowledge origins, with books written almost daily?
- What can be an economic and scholarly impact on stability-only in knowledge origins?

KNOWLEDGE ORIGIN PROBLEMS K.III

When do individuals know or decide one of the positions in epistemology? Do they decide after a problem occurs, before it occurs (preventative epistemology), after ignoring the problem, or in denying the problem?

KNOWLEDGE ORIGIN PROBLEM MONISM

People are alert and react to solve knowledge origins problems after occurring. They are alert to the problems in empiricism, rationalism, and Kant

(1987). Once solved, they again wait for the next problems to occur to solve in knowledge origins.

Alert-reactive problem solving may argue for empiricism. Yet when evidence suggests knowledge originates from within, the empiricist may be confused, deny, or rush to solve the issue. A person who does not believe or understand the child prodigy will need to rethink knowledge and the gifted child.

At the other extreme, adults who believe strictly in innate ideas will get confused when realizing experience is necessary for certain knowledge. They never tasted a lemon and suddenly find they need to taste a lemon, after which they find it sour.

Leibniz and Descartes differed on innate tendency and ideas. For Leibniz, people have innate tendencies (Weiner 1951). They may become mathematicians, physicists, or accountants, depending on circumstances whereby their quantitative skills are developed. Descartes argued that we have innate knowledge well developed. A person will necessarily become a mathematician instead of a physicist, or a chemist instead of a biologist.

KNOWLEDGE ORIGIN PROBLEM PHENOMENOLOGY

We prevent knowledge problems before they occur. The problem solver seeks to solve problems after they occur. However, this could lead to endless cycles of encountering and solving problems. This view assumes that problems will and should always occur. Prevention believes that we can learn from experience, from problems, and might be able to stop problems before occurring. For Kant (1987), a knowledge origin problem without a person is blind, and a person without a problem is empty.

Knowledge origin problem prevention takes a step back. Prevention studies human behavior and is open to new ideas and experiences. Problem prevention in knowledge origin assumes that some people learn better or faster than others. They have seen this. Some people also learn some things better than do others. And individuals exist who simply cannot seem to learn even simple ideas.

In knowledge origin prevention, scholars will develop and teach strategies to watch and diagnose slow and fast learners, and those who learn some topics relatively easily while unable to study other subject matter.

KNOWLEDGE ORIGIN PERSON-PROBLEM DUALISM

We ignore and then react to knowledge problems. Society can ignore and even condemn or ostracize the slow learner. Educators and others may wonder why children and even adults are slow learners. The adults are ignoring psychology and human nature. Suddenly, a crisis may occur through a civil rights or social justice movement demanding an objective, open-minded perspective on learning itself.

KNOWLEDGE ORIGIN PERSON POSTMODERNISM

We deny knowledge problems occur. This position could well occur in a very rural community, a monastic situation, or ancient tribe. Illiteracy can run rampant in such an environment.

Some religious movements can deny the need for education beyond scriptural training or indoctrination.

STUDY QUESTIONS

- Explain the consequences if philosophers simply believe that we must only be alert and reaction to knowledge origins problems, instead of collaborating with psychologists and others on laboratory research.

- How would problem denial in knowledge origins impact on scholarly research?

EXERCISES

The following exercises, when completed, are to become small chapters.

1. Inside teacher and student twofold theme, innate reality means reason and emotion twofold theme.

2. Within lab and classroom twofold theme is pedagogy reality, meaning online and face-to-face twofold theme.

3. Within online and face-to-face twofold theme is the twofold theme of data and theory.

4. Within data and theory themes is theoretical reality of special theory and general theory.

5. Inside special and general theory are parts and isomorphs.

6. Inside online and face-to-face ideas is anatomic reality, meaning manual and mental ideas.

7. Inside manual and mental ideas is library context reality, meaning online and online/brick-and-mortar ideas.

8. Inside online/brick-and-mortar or hard copy ideas is library content reality, meaning books and philosophy/library shelf (organization) ideas.

CHAPTER TWELVE

INTERDISCIPLINARY REALITY:
DISCIPLINES AND PHILOSOPHY

KEYWORDS

metadiscipline: Philosophy as a discipline organizing, justifying, eliminating, and creating discipline.

metaphilosophy: Philosophical inquiry into the nature of philosophy.

qualitative ergonomics: Human factors engineering designing authority, professionals, and people to take into account human ability and limits.

nonqualitative ergonomics: Human factors engineering designing technology to take into account human ability and limits.

Inside the ideas of books and shelves in the previous chapter's exercise is interdisciplinary reality of disciplines and philosophy ideas. These two are the traditional perspective or definition of philosophy. Books and shelves were philosophy in terms of brick-and-mortar (and perhaps online) library arrangement of information.

But brick-and-mortar and even online libraries contain disciplines. Hard copy books in the traditional library are of philosophy as we know it (inquiry into reality, etc.) and of all other disciplines. Philosophy may well be the metadiscipline, the discipline looking at all disciplines. Library philosophers decide on how to arrange the online or brick-and-mortar libraries and information systems. They work in libraries and help people find books and other information.

The inquiry philosopher will debate, question, and seek answers to ideas as such, which will then be transferred to the library thinker.

I am referring to philosophy as philosophy here, instead of metaphysics. This is only to avoid the appearance of wiping out the term "philosophy." What bothers me is that philosophers acknowledge branches including metaphysics, epistemology, ethics, and the state. This suggests that we have knowledge, ethics, the state, and other branches, and then we also study reality (metaphysics).

Is reality something other than knowing, ethics, and the other branches? It reminds me of the mind-body problems in Descartes, and Ryle and Ricoeur's separate efforts to resolve it. While Descartes has the mind-body problem, philosophy does not have a nonreality-reality problem. All branches—metaphysics, which studies reality, and epistemology, ethics, state, and so on, which study nonreality, or fields not associated with "the real"—are seen as equal. If philosophy does not have the nonreality-reality problem, the problem is, indeed, the theory-application problem. Theory is general metaphysics, application is derived metaphysics in terms of remaining chapters. Let's stick with Ryle's view of resolving the mind-body problem, and then apply that to what I see as the nonreality-reality, derived-general reality issue. Ryle sees body and says seeking mind is a category mistake. I argue that seeing ethics, knowledge (and other branches), and then talking of reality is a subset of the category mistake: a branch mistake. Reality is not other than knowledge, ethics, and so on.

It is their general theory. Each of these (epistemology, ethics, etc.) is real. They are not unreal. But metaphysics has abstract options underlying, as I note, underlying and derivative through, the other topics. Heidegger speaks of "being" as presence for everything. All things "are." Metaphysics, for me, is homological or isomorphic, being the same shape found in various sizes for each branch. It seems reasonable that metaphysics (philosophy) ought to be general and derived metaphysics, instead of there being metaphysics and then other branches. Philosophy would be general or theoretical, and applied or derived wisdom. Seeing knowledge, ethics, and so on is seeing reality in a derived sense. Seeing the branches is seeing wisdom in a derived sense.

STUDY QUESTION

- Explain why metaphysics should not be just another branch of philosophy.

DISCIPLINES AND PHILOSOPHY L

DISCIPLINARY MONISM

One reality exists in interdisciplinary monism. This disciplinary reality is totally reducible to the sum of disciplines independent of philosophy. Here, disciplines are alone, and philosophical inquiry does not exist or has become irrelevant. Extreme and ongoing specialization seems the rule, perhaps some interdisciplinarity can occur.

Jerry Jacobs (2013), however, believes that ongoing, serious boundary crossing does occur, without mentioning philosophy as a key player. Philosophical inquiry becomes all but useless at worst, or is simply another discipline. Scholars are in the arts and sciences, others in technology and professions. Disciplinary specialists look at the world as the sum of areas of knowledge, each area as the jurisdiction of a specialist. Philosophy has no place, because it lacks the empirical perspective of research and gathering of data from the real world.

That limited view of philosophy is ironic, because at the very least, library science books speak about metaphysical positions. Readers find references to positivism, existentialism, phenomenology. Librarians (Radon 1996) talk of Hegel, Kant, and other thinkers.

Disciplines "alone" suggests that philosophy is not the career to which a scholar ought to aspire. The typical college undergrad has a better chance studying literature, languages, music, and other soft culture. Studying or majoring in philosophy will get the student nowhere. Indeed, a strict or literal interpretation of disciplines without philosophy means that philosophy does not exist. Such is the attitude of many even within philosophy. If sufficient numbers of philosophy departments close, and interest in philosophical literature significantly declines or disappears, the field may be seeing its final days. Knowledge is then reducible to the sum of disciplines in arts, sciences, and technology.

DISCIPLINE PHENOMENOLOGY

Disciplinary embodied is the view that the arts, sciences, and technology, while important, are within the philosophical context. Each discipline is at least partially due to the philosophy of that discipline. Scholars believe or assume the philosophical perspective that a sociological, ethical, political, physical, mathematical method and content are valid. This does not mean sociology is distinct from economics. Economics is a social phenomenon. And sociology studies the idea of production of goods and services as a cultural, group activity. Einstein (1931) argues for disciplines embodied. He asked California Institute of Technology students, and I repeat this in the next chapter, to study but always integrate science and technology within the framework of human benefit. Science and technology need the humanities, or art broadly speaking. But all art and science, all the arts and sciences need philosophy as a humanizing foundation. A Kantian (1987) view would be that disciplines without philosophy are blind, and philosophy without disciplines is empty.

Einstein's thoughts regarding the human dimensions of science and technology resonate with MIT officials Jerome B. Wiesner (Conference Board 1966), James R. Killian (1966), and Vannevar Bush (prototype issue). Engineers ought to learn the humanities and philosophy, and must also work with philosophers and humanists. According to ergonomics, engineers do this to the extent that they are ergonomics experts and civically minded engineers. I see qualitative and nonqualitative ergonomics emerging.

Disciplines embodied gives philosophy the task of orienting and organizing disciplines into a humane whole. As philosophy does this, we see the field of metaphilosophy. Metaphilosophy is that aspect of philosophy analyzing the reasons for philosophy.

We need to be careful about analyzing and philosophizing about philosophy. If metaphilosophy as about philosophical method, this could be counterproductive, and we get into an infinite regress about metaphilosophy. Metaphilosophy could become meta-metaphilosophy: what are the methods seeking the methods of philosophy. Taken too seriously, metaphilosophy can have no limits and be an infinite regress unless we wish to stop at some point. The stopping would be a judgment call. We want to stop somewhere before searching about the methods of the methods of the methods of philosophy.

Embodied disciplines of technology/science/art picture unity with varying interpretations of philosophy's interdisciplinary role. Boulding (1968) argues for the image as tying together the disciplines between solipsism and empiricism. For him, the whole-part relationship runs throughout disciplines.

Bertalanffy (1968) sees quantitative unity bringing disciplines together, perhaps as reductionism through *General System Theory*. He appears to foresee Edward O. Wilson. Wilson's (1998) *Concilience* calls for the sciences and humanities to come together, most likely in terms of a "scientific" context. *The Oxford Handbook of Interdisciplinarity* (Frodeman et al. 2010) spells out varying efforts to bridge disciplinary boundaries.

STUDY QUESTIONS

- Compare discipline-only with discipline embodied.
- Predict philosophical inquiry if metaphilosophy turns into an infinite variety of meta-metaphilosophy.
- Explain whether disciplines can become unified and coherent without philosophy.

PHILOSOPHY AS INTEGRATIVE

More integratively, my present work sees metaphysical themes of object-subject, change-stability, and problem-person, tying all knowledge and disciplines. Technology, art, and science are each qualitative and quantitative. And the ergonomics' position or model helps us see that the objective ought to always be subject-friendly.

While philosophers will like my defending the subject matter, they could well disagree or at least question philosophy's power or intent to integrate knowledge. Disagreement and at least questioning could come especially from postmodernists, especially followers of Jacques Derrida (1976). Postmodernism and deconstruction, denying the "author," will express serious skepticism as to unity in knowledge, whether that integration is from philosophy or any field.

I understand postmodernism's skepticism. Subjectivity and objectivity are part of reality, though a postmodernist or decontructionist may insist objectivity is minimal if real at all. With a topic that is part of the system, someone can easily become selective and choose that idea or topic as the only reality. Thus, many things are real or at least derivatively so. One can easily select one of the things as the only "reality." Deconstruction decides that because many things are "real," and therefore many "realities," not just one, exist.

Integrative thinkers in philosophy, management, and other fields would join Hicks (1972) who says disciplines are various perspectives of seeing a mountain. They need integration for us to understand the entire ways we use and appreciate the mountain. Ritchelson (2012) points out that disciplines are various perspectives of seeing an enemy or friendly nation within the context of intelligence agencies.

The position that philosophy cannot be a candidate for integrating the disciplines, puzzles me. It was the first "discipline." Early thinkers such as Plato and Aristotle were multifaceted as both social and natural philosophers. Social philosophy becomes what we term the soft culture of arts, humanities, social sciences; natural thinking evolves into what we call the hard sciences of physics, mathematics, chemistry, biology. Empirical expansion bringing about specialization does not necessarily mean the end of whole thinking or interrelated knowledge.

As information explodes, philosophy can transition from being "another discipline," as Mary Midgley (2016) notes, to the fundamental discipline orienting all knowledge. Philosophy is the generic discipline and takes the spot we would call general education, or liberal arts and sciences. The disciplines including technology, sciences and arts, emerged from philosophy. Philosophy does not give us details about the world's specifics but helps us see that and how disciplines emerge and relate. It is interdisciplinary in that sense.

Allan Bloom (1987) finds that disciplines do not relate as they should. But Jerry A. Jacobs (2013) presents what he believes is evidence that traditional arts and sciences disciplines are doing very good work relating among each other, crossing boundaries, and communicating with and influencing each other. Philosophically, Bloom and Jacobs believe disciplines ought to interrelate, and the latter believes they are doing just that without "interdisciplinary" programs. Where Jacobs defends disciplines, John E. Burchard (MIT Bulletin, n. 16) holds that specialization can give insights into the forest of trees.

Tacit in Jacobs and Bloom, then, is the philosophical position that overview is important. Talking about, defending, even criticizing disciplines is interdisciplinary or metadisciplinary. Explicit in my present work, is philosophy's ability as context and framework that and how disciplines interrelate. A.N. Whitehead (1964a) is just as explicit. Disciplines, through philosophy, are not a list of what Jacobs and the business world call academic silos, but "life in all its manifestations" (Whitehead 1964a, 18). Jacobs sees disciplines relating by themselves, not through philosophy.

Ackoff (1960), like Whitehead, sees universities as departmentalized and call for interrelatedness. Kuhn (1963) attempts to integrate political science, sociology, and economics. I am unsure why he does not continue to history, psychology, anthropology, and other disciplines associated with arts, broadly speaking.

As disciplines cross borders and communicate with each other, they find common points and uniqueness. To paraphrase Hillel, if a discipline is by itself, what is it; if it is not unique, then which discipline will be for it? Disciplines are, to paraphrase and simplify Kluckhohn and Murray (1967), like each other, yet unique.

For human factors engineering, common ground ought to be uniqueness-friendly. The ergonomic approach from a qualitative view sees disciplines as philosophy-friendly. Philosophy as synonymous with general education or liberal arts and science gives students and adults an introductory and ongoing, lifelong reintroduction to disciplines and their internal relations.

Says Whitehead, philosophy is the "critique of abstractions" (1964a, 58). He sees abstraction as analysis of wholeness into parts, as specialization. People see "parts" and not the whole of reality. Philosophy helps facilitate an ongoing dialogue between part and whole, abstraction and unity. Does talking of "parts" deny the gestalt? Not at all. The gestalt of reality is a gestalt of gestalts. Unity, Herbert Richardson (1967) points out in his henology, is a unity of unities. Richardson anticipates my book. My first chapter's first section on object and subject unifies the two other sections in the first chapter, and the first chapter unifies the remaining ones, each of which is a unity in its own right. And, the ethics and linguistic chapters unify the first and remaining chapters from the ethical and linguistic perspective.

The 1961–1962 MIT undergraduate bulletin (Burchard, 1961-2. 6) talks of the classroom as the space for "thinking about" what one is doing in the laboratory. In the context of this current chapter, philosophy is the thinking about what people do in technology, science, and art. Philosophy occurs as students generally think about or critique the disciplines. It occurs also each time a discipline specialist critiques data from within that field or specialty, justifying the subject matter.

Don Ihde (1999, 2012) speaks of philosophers doing research and development, or R & D. Thinkers ought engage in public deliberations, even if behind the scenes thinking about society. Philosophy cannot survive by remaining in a secluded cave unrelated to the real world.

Thinking about doing appears more often than we think. MIT (Burchard 1961–62) tells us its faculty includes theoreticians and engineers. The Institute or MIT instills in students that manual skill is less important in the long-run than thinking or theory (Burchard 1961–62). *The Wall Street Journal* carries an article (Byron 2005) reporting that New York City police (NYPD) trains officers to solve crimes by thinking about or studying art. An editorial in *Chemical & Engineering News* (2004) reveals that some scientists and academic officials believe chemistry is but physics and biology, and we can thus split the chemists between the physics and biology departments, while others argue that chemistry is a legit scientific field. The legitimacy of chemistry as a field is therefore a theoretical one based on philosophical assumptions instead of strict chemical knowledge.

PHILOSOPHER AS GENERALIST

Mary Midgley (2016) and Herbert G. Hicks (1972) would be pleased with the idea of philosopher as generalist. Specialists as disciplinarians ought to dialogue with philosophers as generalists or interdisciplinarians. Her article noted earlier is a philosophical version of Henry Winthrop's (1966b) very insightful "Generalists and Specialists". Winthrop's insights of the debate between the two perspectives present a plethora of interdisciplinary ventures, unfortunately omitting the role of philosophy. That omission may well have resulted from the fact that Winthrop is a social scientist, not philosopher.

Navy "SEALs....are generalists, in contrast to Air Force and Army Special Operators in the Ranger regiment and special forces groups (Landau et al 1999)." In the typical SEAL team, if a member is incapacitated, another from the team can take over the duties of the individual who is harmed. Flexibility and general thinking is key.

Philosophy's role in interdisciplinarity is unique. It connects all disciplines by showing that metaphysics as the relations among subject-object, change-stability, and problem-person, run throughout every field of knowledge. Disciplines are related, and form a network.

That philosophy, to be relevant, should learn from and teach other fields, comes across well in Louise Antony's (2016) presidential address to the American Philosophical Association. Philosophy, she notes, ought to learn from the disciplines, and they from it. For example, psychology and philosophy talk about knowledge. Findings from "each field is pertinent to the other." Antony uses the word "continuity" to explain that no field is discontinuous from each others. No man, says, English poet John Donne (2012), "is an island." Antony and Donne resonate with A.N. Whitehead's (1964b) thought that philosophy is the critique of abstractions. Bush (prototype issue) resonates with Whitehead by saying that the future will see increasing specialization, but equally apparent connections among specialties.

Human beings need to abstract or specialize to learn of reality. But philosophy discerns the continuity among all disciplines.

Of course, the skepticism with which students and nonphilosophy faculty meet philosophy courses, even introductory ones, forces many to question an introduction to philosophy as the liberal arts requirement. Beyond Mary Midgley, myself, and some others, most thinkers cannot see philosophy as basic to general education. It is, they might argue, far too abstract. My point, however, is to try integrating such an introduction and general education overview with contemporary, nonphilosophy authors. This can give philosophy some new blood, noting that nonphilosophy is saying in 2017 language what the earlier philosophers often debated or said.

Of course, with a title "debranching metaphysics," philosophy as the core or overview of general education could well have motivated less enthusiasm than I want. As I reflect on making philosophy and metaphysics as palatable as possible without diluting the study of reality as wisdom, the topic of ethics comes to mind. I have noted in the ethics chapter that its details can be synonymous with city planning.

At the start of the ethics or institution's chapter, I said that theoretical metaphysics applies to all chapters, including ethics. On the other hand, because ethical or moral decisions enter when reflecting on the options of object-only, embodied object, dualism, and subject-only, the general theory of metaphysics/philosophy (reality/wisdom), is applied city planning. The derivative reality of ethics is a "general theory" of ethical reflection of which the general theory of metaphysics is derivative ethics. Applied city planning may be a start for introducing metaphysics or philosophy. Eliade (1966), Whitehead (1964a, 1964b), Manfred Clynes and J.H. Milsum (1970) might help point the way.

Eliade's *Patterns in Comparative Religion* (1966) parallel those of some thoughts from biomedical engineering systems (Clynes, 1970) and Whitehead (1964b). Religion, says Eliade, we can and should ultimately study religion in terms of psychology, physiology, sociology, economics, or any other study. None of these or other disciplines stand alone, none of them are isolated from religion. Whitehead (1964a, 18) says, "Life in all its manifestations" would include "algebra, geometry, history, language, literature" and other topics, each following from and relating to the other. Finally, according to Clynes and Milsum (1970) biocybernetics presents a unified view of human beings. Each person is a biochemical, anatomic, physiological, and psychological matrix. Separating any of these as an isolated study is wrong, perhaps impossible.

A unified, general systems approach to disciplines and philosophy means philosophy is isomorphic or homological to the disciplinary thinking. Disciplines are not just juxtaposed but have the same shape as philosophy. They involve the real and its derivatives. An exercise in the previous chapter deals with isomorphs (homologies).

Many generalists say that specialization is bad. But a liberal arts view says embodied specialization is part of human nature, and overspecialization is a distortion to avoid. Burchard maintains specialization is good, neither hurting nor distorting anything or anyone. "Specialization," says Burchard "is here to stay (1961–62)." Translated, do not overdo liberal arts and hurt specialties, because specialization has something to say. Specialization has a place. Bush (Bush, prototype issue) goes further. "We will have more and more specialization, but more connections between specialties" (Bush, prototype issue). More specialties, but correspondingly more articulated general education connecting the specialties. Specialization does not necessarily equal less liberal arts. Relation between liberal arts and specialized study is not necessarily a zero-sum game.

Whitehead resonates with Burchard and Bush. We need abstraction, but Whitehead notes philosophy is "critique of abstraction (Whitehead, 1964)." For Whitehead, abstraction is specialization; we see parts in order to see whole. Whitehead is saying abstraction is here to stay, just as Bush argues that specialization is here to stay. In Whiteheadian terms, Bush would say we will have more and abstraction with correspondingly more connections through critic of abstractions or specialties. Philosophy connects or bridges all the disciplines, akin to John Friedlander (2006) saying that the Reimann hypothesis in "mathematics becomes a bridge across subjects and connecting seemingly disparate ideas…." The present volume does not explore mathematics or the Reimann hypothesis; my point is only to say that Whitehead's view of philosophy parallels Friedlander's position on the hypothesis; both thinkers see something isomorphic or homological that unifies apparently unrelated ideas.

STUDY QUESTIONS

- Explain how philosophy becomes the foundations of interdisciplinarity.

- How would you argue that philosophy should be the foundations of general education?

- Why do so many people not see philosophy as basic to general education?

CITY PLANNING

Reading Eliade (1966) and Whitehead (1964a, 1964b); Ackoff (1961); Clynes, (1970), Hicks (1972), let's try to substitute "city planning" for Whitehead's "life in all its manifestations" (1964a, 18). According to Eliade (1966), religion shows the sacred integrating life. Ackoff (1961) criticizes university departmentalization or overspecialization. Jones and Jones (1975, 11) point out that "no subject can be happily compartmentalized." Every subject matter is a member of what we could say is a fuzzy set: sociology cannot be isolated from economics, religion, or mathematics. Boundaries are fuzzy, never crisp. Clynes and Milsum (1970) note that human beings are physiological-neurologistanatomic-chemical networks. So, seeing people interrelate in the humane city that may not be a monumental task. All five thinkers agree, independently, that human beings and life itself is not fragmented into isolated islands of knowledge. We experience life as people live, work, and play in social groups defined as towns, cities, and the like, as a unified whole. Integrative views of human nature, of life, become an overview in general education or liberal arts, and the geography of where we reside. Wisdom is the selecting of options to reality underlying these disciplines, and they make up our residences as a whole.

My paper (Kazanjian 1970) "Toward a New Academe" proposes a Resource Institute for interdisciplinary research, as with this book. The Resource Institute would be along the lines of Winthrop's Institute for Intellectual Synthesis (Winthrop 1966a).

The reader can see what I am thinking. Academic disciplines are intellectual access to institutions, teaching us knowledge appropriate to those activities and goals. Institutions or ethics are the chapter on ethics. As city planning, philosophy can go from irrelevance and putting people to sleep, to relevance and excitement. Such planning helps us discern the human, unfriendly (total automation), and too-friendly (monastic) sides of institutions.

Renaming philosophy and metaphysics as city planning is not as incredible as it sounds. Palatability certainly can increase. Just as crucial, support within philosophy exists abundantly. No greater a thinker than Plato talks of and names one of his most well-known dialogues *The Republic* (Hamilton and

Cairns 1964). His philosopher-king is ruler. Almost two thousand years later, political thinker Hobbes (2013) articulates the *Leviathan*. Rawls (1971) and Nozick (1973) speak about their ideal states, even if from opposing poles. The hard sciences are not omitted. We do all knowledge, including hard sciences, within the city, urban sprawl, and similar social systems, perhaps excluding the monastery. Knowledge, ecology, and other nonpolitical activities occur within the university situated inside a political, social, economic, cultural context: the human city. This human city rejects, as does ergonomics, the extremes of the cities with mere automation, and monasteries.

Within the civic context, philosophy, if interdisciplinary as I have tried to do in this book, shows the relationship between general education or liberal arts, and the production and consumption of goods and services. Again, this is relationship between thinking about the production of goods and services, and the day-to-day production of those goods and services.

In possibly renaming philosophy/metaphysics as city planning, I do not wish to be described simply as a political philosopher. Nozick, Rawls, and others are political philosophers, but I think of myself as a philosopher. Of course, readers of this book will see my point. This is a philosophy text, not restricted to political theory.

We can also rename philosophy as metaphysics. Reality is prior to wisdom. To repeat, only a real wisdom is wisdom.

This book argues for the case for philosophy/metaphysics, as general education underlying work. It argues also for the work, and the work of studying about work. An alternative title to *City Planning* might be *Metaphysical Options: General Education and Specialized Study*, as with this current chapter. In chapter 1 the object-subject relation underlies change-stability and problem-person. Chapter 1 underlies all remaining chapters, which are derived from chapter 1. Thus, object-subject relations, which I have called secondary general theory, underlie all knowledge, specialized study, and work. Reality, as object-subject, ties everything. Metaphysics as general theory comes as second, third, and fourth general theories.

The term "city planning" requires clarification. One of my exercises in chapter 9 is town and gown. The city can include the town where we produce goods and services, and gown as the school area and time for production of thinking about the production of goods and services. "City" can mean town, or town and gown as an entity, while "planning" is either those leaders in town who govern, or academics in gown who teach in gown and award degrees. In this way, this book can serve as part of gown, but not at the exclusion of town government leaders. Thinking about the production of goods and services is academia, or is the general education part of the gown. Again, I see philosophy (metaphysics) as general education, orienting faculty and students in the disciplines.

Of course, some philosophers, and virtually all nonphilosophers, will doubt if general education can be based on the metaphysical general theory. In response, my effort throughout the chapters has been to show, as with this chapter, how the topics are derived from chapter 1. Exercises also derive from that chapter. Chapter 1 as unified general theory orients disciplines and jobs. Virtually all scholars from other disciplines will deny that their fields and all jobs derive from metaphysics. My take is that subject and object, change and stability, and the preventing, solving or denying of problems, are fundamental to any discipline and job.

Advocates of liberal arts will ask how my or any work on metaphysics can qualify for general education. This book does not include the traditional staples of literature, language, fine arts, music, and religion. It clearly also omits general science, mathematics, physics, chemistry, and biology. Those criticisms are valid. My effort is not that of including the traditional subjects. Indeed, covering them in a single, double, or triple volume is impossible. The present work is only an overview to show that disciplines are related; human beings are interdisciplinary; and philosophy, ethics, metaphysics, and hermeneutics are unified. Metaphysics, in theory and application, is an overview of general education.

The specialist-generalist relation reveals itself in examples. Thinkers and liberal arts advocates might well interpret Ricoeur (1966) as saying human factors engineering (Kantowitz and Sorkin 1968) reintroduces machine into user, academia reintroduces disciplines into philosophy (Midgely 2016; Whitehead 194a), and Judeo-Christian scripture (1 Corinthians 12:4, 1971 KJV), reintroduces diversity of gifts into the body of Christ. In addition, John W. Gardner (1962), might reintroduce excellence into equality, while anthropology (Kluckhohn and Murray 1967), can say sameness is the way to organize differences. Two related points are that Kant might reintroduce percepts into concepts (1987), and Romantic thinkers such as Holderlin (Adler 1998), could state that we must reintroduce Kant's rationalism-empiricism into the romantic and cultural. Philosophers can reintroduce essence into existence. Benjamin Cardozo would reintroduce regulation or law into the Constitution's principles.

Scholars can interpret Gilbert Ryle (1987), saying user is the way to organize machines, spirit is the way to organize gifts, equality is way to organize excellence, whole is the way to organize parts, sameness is way to organize differences, concepts the way to organize perception, and culture the way to organize rational-empirical knowledge. For both Ricoeur and Ryle, liberal arts can be reintroduction of the visible hand into the invisible hand, or that the invisible hand is the way to organize visibility. Put in cybernetic terms, reintroduce feedback into feedforward, or see feedforward as the way to organize feedback. Ryle could well argue that existence is the way to organize the essential. He might also argue that a Constitution is the way to organize laws or regulations.

Nell P. Eurich of the Carnegie Foundation compares corporations teaching about producing goods and services, with the loftier ends of higher education. The aim of higher education is liberal arts and a job. We can interpret Eurich's thought in terms of the generalist-specialist continuum within the academic milieu. General learning teaches "concepts … critical … inquiry and method, history" and "current issues" and "bases for many professions …." (Eurich 1985).

In contrast, corporations and higher education majors teach "productivity and business needs" (Eurich 1985). Liberal arts, general education, and philosophy educate in the *why*, while the major field educates and trains in the *what*, *how*, and *when*. The *why* is continuous with the *what*, *how*, and *when*. The generalist-specialist continuum can find an example or parallel in John Dewey. For Dewey, we ought to sacrifice neither the child for the system, nor the adult authority for the child (Ulich 1971; Noll and Kelly 1970). Authority and freedom go together. Similarly, higher education should jettison neither general learning for jobs, nor specialization for liberal arts. General education ought to provide the "few general principles" of liberal arts (Whitehead, 1964b) underlying knowledge. The present book attempts to do so in terms of its chapters, with the first one basic to all of them. Whitehead does not specify the few general principles, but is defending the liberal arts' position. He resonates with Russell L. Ackoff, who argues that nature is not organized in disciplines the way we find in university compartmentalization (1961)

Chapter one rejects neither general education nor atomism of specialized learning. In sacrificing neither child to adult, nor adult to child, education steers, according to a Deweyian interpretation, between specialization alone and general learning only. Cybernetics as steering, underlies the college and university curriculum.

STUDY QUESTIONS

- Explain how philosophy can be city planning.
- How logical is it to think of a major aim of philosophy to be city planning when Plato, Hobbes, and other social-political-economic thinkers have written about the state?

DISCIPLINE-PHILOSOPHY DUALISM

Two unrelated realities exist, the disciplines as a sum of facts and boundaries, and philosophy. This position involves a strict distinction between the disciplines and philosophy. Where disciplines "alone" denotes that philosophy does not exist, dualism indicates that the field exists, but without any connection to the other fields. That seems to be the case in the common notion regarding philosophy's relevance. Philosophy exists as a field of arguments and discussion, but not as a scholarly pursuit contributing to our knowledge of reality.

Stephen Hawking (1988) laments that philosophy has isolated itself from the disciplines. That isolation was reportedly due to emphasis on linguistic analysis. Philosophy has become, to analytic thinking, simply the analysis of language, instead of more widespread discussion of knowledge, ethics, reality, and other fields in philosophical inquiry. For analytic thinking, language, not metaphysical and other topics, is philosophy's true purpose. Analysis of language is philosophy because clear, simple words are foundations of knowing and wisdom.

Even without linguistic analysis, philosophy is seen as irrelevant to the arts, sciences, and technology. Philosophers are seen as only speculating as to knowledge, broadly speaking, instead of contributing to updating itself through psychological, scientific, sociological, economic, technological, engineering, and other disciplinary insights.

Paul Nash (1968) gives a good example criticizing dualism in liberal arts' relation to specialized disciplines. If we look at philosophy as liberal arts or general education, liberating must, according to Nash, be at "right angles" (Nash 68, 43; Pieper 1993) to specialized learning, and to work itself. In the West, liberal arts started when the Greeks and then the Middle Ages saw manual labor as undignified.

The liberated adult studied mental, intellectual fields such as astronomy, music, art, mathematics: the trivium and quadrivium. But the information explosion meant even these were now jobs and work, and so liberal arts retreated to the study of introductory courses in each field that had been liberal art. Freedom from manual trades evolved into liberation from specialization or overspecialization. In cybernetic terms, liberation liberates or frees the person from atomism, structuralism, dualism, and postmodernism. For cybernetics, it becomes phenomenology. But religion is an excellent source for liberation or liberal arts and sciences. Religion liberates us from evil and steers us toward the good. Hindus, Buddhists, Jains, Taoists, generally involves liberation from matter, time and space. Confucianism means liberation from social disorder. Zoroastrians, Judaism, Christianity, and Islam attempt liberation from ritualism or materialism, and generally escapism. Of course, world-rejecting asceticism means escaping the world, and Christians have monasteries.

PHILOSOPHY POSTMODERNISM

No disciplinary reality exists. Subjectivity as philosophy alone exists. Indeed, different philosophies may exist. If no disciplinary (technological, science, or art) reality exists, then we have postmodernism or deconstruction. Linguistic analysis and existentialism, which for many now means postmodernism, are the main topics.

Philosophy alone is relevant, and disciplines are to be seen only in terms of traditional work done by those holding the PhD in philosophy. Disciplines are all but second-class citizens. Some philosophers feel they are part of academia, and can reach out to other disciplines primarily to teach nonphilosophers the value of philosophy. Such teaching is particularly important to inform science and technology that quantification is almost inferior to philosophy. That attitude is usually from existential orientations. For them, philosophy is not just fundamental to knowledge, but is almost the only field worth studying in any depth. They react against the view that philosophy is done. Done because philosophy does nothing for society. The attitude touches more than philosophy.

This attitude extends to liberal arts and sciences. Industrialized, advancing information societies extol the virtues of engineering, accounting, medicine. Fewer people, especially academics, look at the liberal arts and the well-rounded person as educated. Philosophy and liberal arts share similar public perceptions. The public perceives them as irrelevant at best. Such perception may be more the fault of philosophy and liberal arts, than the public. Philosophy must reach out, influence and be influenced by the disciplines.

Philosophers ought to take modernist hints from academia and law. Management thinker Herbert G. Hicks (1972) says disciplines are various views of a unified reality. Bertalanffy (1968) and Boulding (1968) articulate this unity as general principles underlying data and disciplines. Legal experts remind their members about principles and lifelong learning. Benjamin Cardozo (1965) says statues are no substitute for principles in constitutions. James Doherty (1970) argues that verbiage cannot and ought not replace principles in trial procedure. John Flynn Rooney (1997) calls for judges to have continuing education to refresh skills. Outdated constitutions, little if any lifelong learning, and disorganized and irrelevant data are among issues hindering the judicial process and system. John J. Garland (1973, 55), says computers and reaching out to "other disciplines" can solve "archaic judicial administration, outdated state constitutions, disorganized statue compilations, and the torrent of opinions, regulations and other legal literature." Linking law with other fields develops general education disclosing philosophy, including learning of constitutions. This resonates with Len Young Smith and Dale Roberson (1971) saying that the "jurist Blackstone" called for liberal arts to include the Constitution.

Liberal arts advocates, including the author, believe that their perspective is fundamental for the disciplines and jobs. Philosophers sharing this view argue at every opportunity that philosophy helps us understand human nature and the real world. The disciplines, according to this view, are fine, within the context of philosophy as a holistic vision.

The serious postmodernist will never concur with former US Supreme Court justice Benjamin N. Cardozo. In his *The Nature of the Judicial Process*, Cardozo (1921) talks of the constitution. "A constitution states or ought to state, not rules for the passing hour but principles for an expanding future" (Cardozo 1921 51). Rules valid for the passing hour are true only one time of the day. Principles for now and the future are valid always are true even if different countries have their own principles which do not apply beyond each one's border. Cardozo must have known that national constitutions differ.

Corresponding to Cardozo on the constitution stating principles, Jerome Hall goes further. In criminal law, he states concluding his article, "the ultimate challenge is to construct a universal body of knowledge of criminal law and its administration" (Hall 1973, 31). Philosophy and existentialism, left to themselves, incur the criticism of theoreticians who are open to particulars within universal bodies of knowledge of criminal law and its administration. Unifying theory is fundamental, specialized theories are not. The more unifying a theory, the more real, lasting, far reaching, widely relevant, and universal.

This is modernism in theory and constitutional efforts, a reality that continues toward the future, and ideas or principles that go contrary to constitutional principles, are wrong.

Speaking of postmodernism, two things seem involved. A spatial postmodernism appears to mean that realities are spatial. X is a spatial reality, true for this space, but other spaces have other realities. Substitute culture for space, or a particular location within a culture. Y is a temporal reality, true for this time, but other times have other temporal realities. Substitute various times in a culture, and you find postmodernism saying various times demand different realities.

Hence, different cultures are differing spatial realities. Each culture is valid, each culture is a valid space. Within each culture, the spatial reality has a time reality. A cultural reality might have truths valid at a certain time in the culture, but other truths become valid as they emerge at other times in that same culture or space. That is subjectivity heading for anarchy.

STUDY QUESTIONS

- How could you argue that Stephen Hawking is not entirely correct about philosophy as irrelevant?
- How could you argue that Stephen Hawking is entirely correct about philosophy as irrelevant?

DISCIPLINES-PHILOSOPHY CHANGE AND STABILITY L.I

INTERDISCIPLINARY CHANGE MONISM

Disciplines and philosophy change for their own sake. Here, disciplines emerge, merge, evolve, as an end in itself. New disciplines and ideas in philosophy emerge because writers wish to make money through writing. New texts emerge because a few scholars in an established department believe they have insights sufficiently sophisticated to create another department.

These changes may be fragmentation instead of innovation. We may be heading toward increasingly compartmentalization. According to human factors engineering, creation of new disciplines, and newer views in philosophy, may be the emergence of the user-friendly. The student and professional could be seeing invalid separation of areas of knowledge.

The economic factors enter. Many schools require publication in order that the faculty members gain tenure and professorship. Disciplinary literature, philosophical material, increases only or primarily because the schools demand it and professors want to make more money. Are new titled needed? Schools want publicity. Thus, they insist new titles automatically add to better knowledge.

INTERDISCIPLINARY CHANGE PHENOMENOLOGY

Disciplines and philosophy change as needed. Disciplines and philosophy evolve only when evolution is necessary and adds to knowledge and wisdom. Kant (1987) would argue that interdisciplinary change without stability is blind, and stability without change is empty.

We do not have publish-or-perish under change embodied. Publication is as needed, not just for money, promotion, or indeed retaining one's job.

DISCIPLINES AND PHILOSOPHY CHANGE DUALISM

Disciplines and philosophy never change, then only change. Before the Enlightenment, disciplines were either primitive and simplistic or did not exist. The information explosion went to the other extreme, where knowledge grows almost out of control.

DISCIPLINES AND PHILOSOPHY STABILITY-ONLY

Disciplines and philosophy never change. This was probably the environment or situation before the Enlightenment. Little knowledge, virtually no specialization, few disciplines, and philosophy and theology ruled.

The church was the truth, and influenced philosophical and scientific discourse. Empirical development was unheard of.

STUDY QUESTIONS

- What are the economic implications of professors being forced to publish books?
- What are the implications for knowledge in disciplines and philosophy stability-only?

DISCIPLINES-PHILOSOPHY PROBLEM AND PERSON L.II

INTERDISCIPLINARY PROBLEM MONISM

We are alert and react to problems in disciplines and philosophy after they occur. Only after people reject philosophy or deny the need for interdisciplinarity do we react and try to solve the problem of philosophy's relation to disciplines.

DISCIPLINES AND PHILOSOPHY PROBLEM PREVENTION

We try to prevent problems in disciplines and philosophy. We are proactive and seek to understand and diffuse disciplinary and philosophical problems before they occur. Discussions include the nature of philosophy and its relation to technology, art, and science. Kant (1987) would say interdisciplinary problems without a person are blind, and a person without a problem is empty.

Perhaps the biggest problem here to prevent is where philosophy stands. Does philosophy reach out to technology, science, and art? Or is philosophy concerned primarily with clarifying language, defending mind in the problem of dualism, or dissecting nuances in postmodernism and deconstruction?

Philosophers will need to reach out, learn from, and see where they can benefit technology, science, and art. Similarly, those in engineering, science, and art should be made to feel comfortable talking with philosophers.

DISCIPLINES AND PHILOSOPHY PROBLEM DUALISM

We ignore, and then react and solve problems in disciplines and philosophy. This is especially the case with philosophers, but also with nonphilosophers.

Nonphilosophers perhaps ignore philosophy because of the traditional reason of uselessness. Philosophy does not generate enthusiasm for technology, science, and art. Those in science, art, and technology often need serious ethical problems to occur before reaching out to ethicists or other philosophers.

Similarly, many philosophers do not appear that enthusiastic about technology, science, and art. Some phenomenologists in philosophy seek to update their area through biological and psychological advances. The journal *Neurophenomenology* comes to mind.

INTERDISCIPLINARY PROBLEM POSTMODERNISM

We deny that problems occur in disciplines and philosophy. Disciplines and philosophy may well change, or change embodied in stability. No problems confront the disciplinary and philosophical thinker. That is, no difficulties exist in disciplinary or philosophical discussions. All questions have answers, and no individual sees obstacles to overcome in disciplines or the seeking of reality and wisdom.

STUDY QUESTIONS

- Predict what could happen if philosophers only are alert and react to problems in philosophy's being perceived as irrelevant.

- Explain which of the four options you advocate in dealing with problems regarding disciplines and philosophy.

CHAPTER THIRTEEN

KNOWLEDGE REALITY:
TECHNOLOGY AND SCIENCE/ART

KEYWORDS

hypothesis: A theory or assumption underlying and guiding empirical observation.

postmodernism: Many realities exist and are valid.

heliocentricity: The theory that the earth revolves around the sun.

geocentricity: Theory that the sun revolves around the earth.

Inside disciplines, cognitive reality involves technology and art/science: technology alone, technology embodied, dualism, art/science alone. Technology is application of art and science. Art and science form the theoretical foundations of technology. Engineering can well be synonymous with technology.

Building bridges, homes, high-rises, roads, modifying rivers, and the like, are technology and call for engineers. However, engineers need to study the basics of matter, of the physical world. These are science and theory. Engineers know physics, mathematics, chemistry, and perhaps biology. The enlightened engineer studies the liberal arts in order to see what human beings have done and are doing nontechnically and technologically.

TECHNOLOGY AND SCIENCE/ART M

TECHNOLOGY MONISM

This is knowledge monism, knowledge reality totally reducible to the sum of technological parts or atoms. Technology-only is engineering and other practical topics without science and art. This is application without the theoretical foundations of science and art. For human factors engineering, knowledge monism is science/art unfriendly technology. Schools teach students how to repair technology, perhaps even manufacturing. However, they do not teach science and art as the theory behind technology.

If we put technology apart from science/art, and thus associate ethical, humanistic, and moral issues with science as theory, then technology becomes a strictly "doing" or "building" enterprise almost devoid of human directions. Engineers and technicians do things because they are technologically able to do things. They do not take into account the climatological, social, economic, anthropological, ethical impact on people.

Even if technology acknowledges ergonomics, the human safety and health issue is limited. Ergonomics is allowed to design objects to be user-friendly. But the broader question of qualitative ergonomics as I develop it is ignored. Should we simply design more and more things to be user-friendly? Or should we take the wider humanistic stance that many user-friendly objects may not be socially or culturally beneficial?

Are big cities good if they contain slums, traffic, social unrest, unemployment, and crime? Technology devoid of science/art may well have those results. My chapter on ethics and city planning reflects on the details of what I call technology-only. Details consider suburbs and big cities. Suburbs and small towns could also feel the technology-only impact. Suburbs without sidewalks should rethink the pedestrian's need to walk. People should be able to walk short and long distances instead of relying on the automobile. The bedroom community exemplifies technology-alone. We can build inhuman big cities and suburbs, and so we often do.

James R. Killian (1966), a former MIT official, has warned of the dangers to our cities of a preoccupation with engineering devoid of the human perspective.

TECHNOLOGY PHENOMENOLOGY

Technology embodied means applications of theory in science and art. For technology to succeed, it needs always to be within the context of the theoretical foundations of science and art. For Kant (1987), technology without science/art is blind, and science/art without technology is empty.

The 1987 MIT *Technology Review* published statements by MIT deans, the president, and provost, regarding an extensive review for that time, of the undergraduate curriculum. Said president Paul Gray, technology will not be the major challenge for students and professionals. Instead, the issue will consider "economic, social, and ethical considerations" (Gray, 1987). If the curricular review occurred during 1987, over thirty years before 2018, that difference in time does not invalidate Gray's position that technology arises from and ought to take into account ethics, social sciences, and humanities. Gray's thoughts are not obsolete. Technology, while important in an advanced industrialized world power witnessing increasingly technological changes, will be only part of the problems and questions. Science and technology emerge from cultural, social, anthropological, broadly economic contexts.

Too often, people think of art and science without technology. This, according to technology embodied, suggests that humanities (art broadly speaking) stands or can and ought to stand without technology. But technology is the application of art and science.

Technology applies philosophical and nonphilosophical perspectives we find in science and art. To that end, understanding science becomes important, as does thinking about art. Science can be pure induction (scientific monism), induction based on what Karl Popper (2002) sees as hypothesis (embodiment), and mere personality and community drama as in Thomas Kuhn (1970). Imre Lakatos (2000) attempts to reconcile Popper and Kuhn. Art, broadly speaking, can be the same. There is objective, phenomenological, and purely subjective humanities (humanities, social sciences, the arts, are what the "artists" say it is).

Inside science/art, art colors science. Physics Nobelist, Murray Gell-Mann developed the idea of the quark as fundamental to physics. The word "quark" is from art (Parker, 1988), broadly speaking, and not from science. Gell-Mann is a physicist reading literature as well as science. He had read James Joyce's Finnegan's Wake (2013), and saw a phrase about three quarks. Gell-Mann has surmised that quarks existed in threes, and this matched the phrase in Joyce. Thus, art influences science.

But art/science can also influence technology. The B-29 bomber during World War II that dropped the first atomic bomb, is technology. Its pilot named it the Enola Gay, after his mother. He anthropomorphized or "humanized" the B-29, applying a person's name to the machine. Technicians and lay persons put human names on robots and other machines. The first atom bomb was called "fat man" because of its huge size. The Army had to load it onto the bomber, which could not hold such a big, heavy weapon. As a result, scientists reduced the size and weight, and called the smaller bomb "little boy." Technology builds elementary, high school, college, and university buildings. However, we give these human names: George Schneider Elementary, Lane Tech High School, North Park University, Triton College. In no case do we simply identify a school as being, for example, the high school at Western and Belmont Avenue in Chicago. Human nature is, in part, an anthropomorphizing reality.

TECHNOLOGY—SCIENCE-ART DUALISM

This position is akin to C.P. Snow's (1963) *Two Cultures*. Snow laments the isolation of sciences and engineers from the humanities. Technology-science/art dualism means engineers and other technological professionals fail to communicate with (scientists and those in) art.

SCIENCE-ART POSTMODERNISM

In technology-alone, we find engineers and other professionals devoid of relations with science and art. In science/art-alone, the opposite occurs. Science and art theory is standing alone, without engineering and other professions.

This is an issue in liberal arts and sciences departments. College and universities call their undergraduate departments in most cases, the liberal arts and sciences department. To my knowledge, there is no department of technology, art, and science. The argument for omitting technology may be that science and art are basic to technology, and colleges and universities wish to teach the fundamentals of theory before students learn of technology.

Technology, it appears, is for applications of science and art, in graduate school. However, the impact of technology, of engineering, has become such that we need to help undergraduate students understand the ethics and morals of technology, of the applications of science and art.

STUDY QUESTIONS

- Predict the kind of society in which engineers build things by ignoring people.
- Predict the kind of society in which engineers take art and science into account.
- Explain the results if engineering is eliminated in favor of art and science only.

CHANGE AND STABILITY M.I

KNOWLEDGE CHANGE MONISM

Technology, science, and art change for the sake of change. This is especially true with technology. Computers and handheld or mobile devices seem to change or "upgrade" almost daily. New systems or protocols emerge daily. Society has reduced people to constantly adapt to a newer technology.

Science changes daily, and that may be expected. New knowledge can emerge as a daily factor.

Art in the broadest humanities sense also changes, often dramatically. The humanities introduce scientific, numeric approaches to the social sciences, art education, history, and what the schools may separate as humanities. And the relationships between art, science, and technology change or can change quickly.

KNOWLEDGE CHANGE PHENOMENOLOGY

Technology, science, and art change as needed. For technology, this means changing or advancing our devices only as needed. That may mean introducing a new product on the market perhaps every few years or within a decade, instead of a few times a year.

Daily scientific change may well be good. Embodied scientific change could well mean that scientists are learning more and more of the world around us. MIT president Jerome B. Wiesner well understands the integration of technology, science, and art. He says (Conference Board 1966) that humanists must learn modern science, and scientists and engineers must learn humanities. Both ought to learn about technology.

Art changes with computer activity. By art I will mean soft culture in general. Computers have done much to change soft culture, and one may wonder if those changes are relevant.

Listen to Albert Einstein. He speaks as a scholar in general, not from an ergonomics' view, but his address to students at California Institute of Technology notes that "concern for human beings and their fate must always form the chief interest of all technical endeavors. ... Never forget this in the midst of your diagrams and equations" (Einstein 1931).

What is Einstein saying? He puts science and engineering in a positive context. C.P. Snow's hard culture is good and not evil. Science is good and is not automatically scientism. Everyone ought to be familiar with science and technology. Scientists and engineers ought to be proud of their work. However, science and technology are insufficient by themselves. Research in science and technology ought to eventually be put to use by people having humanity in mind.

This brings in the thoughts of MIT's James R. Killian (1966) and my views on micro and macro human factors. At the least, engineers ought to learn the humanities (art broadly speaking) and human factors specialists take the user into account. At most, as in the previous chapter, technology, science, and art ought to take philosophy into account. There qualitative ergonomics comes in, as the context for human factors engineering.

Vannevar Bush of MIT echoes a similar sentiment, that the "engineering graduate is no longer just a nuts and bolts person, and the science graduate no longer just a laboratory specialist." He points out that MIT has students studying "humanities courses, such as psychology and economics" (Bush prototype issue 56).

KNOWLEDGE CHANGE-STABILITY DUALISM

Technology and science/art are too stable during one time and dramatically change during another time. This perhaps occurred with the Enlightenment. Technological and scientific/artistic advances were virtually unheard of, as all knowledge was under church rule. Then the Enlightenment exploded and empirical research began.

Such dualism occurs even in modern history, in an industrialized nation. Before rocketry and missiles were known and mainstream, the government and academia were unaware of their potential. Virtually no thinking occurred regarding the civilian and military uses of a projectile being shot into the atmosphere.

World War II and Nazi Germany changed that dramatically. We had ignored guided missiles despite Robert Goddard's efforts (Clary 2004). After Adolph Hitler used the V-2, and we invaded and defeated Germany, emphasis on missiles appeared overnight.

KNOWLEDGE STABILITY POSTMODERNISM

Technology and science/art never change. They are stable only. This has been the view of pre-Renaissance times when the church controlled knowledge and life. We are all familiar with the then-pope's warning to Galileo. Galileo defended Copernicus's discovery that the earth revolved around the sun (Velasquez 2014). The pope threatened Galileo to retract his heliocentricity for geocentricity.

STUDY QUESTIONS

- Predict the world if technology changes as an end in itself.
- Explain the results if engineers and humanities scholars do not talk with each other.
- Predict a world where technology, art, and science do not change or advance.

TECHNOLOGY AND SCIENCE/ ART PROBLEMS M.II

Let's see the four ethical positions of how and when we understand the relationship between technology and science/art. Problems will arise as we attempt to understand how technology and science/art relate. Is it ethical to be alert and react to solve technology and science/art problems after they occur, prevent these problems before they occur, ignore and then react to solve the problems, or deny the problems?

KNOWLEDGE PROBLEM MONISM

Scholars are alert and react to solve the problem of people not knowing or understanding technology, science, and art. The uneducated are always present.

Scholars and others are also alert and react to solve the problems of themselves relating technology to science/art. They may not themselves discuss these issues beforehand, but wait for a crisis to occur, perhaps something fatal or degrading to people. Our cities are often deteriorating. Infrastructure collapses, slums exist and perhaps increase. Engineers and technology experts may believe that their fields are adequate. But enlightened professionals will point out the need to prevent instead of prepare for emergencies and reaction.

KNOWLEDGE PROBLEM PHENOMENOLOGY

The young need to learn technology, science, and art as soon. Scholars and schools should prevent misunderstandings and illiteracy as soon as possible. Kant (1987) would argue that a knowledge problem without a person is blind, and a knowledge person without a problem is empty.

Elementary school, high school, and at least some college acquaintance with technology, science, and art is a necessity, not luxury. In 2017, STEM (science, technology, engineering, mathematics) and STEAM (science, technology, engineering, art, mathematics) make efforts toward such integrative education.

KNOWLEDGE PROBLEM DUALISM

Society ignores and then suddenly reacts to the problem of those illiterate about technology, science, and art. This situation occurred the day after the former Soviet Union launched Sputnik, the first artificial satellite. The world, including the United States, experienced a nightmare. The Soviets had beaten America, a world power, by developing and launching the first satellite.

The United States had ignored the Soviets, and now had to react to catch up. It had built and launched its own satellite.

In major cities, water distribution pipes may burst before the cities replace them with larger pipes. Urban governments occasionally ignore electricity until brownouts or power outages occur, until a power crisis hits and millions have no electrical power.

KNOWLEDGE SCIENCE/ART PROBLEM POSTMODERNISM

We deny that technology, science, and art involve problems. This could well be the general attitude of many people in the United States and other countries, especially segments of the Amish community. Much of the Amish and associated groups have no telephones, possibly televisions and other scientific and technological devices.

This could also be the view of many philosophers who believe philosophy is far superior to technology, science, and humanities. For them, problems in disciplines other than philosophy are the fields themselves.

In general, however, they present the image of a people who are technologically, scientifically, and artistically very conservative and in denial.

Technology and science/art problem denial is also part of an advanced civilization such as the United States. Engineers can build cities which become blighted, and believe that human problems do not exist. If these problems occur, they belong to humanists, and not even to scientists, much less engineers.

This stance of problem denial is very close to that of technology-only. Technological problems could result when we look at technology as an end in itself, devoid of the human factor in technical and in broadest human, qualitative terms.

STUDY QUESTIONS

- Predict instances if we only are alert and react to problems in technology, art, and science.
- Explain how you would prevent problems in ethical issues of engineering.

- Predict events if people deny that problems in technology, art, and science occur.

EXERCISES

The following exercises, when completed, are to become small chapters.

1. Inside science/art notion, a reality involves science and art.

2. Science alone, science embodied, science-art dualism, art alone

3. Inside science and art intersection, is the reality involving sciences and arts.

4. Inside technology and science/art idea is the reality involving technologies and sciences/arts.

CHAPTER FOURTEEN

FIELD REALITY:
SCIENCE AND ART

Inside science/art, is what I term *field reality*. This involves the dual themes of science and art. But I must put in a word of explanation for this chapter.

People hear of the philosophy of science, and of scientific method. My effort in this chapter is to note that method cannot be simply an approach or methodological road to science. Science is a goal as the context for method. The relation of science to art is a goal. Scientific methods, often noted as induction, hypothesis, and listening to the community of scholars, seem to ignore the fact that each of these three are being used for a reason. That reason is for us to understand artistic and scientific reality. Any method, and thus a scientific one, is a means toward an end. The end or telos is to understand reality. I shall therefore talk first of the science and art relationship as our goal. Then, I will proceed with scientific method.

SCIENCE MONISM

Science monism is the position that one field exists. The goal is that we understand science as underlying all knowledge. This is science-only. Indeed, scholars call this scientism. Science alone is reflects reality of knowledge (Wilson, 1998). The natural laws of physics, chemistry, mathematics, and biology underlie all other disciplines including arts, humanities, social sciences.

SCIENCE PHENOMENOLOGY

Science phenomenology is the position that science is an embodied field. The goal is to understand science embodied in art. This means that science emerges from, interrelates with, and influences the context or art, broadly speaking. Arts, humanities, social sciences are the "field" of art in dialogue with the field of science. Kant would say science without art is blind, and art without science is empty.

As an embodied field, people ought to study science. Mathematics, physics, chemistry, biology are vital to knowledge and an understanding of reality. Scientific literacy becomes increasingly important to a free society. Computer science could be part of such literacy. Such literacy advances also with links developing among sciences including physics, mathematics, and within biology (Kafatos and Eisner 2004; Kolata 1989). The Christian Science Monitor, July 6, 1976, has an article without the name of the author, "Hurricane Waves." The article notes we are learning to predict hurricane direction and intensity.

Science as embodied also means studying it in connection with art, broadly speaking. Social sciences, humanities, the study of art as in painting, sculpture, the history of art, all comprise the cultural foundations from which hard science (math, physics, chemistry, and biology) emerges. In set theory terms, this is the intersection of art and science. More accurately, it involves science as a function of art, and art a function of science.

The phenomenology of science then can be studied as science, as intersecting with art, or as art. John Allen Paulos (1998) points out a detailed account of embodied science in the art-science intersection. Science and art are a continuum, phenomenologically speaking, though he does not use phenomenology explicitly. The continuum goes from primarily numeric and scientific, to predominantly nonnumeric and artistic knowing. Science is never totally quantitative, art is never completely qualitative.

STUDY QUESTIONS

- What is science as an embodied field?
- Explain the implications of science monism.
- Discuss the implications of science embodied.
- Explain implications of art postmodernism.

SCIENCE-ART DUALISM

Science-art dualism denotes that science and art are two distinct fields. C.P Snow (1963) warns against this. Calling 'two cultures' engineering and humanities, he points out that professionals in either field do not communicate with each other.

Lack of community and thus communication plagues science and art. Snow complains about this. J. David Bolter concurs as his preface to his *Turing's Man* calls for science and art to communicate. Failure to communicate occurs among scientist and artist. It exists also within science. Steven Weinberg (Campbell, 1989) mentions lack of communication between theoretical and applied physicists. Lack of community leads to intelligence agencies not communicating with each other (Odom 2004). A Kantian approach would be that science without art is blind, and art without science is empty. According to Ricoeur, scholars ought reintroduce science into art, and restore embodied science.

Paulos (1998) makes an excellent case for opposing dualism in art and science. Science is primarily the quantitative, art predominantly the qualitative. Scientific truths came to us through human drama instead of dropping from the sky. Richard Kamber (2009) concludes an insightful article in *Common Review* by pointing out that turmoil in the Islamic world, questions of environmentalism, and ethics in the business community require a good understanding of the connection between art and science, which criticizes dualism. In their *Beauty of Fractals* (1986), Heinz-Otto Pietgen and Peter H. Richter bring in the notion that science is good and discloses much, but art helps us appreciate the unpredictable.

Kant, Ricoeur, and isomorphic or homological thinking can overcome what C. P. Snow laments as the two cultures, or as I call it, field dualism of art isolated from science. Start with theoretical phenomenology and the atomistic-existential dialogue or continuum. As Kant might say, atomism without subjectivity is blind, subject without atomism is empty. The Kantian interpretation is the homology or same shape of which we have the derivation that science without art is blind, art without science is empty. Now bring in Ricoeur. He can tell us to reintroduce science into art. Science and art are a continuum instead of discontinuous. Yet, phenomenology can go further to show art as the context of science.

ART POSTMODERNISM

Art postmodernism tells us many fields exist. This is the opposite of scientism or science-alone. If the scientism is the science-only field telling us all human and nonhuman reality is to be seen as only physical, then art postmodernism says no one art or science exists, no one field exists. By definition, any field which a scholar invents is valid.

Postmodernism says scholars can determine as valid any field which a scholar creates, regardless of that area's actual legitimacy. This could mean American, Russian, Chinese, and Italian mathematics are all legitimate. A scholar could create a course on playing cards, gambling, driving autos, skydiving, and so on. Given the notorious nature and implications of postmodernism where any and all ideas are valid, the reader can envision a course on hatred, sexism, racism, and so on.

Pseudoscience, ghosts, telepathy, astrology, magic, faith healing, would all be valid fields of study. Taken seriously, bank robbery, embezzlement, running scams, and pickpocketing could then be established as legitimate things to study, learn, and have as careers.

FIELD CHANGE

FIELD CHANGE MONISM

Science and/or art change is the only reality. They change for the sake of change. No stability, orientation, or direction exists. Science and art can evolve in any way that intellectuals and academic wish. Art postmodernism says all science and art fields would be legitimate; field change monism argues that we ought to have a new science or art field as often as we wish. One implication can be "publish or perish." Academics will publish nonsense, poor research, and the community of scholars would consider this irrelevant production as being valid.

Field change monism is the position of money. Scholars want to simply earn money for publications. Science and art become a strictly or increasingly commercial activity, without true progress or advancement in the fields.

FIELD CHANGE PHENOMENOLOGY

Scientific and artistic change has direction, change as needed, with orientation and purpose. In field change phenomenology, legitimate research has credibility and no scholar is under pressure to create new ideas.

FIELD CHANGE DUALISM

Science and art are stagnant, perhaps as under church control during one period. During a subsequent period, scholars believe they ought to totally jettison the church as completely subjective, and replace it with science and art as purely objective.

FIELD STABILITY POSTMODERNISM

Science and art never change, scientists and artists are always the same. As the opposite of field change monism, art and science stability postmodernism means academia, the government, and industry prohibit any research. Libraries would cease to exist. One implication might be that an institution such as the church could rule all knowledge.

In a secular world, the government could stop research. Thinking and publishing in any field stops, and a secular, anti-religious bias could force theological research and practice to end.

Where field change monism becomes a commercial enterprise, field stability-postmodernism means that scholars and institutions do little or no publication. This position becomes one of field solipsism. Scholars refrain from advancing science and art, and simply believe that they live in a metaphorical or real monastery.

The scientific method, as we shall see later in this chapter, is nonexistent. Observations and scientific approaches to science and art do not see the day. Field stability-postmodernism could be nuanced. Society might well accept research in certain areas of science and art, but prohibit advancement in another or other fields. In 2017, some physicists may believe that string theory is irrelevant, and not really legitimate physics.

FIELD PROBLEM

FIELD PROBLEM-MONISM

One kind of problem exists. Problems to solve in science and art are the only reality. Scientists and artists, broadly speaking, only are alert and react to problems in their fields. A university may insist that String Theory is not a legitimate field of inquiry. The challenge is to foster appreciation for delving into the unknown.

Scholars and laypersons are only alert and react to solve the problem of creationism/evolution debate. No individual thinks ahead as to preventing the debate or controversy.

The creation-evolution problem is another heated issue. Most people are only alert and wait until a crisis occurs between creationists and evolutionists. When a clash happens between religious and scientific individuals (even scientists in the church), individuals either seek a resolution or continue yelling at each other. Each side believes in monism, that the creationist-evolution problem will be endless unless one side clobbers the other. The two sides appear unconcerned that individuals get hurt, and expend needless energy in reacting to what they perceive as the enemy.

FIELD PROBLEM PHENOMENOLOGY

Problems in science and art are embodied. They are not merely out-there, but part of our efforts to prevent reaction. Science and art are to prevent problems in their fields, where possible. Universities and the government attempt to prevent those in science and art from prohibiting research in legitimate fields.

Academics and laity attempt to discuss creationism/evolution in ways whereby they prevent heated arguments going nowhere. The individuals attempt to understand emotionalism and scholarship regarding the creation/evolution issue.

Jesuit thinker, Pierre Teilhard de Chardin, may be what I call a field problem phenomenologist (FPP). He has no problem seeing God and Christ underlying evolution (de Chardin, 1965). The typical field problem phenomenologist does more than be alert and react to solve the problem of creationism and evolution. A scholar will ask the meta-creation-evolution questions. This includes asking what do we mean by God, God's special creation, evolution, Christ, and the like.

Teilhard attempts to show that creation and evolution are not necessarily mutually exclusive. As a theologian of culture, he would be the first to talk of the sacred dimensions of evolution, showing God's and Christ's presence in an evolving universe. A Ricoeurian would argue that we reintroduce evolution (parts, sequence) into creationism. Evolution need not mean God does not exist. Creation can denote that human beings evolved from simple cells toward becoming God's special creation. This requires rethinking and redefining special creation.

FIELD PROBLEM DUALISM

This position involves two distinct field problem realities. We initially ignore, then react to solve scientific and art problems. For creation and evolution issues, people will ignore religion's relation to science until a serious debate occurs, and participants are throwing metaphorical rocks at each other.

FIELD PERSON POSTMODERNISM

Problems do not exist. Persons alone are real. Any person's view is valid. Scientific and artistic problems, problems in understanding science and art, do not exist. The government and academia do not see it a problem if they insist that legitimate areas in science and art ought not have research. Individuals see no problem teaching creationism or evolution. For them, teaching or not teaching one of these is a nonissue.

The postmodern position in creation and evolution becomes almost uncanny. In postmodernism, racial equality and sexual justice, are equally justified along with racism and sexism. Contradictory views are compatible. Eventually, right and wrong go out the window.

SCIENTIFIC METHODOLOGY REALITY: METHOD AND AMETHOD

I have discussed science monism, science phenomenology, science-art dualism, and art postmodernism. This taxonomy proceeds from the notion of science-alone, science in the context of art, science distinct from art, and art-alone. Integral to science, is the scientific method. I will leave for a future work my question as to why we have a scientific, but not artistic method. Technically, scientific and artistic research is nonetheless intellectual, scholarly effort. All academic, and probably other inquiries, ought to be objective, instead of processes which a church or other authority controls. What we call the scientific method would also apply to all intellectual endeavors. I, therefore, question the restrictive term "scientific method." My inclination is to have an intellectual method or a scholarly method.

Scientific method comes into play. First, method and goal are dual themes, but I will restrict myself to method. Method can be method monism, phenomenology, dualism, and method postmodernism (Feyerabend 2010). This is especially true for scientific areas, but applies to art. Matteo Motterlini's (1999) compilation of letters exchanged between Feyerabend and Imri Lakatos's idea regarding method sheds less light on the latter two than I would want.

Method monism is the position that one method or approach exists in any inquiry, questioning, research, or investigation. Scholars and nonscholars may use induction, hypothesis (Popper 2002), or paradigm shift (Kuhn 1970), for any and all investigations.

Specifically and more accurately, monism in inquiry would involve only induction, or only hypothesis, or only the paradigm shift with community of scholars.

Induction looks at many events and generalizes. Hypothesis considers one or a few observations out of the ordinary, and tries to determine a reason. Paradigm shift argues that science (or any inquiry) is always a human effort. Scientists and arts people, engineers and philosophers, are first of all human beings. Knowledge comes not from objective gathering the facts, or observation and hypothesizing, but from listening to authority in terms of the community of scholars.

According to monistic method, the inquirer chooses one of these approaches, and rejects the other two, every time and every place. Thus, scientific or any intellectual investigation is collecting data and is data-driven, or it is hypothesis, or it is the listening to what the community of scholars say.

Method phenomenology means that the inquiry is embodied. Investigation is not just induction, or only hypothesis, or only community of scholars. Each of the three is valid at some point. If we observe the same phenomenon or event over a period of time, or ask many people their opinion of something or someone, induction occurs resulting in generalization. On the other hand, a friend or stranger is limping, or a store is on fire, or a crime is committed. Hypothesis enters. Our hypothesis is the limping is due to pain in the leg. This may be turn out to be a bad back. The fire may be arson or an accident. A crime may be committed by a local resident or someone living miles away;

an amateur or a professional criminal. Finally, an asteroid is headed our way. Astrophysicists and astronomers believe it no danger to earth. People believe them because they are the experts. Neither induction nor hypothesis is possible. To paraphrase Kant, method without questioning the method is blind; doing science without accepted methods is empty.

Police science is an example of phenomenological scientific method. Good cop/bad cop procedure occurs when one police officer (uniformed or detective), or FBI agent, or any federal law enforcement agency, interrogates aggressively or threateningly, while another tries the friendly approach.

Pedagogically, a teacher tries film, book reading, student presentations, field trips, etc. as diverse methods to motivate students. One method cannot be monistic. For Kessen (1966), the teacher must organize the ways in which students can learn. This is a combination of lectures, questions and answers, perhaps powerpoints and films, field trips, project to be done outside class. The R.L. Moore (Wilder, 1982) method of questioning the students comes into play. It is a contemporary version of the Socratic Method.

Method dualism denotes two distinct methodological realities occur. One is no methodology, the other is monistic methodology.

Method postmodernism means many methodological realities exist. Perhaps Feyerabend (2010) is the most famous thinker along these lines, with his *Against Method*. His view has been called methodological anarchy. However, his position persuades us to rethink what he is saying.

Feyerabend's influential work mentions his position of anarchism. If this means he is against any traditional method, trouble starts. Nowhere does he say that he is against induction, hypothesis, and paradigm shifts as monistic. That is, he does not indicate that induction, hypothesis and paradigm shift are three methods he opposes. To say that Feyerabend is against method seems to suggest a scientist may or ought to enter a lab, approach a telescope or other instrument, and do as he pleases. Do as you please in a chemistry lab and an explosion starts.

Unless he is tolerating destroying the lab or any scientific and artistic research, he should have been clear in his introduction or preface as to the word *against*. If I rewrote his introduction or preface, I would be clear. I would start the preface or introduction by noting that intellectuals imply induction, hypothesis and community of scholars are monolithic. That is, adherents to each of the three imply that scholarly endeavor, especially science, is only induction, hypothesis, or community. I would then argue that each has a place, but cannot and ought not be universal, at all times and places. His book, *Against Method* ought start with the fact that induction, hypothesis, and community of scholars are three traditional methods where proponents of each believe their method is the only one we ought use every time and every place. Then, Feyerabend ought to indicate the meaning of anarchy or being against method. If he is arguing against any method, any scientific experiment will conclude with failure, explosion, or anything bad. On the other hand, if he argues against a monistic approach to each of the three methods, then we are safe.

The phenomenological method in science is a complex. Feyerabend could be saying that induction, hypothesis, and community of scholars each has a place in investigations. If this is the case, he is not against method, but against monistic method. His book ought start clearly stating the three methods, and that he is against fixation on only one method, and not against all methods. He is probably in favor of a combination of methods, and in accept chance or serendipity.

Feyerabend may mean that countless methods exist, or that these three methods are mutually exclusive. Such exclusion, in anarchy, implies that in the long run, many realities exist, and that the universe or life is unconnected. Planetary movement is totally independent of general principles regarding events on the planets, and these are totally independent of what astronomers say.

If Feyerabend believes in methodological anarchy, he has strong critics: Hicks (1972), Clynes (1970), Bertalanffy (1968), Boulding (1968), to name a few, all of whom believe that disciplines and all aspects of reality are connected. Life is general principles underlying particular events (phenomena, observations), causes and reasons for events requiring hypotheses, and authorities in communities of scholars telling us about aspects of reality.

In a sense, Feyerabend's and Lakatos's notion of anarchy could go to an extreme. If by anarchy they mean postmodernism and any theory is valid in science, then they are the polar opposite to an intriguing interpretation of methodological monism. That is, I listed induction-only, hypothesis-only, and community of scholars-only as methodological monism. Yet, let's not forget church monism. The church before the Enlightenment proclaimed the virtues of spirituality and was against science. Copernicus and Galileo are classic examples of the church demanding to be the authority concerning all knowledge.

Where the church, induction, hypothesis, and paradigm shift monism mean only one sacred and secular method, then postmodernism means every method is justified. Even methods that will conclude in destruction, chaos, and hate are considered good.

METHOD CHANGE MONISM

One methodological change reality exists. This position denotes change in methodology for its own sake. Scholars change methods whether or not they need a new one.

Scholars do more and more research with animal and human subjects. The insistence that ethics has a role to play in method change, provides evidence that researches ought not merely do experiments on animals and human for the sake of experimentation.

Monism disregards human nature. It can also disregard any living organism. Method monism gets out of hand if scholars treat animals and human as though these are merely objects.

METHOD CHANGE PHENOMENOLOGY

Method change is embodied. Change in method is as needed.

This is especially important in fine tuning induction, hypothesis, and community of scholars. Each requires constant refining.

First, induction requires proper sampling, modeling, and prediction ability. Induction involves the issue of how big a sampling we can or ought to take. The bigger the number of variables, the seemingly better. And Baysian and Frequentist theories set in. For Baysians, induction is a combination of frequency plus the unknown. I attended a gathering every week for five years. So predictable was this, that another attendee one day tapped me on the shoulder and noted that he knew he could count on me attending that day. Then, I was suddenly asked to be an usher.

That meant I would no longer be just another attendee.

Frequentists would have had a problem. My frequent attendance suddenly stopped. I was attending weekly. However, behind the scenes, some ushers retired, and the administration sought an usher. I was attending regularly and thereby qualified to be an usher. The Frequentist observes the events, and perhaps ignores activities seemingly unrelated to the frequency of events.

Second, hypothesis demands adequate, careful diagnosis. I saw a friend at a picnic. He was limping. Apparently, he had leg problems. I asked how his leg was. My friend responded that his leg was fine. His issue was a bad back preventing him from walking well. My hypothesis was wrong.

Improvements in medical diagnosis advance health. Ordinary illnesses involve relatively adequate determinations of the cause. Over time, psychiatric, blood, urine, bone, MRI, and other tests can probably pinpoint the problem of a sickness. Idiopathology can be a more complicated issue. A disease or behavior has unknown causes. Medical professionals try to improve methods of developing a hypothesis for understanding the cause previously unknown.

As medicine and hypotheses about illness develop, puzzles remain about how some diseases disappear. Some cancers seem to be in remission. Some remain but without symptoms.

Third, perhaps trickiest of all, what do we mean by community of scholars, and how does personality enter into our conclusions? A professional group announces that they conclude a behavior is or is not a crime. Their professional status persuades us to believe what they say.

However, was the professional under pressure to make the conclusion? A lobbying organization could have influenced the professionals' decision. For Thomas Kuhn, intellectuals are first of all human beings. They can be wrong for any reason.

Scientific issues and statements are perhaps more important than in art, broadly speaking. Scientists perhaps have greater implications. Announcements about cancer, the climate, and other physical and psychological topics could affect us more than will statements about the nature of painting, ethics of films or movies, and whether a play is too sexually provocative.

Method change phenomenology is an ethical approach to experimentation. Where method monism can mistreat animal and human subjects, method phenomenology takes the animal and human into account. Method change monism forces people to be subjects, or puts them in experiments without their knowledge. On the other hand, method change phenomenology seeks volunteers.

Obviously, human beings can volunteer. But until we can communicate with animals as we do with people, volunteering is impossible with living things other than people. The very most that researchers can do with nonhumans is to treat them ethically.

Method change phenomenology brings into mind physics. Murray Gell-Mann once observed that difficulty of isolating the quark might have an answer. Asked Gell-Mann, "will some unknown young scientist find a new way of looking at fundamental physics that clarifies the picture and makes today's questions obsolete" (Calder, 1977)? A bright, creative physicist could well develop an experiment to discern the quark. This would mean an experiment of which we are presently unaware. My interpretation of my friend, Doug Binckly's explanation of why we cannot isolate the quark, is that it is embedded as part of a network from which it cannot be isolated. The quark apparent cannot stand alone.

Where method change monism says simply change for its own sake, method change phenomenology argues that we do so as needed. And when we need to change and cannot find an answer, a bright unknown scientist might have the answer. Or, a bright known intellectual from any field may have a point from which a field can benefit.

However, this does not mean the idea is totally subjective. It would involve something of modifying existing methods and techniques. Christopher Columbus could not envision Global Positioning Systems, television, radio, or other scientific developments. Eventually, electronics came into being, but were expansions of previous, embryonic research. Novelty is not total novelty.

METHOD CHANGE DUALISM

Scholars make no change in method during one time, and then changes that are unnecessary during another time.

Implications of method change dualism denote going from no research to mere research. We would live in a monastery during an initially period, and unethical studies and experiments thereafter.

METHOD STABILITY POSTMODERNISM

Many methods, any method, is valid. No method changes, even when situations demand change.

Interpreted as anarchy, method stability postmodernism, would leave to inability to progress, and could mean disaster. The postmodern scientist walks into a lab and destroys it through carelessness. Such scientists also may use sophisticated instruments in a careless way, resulting in experiments giving the wrong conclusions. The researchers, intentionally or unintentionally are doing what they please instead of following rules, caution, and attention.

Feyerabend, if interpreted as anarchic, would favor or at least tolerate unethical method. This leads to unethical experimentation. If he is against 'objective' or universally accepted methods including induction, hypothesis and the community of scholars, his efforts could well lead to justifying moral and immoral experiments. His intentions and philosophy of science appear restricted to 'subjective' methodology.

Looking at Feyerabend, a careful analysis reveals what I would term method solipsism. He advocates a scientist or artist, employing their own approach, which would not necessarily be universally desirable. Solipsism appears, by definition contrary to postmodernism. Postmodernism means many realities exist, solipsism that one reality, the self, exists. However, both are subjectivity. In either case, the person generates, accepts, or follows his or her own method.

The solipsist follows his or her own method and says other selves do not exist. A postmodernist concedes other selves and methods, but is generating his or her own method, denying an objective position. Solipsism denies selves out-there; postmodernism accepts other selves, but rejects object reality behind other selves. Both solipsism and postmodernism deny objectivity.

If Feyerabend were here today, and promoted an anarchic method or approach, he probably could violate the law or ethics and endanger life. He says he is against method. Interpreted in an undesirable way, his position might be that of careless, and illegal or unethical method. Being literally against method gives the appearance of desiring to live as a hermit, a monk in a monastery, or otherwise simply doing nothing.

Of course, this is a derivative of postmodernist metaphysics, where racism and sexism are as valid as equality and justice. This is not to single out Feyerabend, but to point to a danger in an important field—scientific experimentation.

METHOD PROBLEM MONISM

One method problem exists. People only are alert to react to solve problems in method. If induction, hypothesis, or community of scholars produces no results, investigators solve the problem by changing the method. Investigators change a possibly dangerous method if and when danger or fatality occurs to people or property.

Intellectuals may have been looking in the wrong places. Yet, they were doing so, satisfied by the notion that if something went wrong, they would start looking in the correct direction. Method problems will always exist. Prevention is not needed. People will get hurt, property damaged, but solutions solve these obstacles. As long as investigators 'pay the insurance premiums,' literally or figuratively, the insurance company will pay the bill.

METHOD PROBLEM PHENOMENOLOGY

Methodological problems are embodied. Scholars try to prevent problems in methodology. Communication exists among all investigators. Scientists, all is art, broadly speaking, and subfields in science and art, ought to be in the community. Jeremy Campbell (1989) points out that, according to Steven Weinberg, a lack of communication and possible biases between astrophysicists and astronomers, prevented discovering a background noise from the Big Bang. Theoreticians believed instruments could detect the noise, those making observations either did not believe this or were not communicating with thinkers. Snow warned, as mentioned, of lack of communication among scientists and those in art or humanities. As noted, Bolter (1984) criticizes communication failure between scientists, humanists, and engineers.

Communications often breaks down in national security. Odom (2003) explains that intelligence agencies need a sense of community to foster inter-agency cooperation and communication.

Claude E. Shannon and Warren Weaver (1971) give us an excellent account of the quantitative dimension of communication. However, sender and receiver, transmitter and recipient in communications, manifest community. Community is the qualitative and intersubjective framework for quantitative communication. Much interdepartmental work needs to be done between academic departments of philosophy, sociology, and communications.

METHOD PROBLEM DUALISM

Scholars ignore methodologic problems, and then react to solve them. In many case, the methodologic problems may be ethical ones. Investigators may cheat on data, mistreat animals, harm human beings, or perhaps destroy the environment. Some could report their careless experimentation to the government. Or, knowledge of deadly or harmful results could reach government or media outlets. The government reaches and demands to know from the investigator what is occurring. The investigator reacts and perhaps changes or shuts down the experiment.

METHOD PERSON POSTMODERNISM

Many and all persons exist, without methodological problems. Thinkers see no problems in method.

Dangerous methods pose no danger. Persons, scientists and other intellectuals may do as they please. In thinking of postmodernism, scholars write much about emotionally and personally offensive ideas. Little if anything is about postmodernism in terms of physical safety.

Terrorism, mass shootings, government and corporate corruption are never part of the definition of postmodernism, from what I see. Given postmodernism's emphasis on topics that are only offensive, I have yet to see a scholarly paper or even letter to the editor on validity of physical and organization harm.

Yet scientific method postmodernism, or method-person postmodernism, would at minimum border on justifying, tolerating, or accepting material and organizational wrongdoing in the name of scientific or other intellectual experiment.

At the most, method monism insists that induction, hypothesis, and community of scholars is each universal. Results can be wrong, but the aim of each of these traditional, socially accepted methods is not blatant, uncaring inhumanity.

An institutional review board, reviewing the ethics of research, might well question Feyerabend and any anti-method position regarding the postmodernist implications. At the very least, such a review board would ask Feyerabend to clarify his use of the phrase "against method."

Such a review board, then, concurs with Kant (Kant 1959). Kantian ethics demands that we treat people as ends instead of means. Kant's view is definitely no postmodernism. Scholars ought to reject the postmodern position that any method is justified in experimenting on people. Ecologically speaking, experimenters must decline a postmodern stance on any experiment on anything: animal, vegetable or mineral. Doing harm by reducing animate and even inanimate nature is wrong."

CONCLUSION

This book will agitate philosophers. At the least it will annoy them. They traditionally associate philosophy with branches, and metaphysics as a branch instead of replacing philosophy. I associated metaphysics as a branch for decades after college. However, as I study metaphysics, ethics, epistemology, and remaining "branches," I find a problem with that organization. This is especially true to relegating metaphysics, ethics, and hermeneutics to just another branch.

Metaphysics is inquiry about reality. This would suffice to move that "branch" to the lofty level as general theory of reality. Reality is prior to all topics, for everything must be real before being a topic. Philosophers may believe this, but do not put metaphysics or the study of reality as the first chapter, and frequently even as the first branch. They also do not emphasize that every other traditional branch is derived reality.

Ethics, epistemology, and the other topics are applied or derived metaphysics or reality. Ethics as ethical reality asks if there is right or wrong. This question, while derived reality, applies back to metaphysics as to which position about reality we ought to accept as ethical. Should we believe a particular metaphysical position? With little hesitation, existentialists will react that that analytics and positivism are unethical. Historically, existentialism emerged as such a reaction to the quantification of people and reality. Epistemology is applied metaphysics, part of what we would call education or psychology, but these are ultimately philosophical.

Interpretation plays a similar role. It is derived reality. Hermeneutics, the study of interpretation, must be real before, or in order to be that field. As derived or hermeneutical reality, interpretation also applies back to reality, to metaphysics. Interpretation asks which position reality is right; linguistic hermeneutics inquires as to which words we ought to accept as meaningful, and do their meanings change? Meaning can be thoroughly the same for all people and need no interpretation, generally uniform with allusions to its history, dualistic, and basically idiomatic. But before we discuss the meaning of words, a discussion of the meaning of reality must occur. Metaphysics is a hermeneutics inquiring into the meaning of reality (object-only, embodied object, dualism, subject-only). Then, linguistic hermeneutics inquires into the meaning of words used to refer to reality. Do we use the word "being," "isness," "atoms," or what, to write about metaphysics?

To debranch philosophy is to reorganize what philosophers have called the branches. Debranching brings philosophy into mainstream organization of general theory and derivations. The derivations or applications are more than a list of topics or institutions. I have organized the applications in a hierarchy, where every topic after metaphysics arises from within that general theory. Further, every successive chapter and exercise arises from within the previous chapter or exercise. The hierarchy puts metaphysics as the study of reality as the first chapter. That chapter reveals the top idea, the fundamental notion in philosophy: reality. It is the highest form of wisdom. This fundamental notion of wisdom consists of two themes, objectivity and subjectivity. All other topics from predictive reality to inflation and deflation in discussing truth, are derivative wisdom and reality. As derivative wisdom and reality, they are derivative twofold themes.

The typical philosophy or any book shows a list of chapters. The chapters are generally a list of topics; philosophy books explore its branches. To my knowledge, no philosophy book has chapters emerging from and contained within previous ones.

Let me clarify. When I showed a colleague my initial table of contents a few years ago, it contained roughly fifty chapters. This shocked my colleague. He would read thirteen or fourteen chapters, not fifty. But my ideas or chapters formed an internally consistent, flowing taxonomy. What to do? I decided that instead of cutting out nearly forty chapters, I would turn those into exercises. Thus, in a given chapter, what would have been the next chapter is the now that chapter's first exercise.

My view in this book is different. Within or inside each chapter is the germ of the next one. In other words, the chapter on ethics talks of outer-worldly ascetics rejecting and inner-worldly ascetics accepting but transforming society. The following chapter on gemeinschaft and gesellschaft, family and specific roles is a subset of ethics, further articulating the meaning of family and jobs within society and matter.

My effort is probably sets and subsets. Chapter one is the set, chapters two through fourteen are subsets.

Each chapter integrates traditional metaphysics. That involves the spectrum from atomism and structuralism, to postmodernism. The second session of each chapter integrates this with process and stability. My point is the atomism, structuralism, through postmodernism, denotes options in change and stability. Atomism, structuralism, through postmodernism (1) change alone, (2) change as the evolution of a stability which is atomism, structuralism, or any option through postmodernism, (3) dualism, and finally (4) do not change. The final section means that potential problems exist in discussing and understanding each chapter. Do we (1) react to, (2) prevent, (3) ignore and react to, or (4) deny, problems?

Readers may well consider whether this approach is another in the list of types of philosophy. Thinkers have given us logical positivism, linguistic analysis, pragmatism, existentialism, solipsism, skepticism, and phenomenology. Philosophers have put forth process thinking, deconstruction, poststructuralism, postmodernism.

To the extent that we can reasonably define any of these, I see some truth in each. In that sense, I like to think of unified philosophy.

The insertion of human factors engineering will be a surprise to many philosophers. Philosophy acknowledges the philosophical basis of technology. But no philosophy book of which I am aware, has formally integrated the field with human factors or ergonomics.

However, I find a major unity of philosophy and human factors engineering. Theoretical metaphysics talks of the object and subject. If objectivity or object is the external world, the environment, and subjectivity is the human, social dimension, a connection emerges between human factors and philosophy or metaphysics.

Theoretical metaphysics helps show the connection. That metaphysics includes objectivity alone, objectivity embodied, object-subject dualism, and subjectivity alone. Again, I am restricting myself to those four positions. Objectivity alone excludes subjectivity. Human factors talks here of the user unfriendly object. Objectivity embodied is phenomenology, taking subjectivity or the human into account. In dualism, objectivity and the human are two distinct realities. Finally, subjectivity alone denotes the human factor without the environment's functions.

Semantics and language enter. Where metaphysics speaks of the existential or subjective factor coloring the objective, human factors talks of the human factor of the environment. Where metaphysics tells us of the object being value free, ergonomics mentions the user unfriendly. There seems no parallel between dualism and human factors terminology. But where metaphysics mentions subjectivity alone, human factors tells us of the user too-friendly.

HUMAN FACTORS: THEORETICAL, MICRO AND MACRO

Theoretical and applied metaphysics or theoretical and applied philosophy has a human factors parallel. Theoretical metaphysics or philosophy can be theoretical human factors. This is the most abstract view of human factors engineering. Micro human factors can mean all applied metaphysics where we see the relations between object and subject. Macro human factors would mean city planning. Here, we design the object as the city, containing all micro objects.

Micro ergonomics or human factors will consist of reverse human factors. This is the design or adjustment of the person to technology, any object, or other person. Examples includes police bomb squads adjusting to a bomb, people adjusting to the weather, students to a career, the military to nuclear, biological, or chemical weapon.

Theoretical metaphysics, speaking of analysis or objectivity and lifeworld or subjectivity, brings us to philosophy and game theory. Analysis denotes parts; the lifeworld discloses the whole or pre-reflective. Game theory tells us about responses to the other participants in competition. If game theory deals with strategy and responses, these need not be to serious situations. Any response to a participant or inanimate situation can mean expanding game theory to a nonlethal problem or normal affair. I see game theory as serious response to a lethal situation, but within also the casual response to a normal daily context. The former can be ice on the road or a suspicious person to avoid, or the enemy, or something dangerous in business. The casual might be trying to cross the street when suddenly the light changes to red and we must stop.

Another example of the casual situation could be how to respond to a friend's or loved one's conversation or gestures during the typical day. This is typical intersubjectivity.

Throughout this book, readers will have noticed I have defined the lifeworld as method/approach, and geography. We can approach or study atomistic alone, atomistic embodied, dualistic, and lifeworld alone society in terms of (atomistic) analysis alone, analysis embodied, or subjectivity alone: reflection alone, embodied reflection, or pre-reflection alone. What are we approaching or studying? Our aim is to study the geographical lifeworld. Philosophy looks at the totally automated city, humane city where motion or parts are integrated in human terms, a dualism of monastery and automated city, and monastery or humane city alone.

A totally automated city might well, in 2018, mean a place of complete artificial intelligence, automation, and online activity. Human beings are rarely seen interacting with each other.

Serious game theory is reductionism or analysis alone, probably putting everything online. Lifeworld alone as game theory could be the monastery, or pre-reflective approach alone.

With philosophy as the options of theoretical and applied monism, phenomenology, dualism, and postmodernism, philosophers are able to clarify the subject-matter's future. Objections to philosophy's importance to society appear to follow an essential line of criticism. Philosophical reflection does little or nothing. The arts and sciences, technology, provide for a better life. What does philosophy offer? From the practical perspective, little to nothing.

However, think about the workplace. Work is the choosing and implementing of production and consumption of goods and services. Without such goods and services, civilization stalls, perhaps stops. Where does philosophy fit in? It believes that we ought to choose the correct and ethical ways of producing, distributing and consuming. Someone has said philosophy does not bake bread, but baking manifests the belief that making bread is meaningful and necessary. Having said this, the workplace is more than just baking bread. We occasionally, periodically, pause to think about how, why, where, when, and who, of baking, or working. How do we bake? Who bakes? Why? Where do we bake?

Beyond the workplace, philosophy is reflection on what we are doing in life. Its central questions are the "big ones." What is real? What is the source of knowing? What is right and wrong? How is the state originated?

The first question helps us determine whether reality is quantitative, human, or some combination. By thinking about the sources of knowing, philosophers help us understand whether knowledge is innate, experiential, or a combination. Discard right and wrong and we can be on the way to ending civilization. How the state originates enables us to discern whether society is natural, artificial, or a combination.

One aspect of the preceding paragraph is the notion of gaining and recording knowledge. Human beings do not just walk around knowing everything. Our capability of knowing is limited. Much of what we know is stored. Books, journals, encyclopedias, maps, and other material form the library.

Philosophy is like the library shelves. It organizes knowledge. Organization includes the way we manage and locate information about reality, knowledge itself, society, ethics, and the multitude of subsystems.

Inside the books on shelves, we find literature on knowledge itself. Philosophy helps us reflect on technological, scientific, and artistic knowledge or disciplines. This reflection provides the basis of interdisciplinarity—connecting knowledge. The foundations of such unity, according to Alfred North Whitehead (1964), is the analytic-wonder dialogue. He eloquently, simply states that philosophy starts in wonder, proceeds with analysis, and in the end, wonder remains. In understanding technology, science and art, we are awed, then objectify, finally continue to wonder.

Whitehead is speaking about the lifeworld approach which underlies knowing and life. Many thinkers, as in General System Theory, eiconics, and the like, call this the homological or isomorphic way. The analytic-lived approach is the same shape or homo-logos, isomorph, of which all disciplines are variations. As we mentioned earlier, Mary Midgley believes that philosophy is not a discipline among others, but their inherent orientation. This sounds very close to Martin Heidegger's (Heidgger, 1966) notion that being underlies and is manifest through Dasein or possibility of human nature, around which we see the sum of beings. Being is not the sum of beings.

Whitehead anticipated homological or isomorphic interdisciplinarity, and Heidegger. From the perspective of Whitehead, "if a few basic principles are found underlying all knowledge, that is economy of thought" (1072b). Metaphysical options run throughout all chapters in this book, and the chapters, in turn, run throughout the disciplines.

Those options help us with observing and thinking about the city around us. Observe buildings, traffic, streets and sidewalks, buses, bikes, bridges, parks, and parking of cars. Experience or observe social events, and the programs which ushers distribute about them. Listen to and reflect on conversations. Are each of these objects and events atomistic, structural, humane, dualistic, postmodern?

Put another way, are buildings ornate or simply form follows function? The former is more human and eye-catching. The latter more or less glass and steel, sterile. Those opposites are atomistic and phenomenological. Streets may have lanes only for cars and buses, or include bicycle paths. Those streets without bike paths ignore the biker, but those with paths take the biker into account. Acknowledging bikers is phenomenological because the city takes them into account, ignoring them is atomistic since it forces them to only walk, take a bus, or drive a car. Identifying ourselves during transactions in the big city can be annoying. Go to a bank and deposit or withdraw money. You need to produce a photo ID. Or you are at a store paying for goods. The store does not require an ID, but may want a card or other item identifying you, which you swipe or insert on a computer.

During the 1950s, these forms of identification may not have even existed. Our increasingly anonymous society requires an external, totally objective means of verifying your identity. The banker, cashier, store owner, do not know you. Even if they recognize you, the computer requires a record of your transaction. All this is atomistic. Culture has reduced you to an object. Philosophy helps you understand this, and it enables you to compare reductive, urban culture with the opposite: the monastery. Reflection on metaphysics then gives us the framework to see a town or city somewhere between a monastery and anonymous big city or equally problematic bedroom community.

Whitehead compares philosophy with architecture and construction work (1964a). He argues that philosophy builds cathedrals before workmen move the first stone. Workmen move the first stone because they are able, but also the architect has decided that a cathedral is to be built, and built with stones instead of lumber. In Whiteheadian thought, philosophy may be chronologically before activity, but it is also the principles and options underlying all action. Action is the unfolding of the option we choose.

ETHICS

Chapter one said that theoretical metaphysics is foundational to remaining chapters. As such chapters two to fourteen are derived metaphysics. But chapter seven is theoretical ethics, applicable to all other chapters including the first one. This denotes a relationship between metaphysics and ethics. Such a claim, or even suggestion, goes against the grain of traditional philosophy. I know of no philosopher who has believed such an intimate connection between metaphysics, philosophy, and ethics. Traditional philosophy as the love of wisdom sees metaphysics as inquiry into reality, not right and wrong. It views ethics as asking about right and wrong, not the nature of reality.

However, take another look at theoretical metaphysics. Options exist. As I mention many times, this book restricts itself to four of them: objectivity (atomism and structuralism) alone, objectivity embodied, subject-object dualism, and subjectivity (postmodernism, existentialism) alone. In at least one case, that of existentialism or subjectivity alone, thinkers argue that atomism and structuralism are unethical. I should point out that the existentialists are rarely explicit.

Existential philosophers argue mainly that almost any reductionism, or any structural emphasis, is against human nature. To be ethical is for a human being to do something in the interest and for the good. This may be the good according to God, nature, or specifically human nature.

A unified general theory of ethics claims four options: doing without ethics; doing through ethics; only ethics, followed by only doing; and ethics alone without doing. That unity then sees change alone where ethics differ for the sake of differing, change embodied meaning ethics are differing as needed, change-stability dualism (ethics does not change, and then only changes), and ethical stability alone. Finally, problems confronting us when being ethical will always exist, potential problems will be here at all times, people ignore and then react to solve problems in ethics, and they deny problems exist.

Metaphysical purist may argue against this wide ranging definition of ethics. They may insist that ethics cannot be intimately involved with metaphysics. My point is that any branch of philosophy must be real in order to be a branch. And that with reality consisting of at least four options, these options have major implications for our behavior. As such, the options most likely constitute ethical dimensions.

Human factors engineering is *ipso facto* an ethic. Designing environment, whether persons or objects, for persons or objects, has implications for individuals. A user unfriendly table can be difficult or dangerous for the person to use. Poor training of police or military as they deal with bombs and other weapons directed against them or the general public can lead to death or injury to the law enforcement or uniformed and civilianclothed armed service member.

To my knowledge, human factors engineering or ergonomics has never been a topic in an ethics text. Such texts consider numerous issues such as abortion, homosexuality, animal rights, ecology, euthanasia, lying, and pornography. Texts and organizations in business ethics ask students to think about equal pay, management-labor disputes and issues, automation, and gender and the workplace. The nearest that business ethics comes to ergonomics are discussions regarding workplace conditions. OSHA, the Office of Safety and Health Administration, attempts to respond to such problems. The EPA or Environmental Protection Agency, responds to hazardous conditions in the air, including air pollution.

As mentioned in earlier, traditional ethical theories seem to need correction. Ethics text talk of generally six theories: divine command, natural law, virtue, duty, egoism, and utilitarianism. But examination of each one appears to persuade us to say that there may need to be only two: divine command and natural law. Divine command says being ethical means following God. Natural can include God, but can be atheistic and purely secular. Look at the remaining four theories. Virtue tells us it is ethical to use moderation. This is Aristotle's Golden Mean. Virtue theory is presumably different from egoism. Yet, virtue theory could tell us to be moderate in egoism. Egoism might well denote it is in our interest to be moderate. Virtue is said to differ from utilitarianism. Yet, utilitarianism might say lessening pain and maximizing pleasure can be moderate. It would make little sense to propose being as pleasurable as possible, drinking and eating immoderately. Utilitarianism can be egoism. It may be in my self interest to lessen pain and increase pleasure. As a politician, I can advocate helping the poor simply to get votes.

Being moderate in helping give pleasure for egoist reasons, can well be my duty. That is, natural law or divine command can tell us our duty is to increase pleasure moderately or reasonably, for political (egoist) purposes. God or nature says our duty is to increase pleasure for selfish reasons. Some utilitarians may argue that I cannot use *maximize* and *moderately* or *reasonably* together.

ETHICS AND ECONOMICS

Readers will see that I all but equate unified ethics with economics. This could pose a problem for ethicists and economists. Each professional could well maintain that these are two separate topics. Indeed, an economist professor once insisted that economics has nothing to do with ethics. It is only the choice of resources, and the most efficient way of production, distribution, and consumption. But economics is more. It is not simply mathematics, physics, chemistry, or biology. As a social science, perhaps a humanities, economics is a human activity.

Economics and any activity, involves two things. Both cases mean "doing." Riding a bicycle is more than riding a bike. Teaching and studying mathematics goes beyond pedagogical mechanics. How we get on the bike and pedal is primarily mechanics, not necessarily ethics. Whether the bicycle is ours or stolen, is ethics. Teaching and studying mathematics is primarily mechanics, not necessarily ethics. However, whether we are teaching intentionally to mislead, or studying by having stolen a math book, brings in ethics.

Merely doing something can become unethical, if we are going through ritualistic motions. Ritual is probably good, but unethical if meaningless or excessive. On the other hand, doing nothing becomes unethical in that people stop functioning. Harvard's Daniel Bell (1976) warns against behaving without ethics and committing oneself exclusively to ethics. His argument reveals a phenomenological bent.

Because human activity concerns choice, production, distribution, consumption, and ecological responsibility, economics comes to hold a major ethical component, and the reverse. Speaking of ethics almost necessarily involves economics. As I read economics books, what strikes me is their language of micro- and macroeconomics, and often complex mathematics. Economists call the mathematical portion econometrics. My chapter on ethics as economics tacitly indicates that both topics—morality and production of goods and services—must start with an integrated view.

Economics is typically value-free. Texts do not warn us against excess technology, or admonish us against overdoing automation. They do not compare big city economics, robotics, anonymity, and the bedroom community of 2018 with the moderately sized city or small town of 1950. Textbooks do not compare any city with the monastic life. At most, libertarians and anarchists such as Robert Nozick and Friedman speak of social and political justice, and the economic implications of free enterprise, perhaps comparing them with those of central planning and regulation. My chapter on economics and ethics implies four options: over-regulation, regulation, dualism of deregulation and overregulation, and deregulation as an end itself.

PHILOSOPHY AS INTEGRATIVE

I have tried to make it no secret that my view of philosophy is inclusive. Gary Gutting (2012) argues that philosophy is relevant because it provides help with ethics. But philosophical inquiry is interdisciplinary. Plato was a social and natural philosopher. Aristotle did ethics, but also metaphysics, logic, politics, and more. Whitehead touched on almost everything conceivable in knowledge. Readers will notice, and professional philosophers could well object to, my referring to an extensive nonphilosophical bibliography.

Topics and disciplines of human factors engineering, anthropology, espionage, game theory, sociology, economics, psychology, manifest philosophy. This text does include sections or even a chapter on hard science. No chapter deals with physics, chemistry, mathematics, or biology. Chapters twelve and thirteen have references to unifying ideas within and among biology, math, physics, and meteorology. Philosophy benefits when scholars discern interdisciplinarity, and philosophers listen to and incorporate these into philosophical discourse.

Philosophy is undoubtedly the earliest topic of study. Earliest thinkers of the East and West speculated about reality, knowledge, ethics, beauty, and the state. As knowledge expanded and information crystallized—especially in the West—technology, sciences and arts emerged. For many scholars, these disciplines should replace philosophy. Intellectuals appear to insist that Enlightenment and modern research is empirically answering, or making serious progress toward solving, questions about which philosophy has speculated.

But those questions remain. Scholars continue to debate the nature of reality, origins of the state, sources of knowing, issues of ethics. Stewart and Mickunas (1990) remind us that abortion is not a question of biology, but of philosophical contexts and assumptions. Similarly, whether and how arts, sciences, and technology connect is a philosophical issue. Euthanasia, war, symmetric and asymmetric conflict, universal health care, and whether college is for everyone are philosophical questions.

If philosophy is the earliest topic of inquiry, it is foundational. My chapter titles attempt to emphasize that. These titles are reality, linguistic reality, truth reality, truth theory reality, and so on. Reality is fundamental, others are derived reality. No philosophical writing of which I am aware looks at epistemology, ethics, the state, and so on as isomorphically or homologically derived from metaphysics, as derived reality. Of course, equating theoretical metaphysics with theoretical human-factors engineering and suggesting that other disciplines are micro- and macro-human factors may well delight technology professionals, especially engineers. Source of knowledge is knowledge origin reality but also microergonomics; the origin of society is social origin reality and micro human factors engineering, and ethics or ethical reality, probably synonymous with economic reality, is macro human factors.

Philosophy, instead of retreating into a cloister, needs to open to dialogue with the scholarly, governmental, and corporate world. Seen in a larger framework, philosophers ought to note that presidents, Congress, and the United States Supreme Court, are philosophizing. They are debating national and world issues, and not directly producing goods and services. Corporate executives at the highest levels of business are not directly producing goods and services, but making philosophical decisions. These leaders are concerned with laws, regulations, who to hire, how to deal with employees, and ways to organize and reorganize their companies. Universities are developing and teaching knowledge, hopefully also wisdom. Think tanks are discussing policy.

Dialogue ought not to connote that philosophy is only applied. Research and development (R&D) departments of corporations engage in producing ideas for future production of goods and services. Think tanks are R&D institutions. Think tanks and corporate research and development departments justify the need for theory, experimentation, and human activity not immediately related to production of goods and services. Philosophers ought to talk with all nonphilosophers, theoreticians and practitioners. A philosopher engaged in linguistic analysis can continue in his or her efforts, but should converse with anthropologists, poets, novelists, computer specialists, mathematicians, and existential and phenomenological colleagues. Existential thinkers should never avoid speaking with linguistic analysts, logical positivists, computer professionals, mathematicians, anthropologists, and the same list of people with whom analytical thinkers converse.

If, as Midgley, Whitehead, and I argue, philosophy is foundational to technology, sciences, and arts, then it holds more than departmental and disciplinary status on the campus. Technology, science, and art can have deans and chairs. However, philosophy would have a higher office. Philosophical assumptions underlie the disciplines. Society and academia assume or believe that technology, science, and art ought to be areas of study. John Cassidy (2015, p. 84) gives a good defense for attending college and studying liberal arts, which one can interpret as arguing for philosophy. Studying for jobs is fine; education in philosophy, liberal arts, or general education helps with life as a whole as a context for work. Where, then, might we put philosophy?

Philosophy would not be a department under a dean or chair. Instead, the preceding paragraph implies, philosophy probably ought to be under a vice provost. At the very least, a vice president must be head of a philosophy office. That status connotes that academia talk about the philosophy office, not the philosophy department. Unquestionably, nonphilosophy faculty and administrators could react with mass hysteria, serious complaints, and powerful objections. Those characteristics and descriptions may be anywhere from unfounded to exaggerated. Yet, nonphilosophers might not be happy with a philosophy entity having academic and administrative power over them, or even its leader or head being associate provost. In their view, one discipline does not organize or manage another. But this work has never said that philosophy is a discipline among others.

Dane Ward (2017) envisions the future academic library as an integral part of a college and university's total operations. "Changes in academic libraries," notes Ward, would fully influence and impact "activities, relationships, and changes in other departments" (Ward 2017, A44). Philosophers might well argue for the same situation regarding philosophy. The future philosophy office (or department?) will be integrally networked with all academic departments, and operations.

The previous pages and chapters have argued that disciplines exist for two reasons. One is empirical research. This appears in books and disciplinary literature. The second is actually foundational to empirical research. That is the assumption, the philosophical belief, that empirical research, and thus any discipline, is legitimate.

Philosophy's importance is akin to that of human resources, the treasurer, comptroller, public relations, public safety, and related administrative offices. Every employee of the university or college reports to human resources, treasurers, and other executive departments or offices."

Will philosophy be called metaphysics, and the two of them equivalent? Should philosophy, the love of wisdom, combine with metaphysics, the study of reality? This could result in physiosophy, or reality as wisdom.

To the extent that each chapter, and thus technology, science, and art, derive from fourfold patterns (monism, phenomenology, dualism, and subjectivity), philosophy assumes the role of the foundations of liberal arts and sciences, of general education.

REFERENCES

Ackoff, Russell. 1960. "Systems, Organizations, and Interdisciplinary Research," *Yearbook of the Society for General Systems Theory* 5.

Adams, Jack A. 1989. *Human Factors Engineering*. New York: MacMillan.

Adams, Jack A. *Human Factors Engineering*. New York: MacMillan: 1989.

Adams, James Luther. 1973. *Paul Tillich's Philosophy of Culture, Science & Religion*. New York: Shocken.

Adler, Jeremy, ed. 1998. *Hoderlin, Fredrich: Selected Poems and Fragments*. Translated by Michael Hamberger. New York: Penguin.

Ambrose, Stephen. 1998. *Citizen Soldiers*. New York: Touchtone.

Ammerman, Robert R., ed. 1965. *Classics of Analytic Philosophy*. New York: McGraw-Hill.

Anft, Michael. 2017. "The New Urban Science: Big Data and big dollars are transforming the field. But where is the big idea?" *The Chronical Review: The Chronicle of Higher Education. Section B* (August 4).

Anglin, Jeremy M. 1973. *Beyond the Information Given*. New York: Norton.

Antony, Louise. 2016. "Things Oughta Make Sense," Presidential Address, American Philosophical Association, Proceedings and Addresses of the American Philosophical Association, University of Delaware–Newark.

Applebaum, Stanley. 1996. *English Romantic Poetry: An Anthology*. New York: Dover.

Aquinas, St. Thomas. 2001. *Summa Theologica. I-II, Question 7*.

Aristotle. 1999. *Nicomachean Ethics*, 2nd ed., trans. Terrence Irwin. Indianapolis: Hackett.

Audi, Robert. ed. 1993. "Nyaya," *Cambridge Dictionary of Philosophy*. Cambridge, Cambridge University Press

Audi, Robert., ed. 1993. "Kant," in *Cambridge Dictionary of Philosophy*. Cambridge: Cambridge University Press. Ayer, A.J. 1959. *Logical Positivism*. New York: Free Press.

Ayer, A.J. 1959. *Logical Positivism*. New York: Free Press.

Bamford, James. 2002. *Body of Secrets*. New York: Anchor.

Barnett, Lincoln. 1966. *The Universe and Dr. Einstein*. New York: Bantam.

Barrows, Christine. 2012. "Understanding the Role of Parochial Control in a Disadvantaged Brooklyn Community." Presentation at the American Sociological Association. Las Vegas, NV.

Baum, Rudy M. 2004. Editorial, *Chemical & Engineering News* (October 11).

Beilock, Sian. 2015. *How the Body Knows Its Mind*. New York: Atria.

Bell, Daniel. 1976. *The Cultural Contradictions of Capitalism*. New York: Basic Books.

Bellman, Richard. 1962. "Dynamic Programming, Intelligent Machines, and Self-Organizing Systems." Polytechnic Institute of Brooklyn Symposium on Mathematical Theory of Automata.

Benesh, Peter. 2002. "Innovate: Col. John Boyd's Creativity Changed Military Air Strategy the World Over." *Investor's Business Daily* (October 30).

Berger, Peter L. 1967. *The Social Construction of Reality: A Treatise on the Sociology of Knowledge*. New York; Anchor.

Bergmann, Jonathan, and Aaron Sams. 2012. *Flip Your Classroom*. Eugene OR: International Society for Technology in Education.

Berkeley, George. 1897. *A Treatise Concerning the Principles of Human Knowledge*.

Bertalanffy, Ludwig von. 1968. *General System Theory*. New York: George Braziller.

Blanning, Tim. 2012. *The Romantic Revolution*. New York: Modern Library.

Blanshard, Brand. 1980. "The Philosophy of Brand Blanshard." In *Library of Living Philosophers*, edited by Paul A. Schilpp. LaSalle, IL: Open Court.

Bloom, Allan. 1987. *The Closing of the American Mind*. New York: Paperback.

Bobbs-Merrill: 1959.

Bolter, J. David. 1984. *Turing's Man*. Chapel Hill: University of North Carolina Press.

Boss, Judith A. 2014. *Ethics for Life*. New York: McGraw-Hill.

Boulding, Kenneth. 1968. *The Image*. Ann Arbor: University of Michigan Press.

Brooks, Rodney. 2017. "The Seven Deadly Sins of AI Predictions." *The MIT Technology Review* 120, no. 6. November/December).

Buber, Martin. 1970. *I and Thou*. New York: Scribner.

Bukatko, Danute, and Marvin W. Daeler. 2004. *Child Development: A Thematic Approach*. Fifth Edition. Boston: Houghton.

Burchard, John E. *This Is MIT: Massachusetts Institute of Technology Bulletin*, Cambridge, Massachusetts. Undergraduate Catalogue Issue for 1961–1962.

Burns, James MacGregor. 1979. *Leadership*. New York: Harper.

Burrows, William E. 1986. *Deep Black*. New York: Harcourt, Brace, Jovanovich.

Bush, Vannevar. "A Conversation," Prototype Issue. *International Science and Technology*.

Bush, Vannevar. "Thinking Ahead with Vannevar Bush," *International Science and Technology: Prototype Issue*.

Byron, Ellen. 2005. "To Master the Art of Solving Crimes, Cops Study Vermeer." *The Wall Street Journal* CCXLVI, no. 18 (July 27).

Calder, Nigel. 1977. *The Key to the Universe.* New York: Viking.

Campbell, Jeremy. 1989. *The Improbable Machine.* New York: Simon & Schuster.

Camus, Albert. 1991. *The Myth of Sisyphus and Other Essays.* Translated by Justin O'Brien. New York: Vintage.

Cannon, Martin J. *Management: An Organizational Perspective.* Boston, MA; Little Brown and Company: 1977.

Cardozo, Benjamin N. 1921. *The Nature of the Judicial Process.* New Haven, CT: Yale University Press.

Cardozo, Benjamin. *The Nature of the Judicial Process.* 1921. New Haven: CT: Yale University Press.

Carnap, Rudolf. 2005. *The Logical Structure of the World.* LaSalle, IL: Open Court.

Cassidy, John. 2015. "College Calculus." *The New Yorker* (September 7).

Cerami, Joseph R., and Jay W. Boggs, eds. 2007. *The Counterinsurgency and Interagency Warfare: Stability, Security, Transition, and Reconstruction Roles.* Strategic Studies Institute.

Chapanis, Alphonse. 1960. "Human Engineering," in *Operations Research and Systems Engineering*, ed. Charles D. Flagle, William H. Huggins, and Robert H. Roy. Baltimore: Johns Hopkins University Press.

Chomski, Noam. 1998. *On Language.* New Press.

Clark, Mary T., ed. 1972. *An Aquinas Reader: Selections from the Writings of Thomas Aquinas.* New York: Doubleday.

Clary, David. 2004. *Rocket Man: Robert Goddard and the Birth of the Space Age.* New York: Hachette.

Clynes, Manfred and J. H. Milsum. ed. *Biomedical Engineering Systems.* New York: McGraw-Hill.

Clynes, Manfred. 1970. "Toward a View of Man," in *Biomedical Engineering Systems*, ed. Manfred Clynes and J.H. Milsum. New York: McGraw-Hill.

Cohen, Arthur A. 1998. "Why I Chose to be a Jew." In *An Arthur A. Cohen Reader: Selected Fiction and Writings on Judaism, Theology, Literature, and Culture*, edited by David Stern and Paul Mendez-Flohr. Detroit: Wayne State University Press.

Conference Board. 1966. *The Challenge of Technology.* Annual Conference on Science and Humanities, November 30.

Conklin, John. 1995. *Criminology*, fifth edition. Boston: Allyn & Bacon.

Copelston, Frederick. 1993. *History of Philosophy.* New York: Image.

Cornford, F.M. 1953. *Before and After Socrates.* London: Cambridge University Press.

Corrado, Michael. 2008. *The Analytic Tradition in Philosophy: Background and Issues.* Booksurge Publishing.

Cox, Harvey. 2013. *Secular City*. Princeton, NJ: Princeton University Press.

Crawford, Matthew B. 2009. *Shop Class as Soulcraft*. New York. Penguin.

Dale, Rose. 2017. "Letter to the Editor." *Philosophy Now*, no. 121 (August/ September).

Daly, Herman, and John Cobb Jr. 1969. *For the Common Good*. Boston: Beacon.

Darwin, Charles. *The Origin of the Species*. New York. Signet. 2003.

Davies, Paul. 1985. *Superforce*. New York: Simon & Schuster.

Davis, Fred. 1972. "The Cab-Driver and His Fare," in *The Social Dimensions of Work*, ed. Clifton D. Bryant. Englewood Cliffs, NJ: Prentice-Hall.

Davis, Martin. 1997. *Game Theory*. New York: Dover.

Dawson, Raymond, trans. 2008. *Confucius: The Analects*. Oxford: Oxford University Press.

de Chardin, Pierre Teilhard. *The Phenomenon of Man*. 1965. New York: Harper.

Deane, S.N., trans. 1962. *Saint Anselm: Basic Writings*. LaSalle, IL: Open Court.

Dennett, Daniel. *Darwin's Dangerous Idea: Evolution and the Meanings of Life*. New York. Simon & Schuster. 1996.

Derrida, Jacques. 1976. *Grammatology*, trans. Gayatri Chakravorty Spivak. Baltimore: Johns Hopkins University Press.

Descartes, René. 1999. "Letter," in *The Philosophical Writings of Descartes*. Vol. 3, ed. John Cottingham, Robert Stoothoff, and Dugald Murdoch. Cambridge: Cambridge University Press.

Doherty, James. 1970. "A Few Suggestions for Handling Criminal Appeals." *Case & Comment* 75 (1).

Doniger, Wendy and Brian K. Smith. trans. 1991. *The Laws of Manu*. London: Penguin.

Donne, John. 2012. *Meditation*. Vol. XVII, *The Best of John Donne*. New York: CreateSpace.

Douglas, John. 1995. *Mind Hunter*. New York: Simon & Schuster.

Drucker, Peter F. 1974. *Management*. New York: Harper & Row.

Dubrin, Andrew J. 1974. *Fundamentals of Organizational Behavior*. New York: Pergamon.

Dunkelman, Marc J. 2014. *The Vanishing Neighborhood*. New York: Norton.

Eddy, Mary Baker. 1934. *Science and Health with Key to the Scriptures*. Boston: Christian Science. Publishing Company.

Edmonds, Patricia. 2017. "Genius," in *National Geographic*, May.

Einstein, Albert. 1931. Address to Students, California Institute of Technology. I appreciate California Institute of Technology for making available to me a copy of this address. I initially learned of it through its appearance in the prototype issue of International Science and Technology.

Eliade, Mircea. 1966. *Patterns in Comparative Religion*. Cleveland, OH. World.

Eurich, Nell P. 1985. *Corporate Classrooms: The Learning Business.* Princeton, NJ: The Carnegie Foundation for the Advancement of Teaching.

Feyerabend, Paul. 2010. *Against Method.* London: Verso.

Fitzpatrick, B. 1997. "Some aspects of the work and influence of R.L. Moore." In *Handbook of the History of General Topology Volume 1,* edited by C. E. Aull and R. Lowen. Kluwer Academic.Available through EAF on CD.

Flower, Clair. 2008. "Living with dying: Reflections on Family Music Therapy with Children Near the End of Life." In *Music Therapy with Children and Their Families,* edited by Amelia Oldfield and Claire Flower. London: Jessica Kingsley Publishers.

Foner, Eric. 2010. *The Fiery Trial: Abraham Lincoln and American Slavery.* New York: Norton.

Friedlander, John. 2006. "Stalking the Reimann Hypothesis." *Notices of the American Mathematical Society* 53, no. 8 (September).

Friedman, Milton. 2002. *Capitalism and Freedom.* Chicago, IL: University of Chicago Press.

Frodeman, Robert, Julie Thompson Klein, Carl Mitchem, eds. 2010. *The Oxford Handbook of Interdisciplinarity.* Oxford: Oxford University Press. Gadamer, Hans-Georg. 2013. *Truth and Method.* London: Bloomsberry.

Gadamer, Hans-Georg. 2013. *Truth and Method.* Trans. Joel Weinsheimer and Donald G. Marshall. London: Bloombury Academic.

Gafter, Amanda. 2016. "The Case Against Reality." *The Atlantic* (April 25) Cf. Mark, Justin T. et al.

Gaines, Larry, and Roger Leroy Miller. 2012. *Criminal Justice in Action.* Belmont, CA: Wadsworth.

Gannon, Martin J. *Management: An Organizational Perspective.* Boston: Little, Brown and Company. 1977.

Gardner, John W. 1962. *Excellence.* New York: Harper.

Gardner, John W. 1965. *Self-Renewal.* New York: Harper.

Garland, John J. 1973. "Computers and the Legal Profession." *Hofstra Law Review* 1 (1).

Geach, Peter, and Max Black, trans. 1980. *Philosophical Writings of Gottlob Frege.* Blackwell Publishers.

Gendlin, Eugene T. 1981. *Focusing.* New York: Bantam.

Giddens, Anthony. 1984. *The Constitution of Society.* Berkeley, CA: University of California Press.

Gilb, Corinne. 1967. "Testimony." In *Full Opportunity And Social Accounting Act Hearings Before the Subcommittee on Government Research of the Committee on Government Operations, United States Senate Ninetieth Congress, First Session on S. 843.* Washington, D.C.: U. S. Government Printing Office.

Giles, Herbert A. *The Religions of Ancient China.* New Hampshire; Books for Libraries Press. 1969.

Godfrey, J. E. Drexel. 2006. "Ethics and Intelligence." In *Ethics of Spying: A Reader for the Intelligence Professional*, edited by Jan Goldman. Lanham, MD: Scarecrow Press.

Gottheil. Fred. 2009. *Principles of MicroEconomics: Sixth Edition*. Mason, OH: South-Western Cengage Learning.

Gray, Paul. 1987. "Seeking Educational Synergy." *MIT Technology Review* (October).

Greene, Stephen G. 1999. "Stemming the Tide of Urban Sprawl." *The Chronicle of Philanthropy* XI, no. 8 (February).

Grene, Marjorie. *The Philosophy of Biology*. New York. Cambridge University Press. 2004.

Gutting, Gary. 2012. "Philosophy—What's the Use?" *New York Times: Opinion*, July 25, 2012.

Haldane, Elizabeth S. 1968. *The Philosophical Works of Descartes*. Vol. 1. London: Cambridge University Press.

Hall, Jerome. 1973. "Perennial Problems of Criminal Law." *Hofstra Law Review* 1 (1).

Hamilton, Edith, and Huntington Cairns. 1964. *Plato*. New York: Random House.

Harrison, Brigid Callahan, Jean Wahl Harris, and Michelle D. Deardorff. 2013. *American Democracy Now*. New York: McGraw-Hill.

Hartschorne, Charles. 1991. *The Logic of Perfection*. LaSalle: Open Court.

Harvard Dialect Survey. 2002.

Hawking, Stephen. 1988. *A Brief History of Time*. New York: Bantam.

Hegel, G.W.F. 2003. *The Phenomenology of Mind*, trans. J.B. Baillie. Mineola, NY: Dover.

Hegel, G.W.F. 2003. *The Phenomenology of Mind*. Trans. J. B. Baillie. Mineola, NY: Dover.

Heidegger, Martin. 1966. *Being and Time*. New York: Harper.

Hertz, David. *Faith of Our Fathers*. New York: Basic Books. 1984.

Hicks, Herbert G. 1972. *The Management of Systems: A Systems and Human Resources Approach*. New York: McGraw-Hill.

Hobbes, Thomas. 1982. *Leviathan*. New York: Penguin. Hopfe, Lewis M., Mark R. Woodward, and Brett Hendrickson. 2009. *Religions of the World*. Boston: Pearson.

Hook, Steven W. 2017. *U.S. Foreign Policy*. Los Angeles, CA: Sage.

Hume, David. 1985. "On the Original Contract." In *Essays, Literary, Moral, and Political*. New York: Liberty Fund.

Hunter, A. 1985. *"Private, Parochial, and Public Social Orders: The Problem of Crime and incivility in Urban Communities,"* edited by G. Suttles and M. N. Zald. The Challenge of Social Control. Ablex Publishing.

"Hurricane Waves." *The Christian Science Monitor*. July 6, 1976.

Hursthouse, Roselind. 2002. *On Virtue Ethics*. New York: Oxford University Press.

Husserl, Edmund. 1970. *The Crisis in European Sciences and Transcendental Phenomenology*. Evanston, IL: Northwestern University Press.

Ihde, Don. 1999. *Expanding Hermeneutics: Visualism in Science*. Evanston: Northwestern University Press.

Ihde, Don. 2012. *Experimental Phenomenology, Expanded 2nd Edition: Multistabilities*. SUNY Press.

Jacobs, Jerry A. 2013. *In Defense of Disciplines*. Chicago, IL: University of Chicago Press.

Johnson, Brian Aaron. 2018. Fire Prevention Blueprint. ThatCodeCoach.com: 2018.

Johnson, D.M. 2011. *Socrates and Athens*. New York: Cambridge University Press.

Johnson, Richard A., Fremont E. Kast, and James E. Rosenzweig. 1967. *The Theory and Management of Systems*. New York: McGraw-Hill.

Johnston, Charles. 2016. *Tao Te Ching*. Khsetra Books.com.

Jones, R. Kenneth, and Patricia Jones. 1975. *Sociology of Medicine*. New York: Halstead Press.

Joyce, James. *Finnegan's Wake*. 2013. Important Books.

Kafatos, Fotis C., and Thomas Eisner. 2004. "Editorial: Unification in the Century of Biology." *Science* 303. (27 February).

Kahneman, Daniel. 2013. *Thinking Fast and Slow*. New York: Farrar, Straus & Giroux.

Kamber, Richard. 2009. "Plotting Philosophy's Future." *Common Review* (Fall).

Kant, Immanuel. 1927. *Critique of Practical Reason*. Translated by T. K. Abbott. London: Longmans Green.

Kant, Immanuel. 1959. *Foundations of the Metaphysics of Morals*. Translated by Lewis White Beck. New eYork.

Kant, Immanuel. 1987. *The Critique of Pure Reason*, trans. Norman Kemp Smith. New York: MacMillan.

Kantowitz, Barry H., and Robert D. Sorkin. 1968. *Human Factors Engineering*. New York: Wiley.

Kast, Fremont E., and James E. Rosenzweig. 1970. *Organization and Management: A Systems Approach*. New York: McGraw-Hill.

Kaufmann, Walter. 1970. *Martin Buber: I and Thou*. New York: Scribner.

Kazanjian, Michael M. 1970. "Toward a New Academe," *Hearings Before the General Subcommittee on Education of the Committee on Education and Labor, House of Representatives, Ninety-First Congress, Second Session on H.R. 517, H.R. 776, H.R. 9866, H.R. 10833, and H.R. 11546, p. 1380.*

———. 1971. "Theology of Culture: Religious Dimensions of Secularity." *Delta Epsilon Sigma Bulletin* 16 (1).

———. 2002. *Phenomenology and Education*. Amsterdam: Rodopi.

———. 2015. "DeBranching Philosophy: Spies, Carpenters, and Philosophers Toward Reorganizing Metaphysics, Ethics, and Epistemology." Behavioral Social Science Colloquium, Triton College, River Grove, IL.

Kerstetter, Wayne. 1985. "Who Disciplines the Police? Who Should?" In *Police Leadership in America*, Edited by William A. Geller. New York: Praeger.

Kessen, William. 1966. "The Strategy of Instruction," in *Learning About Learning: A Conference*. ed. by Jerome S. Bruner. Washington, D.C.: United States Government Printing Office. United States Department of Health, Education, and Welfare.

Kessen, William. 1966. "The Strategy of Instruction," in *Learning About Learning: A Conference Report*, ed. Jerome S. Bruner. Washington, DC: US Department of Health, Education and Welfare.

Kierkegaard, Soren. 2003. *Fear and Trembling*, translated by Alastair Hannay. New York: Penguin.

Kilcullen, David. 2010. *Counterinsurgency*. Oxford: Oxford University Press.

Killian, James R. 1966. "Lift the Human Spirit," in *College Life*, ed. C. Gilbert Wrenn, Norman T. Bell, Richard D. Burckhardt, and Victor B. Lawhead. Boston: Houghton-Mifflin.

Kluckhohn, Clyde and Charles Murray. 1967. "Personality Formation: The Determinants," in *Personality in Nature, Culture, and Society*. ed. Clyde Kluckhohn and Charles Murray. New York: Knopf.

Kluckhohn, Clyde, and Charles Murray. 1967. "Personality Formation: The Determinants," in *Personality in Nature, Society, and Culture*, ed. Clyde Kluckhohn and Charles Murray. New York: Knopf.

Kolata, Gina. 1989. "Mathematicians Find Link in Knot Theory and Physics." *New York Times*, February 21, 1989.

Kripke, Saul. 1991. *Naming and Necessity*. New York; Wiley-Blackwell.

Kuhn, Alfred. 1963. *The Study of Society: A Unified Approach*. Homewood, IL: Irwin.

Kuhn, Thomas. 1970. *The Structure of Scientific Revolutions*. Chicago, IL: University of Chicago Press.

Kushner, Harold S. *When Bad Things Happen to Good People*. New York: Anchor: 2004.

Lakatos, Imre. 2000. *For and Against Method*. Chicago, IL: University of Chicago Press.

Lakoff, George, and Mark Johnson. 2003. *Metaphors to Live By*. Chicago: University of Chicago Press.

Landau, Alan M., and Frieda W. Landau, Terry Griswold, D. M. Giangreco, and Hans Halberstadt. 1999. *U.S. Special Forces: Airborne Rangers, Delta & U.S. Navy SEALs*. Oseola, WI: MBI Publishing.

Leamnson, Robert. 2000. "Learning as Biological Brain Change." *Change* (November/December).

Learning Channel. 2007.

Leibniz, Gottfried, Wilhelm. 1951. "New Essays on the Human Understanding," in *Leibniz Selections*. ed. by Philip P. Weiner. New York: Scribners.

Leibniz, Gottfriend W. 1951. "New Essays on the Human Understanding," in *Leibniz Selections*, ed. Philip P. Weiner. New York: Scribner.

Lenin, Vladimir. *Essential Works of Lenin*. New York: Create/Space. 2013.

Levi-Strauss, Claude. 1963. *Structural Anthropology*. New York: Basic.

Levi-Strauss, Claude. 1966. *The Savage Mind*. Chicago: University of Chicago Press.

Levi-Strauss, Claude. 1969. *The Raw and the Cooked*. New York: Harper.

Levine, Alan J. 2008. *The War Against Rommel's Supply Lines*. Mechanicsburg, PA: Stackpole Books.

Locke, John. 1952. *The Second Treatise of Government*. Ed. Thomas P. Peardon. New York: Macmillan.

Locke, John. 1993. *An Essay Concerning Human Understanding*, ed. A.C. Fraser. Oxford: Nabu.

Maimonides, Moses. 2017. *Guide for the Perplexed*. Translated by M. Friedländer. New York: Dover.Marcel, Gabriel. 2011. *Being and Having*. Translated by Katherine Farrer. Old Aberdeen College; Publisher Unknown.

Malcolm, Norman. 1958. *Ludwig Wittgenstein: A Memoir*. London: Oxford University Press.

Mankiw, N. Gregory. 2015. *Principles of Economics*. Stamford, CT: Cengage Learning.

Mark, Justin T., Brian B. Marion, and Donald Hoffman. 2010. "Natural Selections and Verdical Perceptions." *Journal of Theoretical Biology* 266, (2010): 504–515. Cf. Gafter, Amanda.

Marx, Karl and Eugene Kamenka. *The Portable Marx*. New York: Portable Library. 1983.

Maslow, Abraham. 2014. *Toward a Psychology of Being*. New York: Sublime Books: 2014.

Massey, J.L. 1968. "Information, Machines, and Men," in *Philosophy and Cybernetics*, ed. Frederick J. Crosson and Kenneth M. Sayre. *Cybernetics and Philosophy*. New York: Simon & Schuster.

McEachern, William A. 2015. *Econ: Principles of Macroeconomics*. Stamford, CT: Cengage.

McGregor, Douglas. 1960. *The Human Side of Enterprise*. New York: McGraw-Hill.

McKeon, Richard, ed. 1966. *The Basic Works of Aristotle*. New York: Random House.

McKeown, 1966. *The Basic Works of Aristotle*. New York: Random House.

Merleau-Ponty, Maurice. 1995. *Phenomenology of Perception*, trans. Colin Smith. London: Routledge.

Michael, Peter H. 2011. *Remembering John Hanson. New York: Underground Railroad Free Press*.

Midgley, Mary. 2016. "Does Philosophy Get Out of Date?" *Philosophy Now* 103.

Mill, John Stuart. 2005. *Utilitarianism*. New York: Barnes & Noble.

Mill, John Stuart. 2015. *Auguste Comte and Positivism*. Independent Publishing.

Millican, Peter. 2008. *David Hume: An Enquiry Concerning Human Understanding*. Cambridge: Cambridge University Press.

MIT Undergraduate Bulletin, Catalogue. Burchard, John. 1961–62.

Morgan, Michael Hamilton. 2007. *Lost History: The Enduring Legacy of Muslim Scientists, Thinkers, and Artists*. Washington, D.C.: National Geographic.

Moss, Pamela A. 2005. "Understanding the Other/Understanding Ourselves: Toward a Constructive Dialogue About 'Principles' in Educational Research," *Educational Theory* 55 (3).

Motterlini, Matteo, ed. 1999. *For And Against Method*. Chicago: University of Chicago Press.

Munson, Thomas. 1968. *Reflective Theology: Philosophical Orientations in Religion*. New Haven, CT: Yale University Press.

Nash, Paul. 1968. *Authority and Freedom in Education*. New York: John Wiley & Sons.

Natoli, Joseph, and Linda Hutcheon, eds. 1993. *A Postmodern Reader*. Albany, NY: SUNY Press.

Nelson, Cary. 1997. "The Real Problem with Tenure is Incompetent Faculty Hiring." *The Chronicle of Higher Education*, November 14, 1997.

Niebuhr, H. Richard. 1975. *Christ and Culture*. New York: Harper.

Nietzsche, Friedrich. 2014. *Beyond Good and Evil*. Lexington, KY: Millennium Publications. 2014a.

Nietzsche, Friedrich. 2014. *The Will to Power*. Translated by Anthony M. Ludovici. Lexington, KY, Publisher Unknown. 2014b.

Noll, James Wm., and Sam P. Kelly. 1970. *Foundations of Education in America*. New York; Harper and Row.

Nozick, Robert. 1974. *Anarchy, State, and Utopia*. New York: Basic.

Nozick, Robert. 1974. *Anarchy, State, and Utopia*. New York: Basic Books.

Odom, William E. 2004. *Fixing Intelligence*. New Haven: Yale.

Osterburg, James W., and Richard H. Ward. 1997. *Criminal Investigations*, 2nd edition. Cincinnati: Anderson Publishing.

Ottheil, Fred. 2009. *Principles of Microeconomics*. Mason, OH: Cengage.

"Outcome vs. Process Evaluation." *The Personnel Administrator*, November 1978.

Packard, Vance. 1957. *The Hidden Persuaders*. New York: LG Publishing.

Paley, William, Matthew D. Eddy, and David Knight, eds. 2008. *Natural Theology*. Oxford: Oxford University Press.

Paley, William. 2010. *Natural Theology*. New York: Deward Publishing.

Park, Michael Alan. 2008. *Introducing Anthropology: An Integrated Approach.* Fourth Edition. Boston: McGraw-Higher Education.

Parker, Barry. 1988. *Einstein's Dream.* New York: Plenum.

Parsons, Talcott. 1967. *The Structure of Social Action.* Vol. 2. New York: Free Press.

Paulos, John Allen. 1998. *Once Upon a Number.* New York: Basic.

Penkovsky, Oleg. *Penkovsky Papers.* New York: Harper. 1965.

Petraeus, General David H., Lt. General James P. Amos, and Lt. Colonel John A. Nagl. 2007. *The U.S. Army/Marine Corps. Counterinsurgency Field Manual.* Chicago: University of Chicago Press.

Petro, Joseph. 2005. *Standing Next to History.* New York; St. Martin's Press.

Phillips, Chandler Allen. 2000. *Human Factors Engineering.* New York: Wiley.

Pieper, Josef. 1993. *Leisure the Basis of Culture.* New York: Penguin.

Pietgen, Heinz-Otto, and Peter H. Richter. 1986. *The Beauty of Fractals.* Berlin: Springer-Verlag.

Pinker, Stephen. 2003. *The Blank Slate.* London and New York: Penguin. Polanyi, Michael. 1962. *Personal Knowledge.* Chicago, IL: University of Chicago Press.

Podolefsky, Aaron, Peter J. Brown, and Scott M. Lacey. 2009. *Applying Anthropology: An Introductory Reader.* Nineth Edition. Boston: McGraw Higher Education.

Popper, Karl. 2002. *Conjectures and Refutations.* London: Routledge.

Priess, David. 2016. *The Presidents' Book of Secrets: The Untold Story of Intelligence Briefing to American Presidents.* Foreword by George H.W. Bush. New York: Public Affairs.

Putnam, Hilary. 1992. *Realism with a Human Face.* Cambridge: Harvard University Press.

Radon, Rosemary. 1996. *Information Science.* Cambridge: Gower.

Ragin, Charles C. 2000. *Fuzzy-Set Social Science.* Chicago: University of Chicago Press.

Rand, Ayn. 1996. *Fountain Head.* New York: Signet.

Ransom, Harry Howe. 1958. *Central Intelligence and National Security.* Cambridge, MA: Harvard University Press.

Rathus, Spencer A. 2003. *Voyages.* Belmont, CA: Thomson.

Rawls, John. 1971. *A Theory of Justice.* Cambridge, MA; Harvard University Press.

Rawls, John. 1971. *Theory of Justice.* Cambridge, MA: Harvard University Press.

Richardson, Herbert. 1967. "A Philosophy of Unity." *Harvard Theological Review* 60 (1).

Richelson, Jeffrey T. 2012. *The US Intelligence Community.* Sixth Edition. Boulder: Westview Press.

Ricoeur, Paul. 1966. *Freedom and Nature: the Voluntary and Involuntary.* Evanston: Northwestern University Press.

Ricoeur, Paul. 1966. *Freedom and Nature*. Evanston, IL: Northwestern University Press.

Ritzer, George. 1996. *Modern Sociological Theory*. Fourth Edition. New York: McGraw-Hill.

Robinson, Linda. *Masters of Chaos*. New York; Public Affairs. 2004.

Rooney, John Flynn. 1997. "Continuing Education Classes Urged for Judges." *Chicago Daily Law Bulletin* 143 (209).

Roper, Lyndal. 1968. *Martin Luther*. New York: Random House; 2017.

Rousseau, Jean-Jacques. *The Social Contract*. New York: Penguin.

Russell, Bertrand. 1972. *The History of Western Philosophy*. New York: Simon & Schuster.

Russell, Bertrand. 2009. *The Basic Writings of Bertrand Russell*. New York: Routledge.

Russell, Bertrand. 2017. *The Problems of Philosophy*. Createspace Independent Publishing Platform.

Ryan, Alan, ed. 1987. *John Stuart Mill and Jeremy Bentham: Utilitarianism and Other Essays*. New York: Penguin.

Ryan, Alan, ed. 1987. *John Stuart Mill and Jeremy Bentham: Utilitarianism and Other Essays*. New York: Penguin.

Ryan, Alan. 1970. *The Philosophy of John Stuart Mill*. New York: Humanity.

Ryle, Gilbert. 1984. *The Concept of Mind*. Chicago, IL: University of Chicago Press.

Ryle, Gilbert. 1984. *The Concept of Mind*. Chicago: University of Chicago Press.

Samuelson, Paul A. 1973. "From GNP to NEW." *Newsweek*, April 9.

Samuelson, Paul A. 1970. *Economics*. New York: McGraw-Hill.

Samuelson, Paul, and William Nordhaus. 2009. *Economics*. New York: McGraw-Hill.

San Diego Tribune. 1977, July 22.

Sartre, Jean-Paul and Hazel Barnes. 1993. *Being and Nothingness*. New York: Washington Square Press.

Sartre, Jean-Paul. 1969. *Being and Nothingness*. New York: Washington Square Press.

Sartre, Jean-Paul. 2007. Translated by Carol Macomber, edited by John Kulka. *Existentialism Is a Humanism*. New Haven: CT; Yale University Press.

Scheler, Max. 1962. *Man's Place in Nature*. Translated with an introduction by Hans Meyerhoff. New York: Noonday Press.

Schutz, Alfred. 1970. On Phenomenology and Social Relations. Chicago: University of Chicago Press.

Schutz, Alfred. 1970. *On Phenomenology and Social Relations*. Chicago, IL: University of Chicago Press.

Searle, John R. 2001. *Rationality in Action*. Cambridge, MA: MIT Press.

Shallit, Jeffrey. 2005. "Mathematics by Experiment and Experimentation in Mathematics." *Book Review: Notices of the American Mathematical Society*, September.

Shannon, Claude E., and Warren Weaver. 1971. *Mathematical Theory of Communication*. Champaign, IL: University of Illinois Press.

Sharkey, Patrick. 2017. "A Fragile Urban Consensus: Economists and Sociologists Agree: Neighborhoods Matter: Now Comes the Hard Part." *The Chronicle Review: The Chronicle of Higher Education: Section B*, August 4.

Shinan, Avigdor. 1990. *The World of the Aggadah*. Tel-Aviv: MOD Books.

Singer, Peter. 2015. *The Most Good You Can Do*. New Haven, CT: Yale University Press.

Smith, Huston C. 1966. "Death and Rebirth of Metaphysics." In *Process and Divinity: The Hartschorne Festschrift*, ed. William Reese and Eugene Freeman. LaSalle, IL: Open Court.

Smith, Len Young, and Dale Roberson. 1971. *Business Law*. 3rd ed. St. Paul, MN: West Publishing.

Smith, Preston and Donald G. Reinertsen. 1991. *Developing Products in Half the Time*. New York: Van Nostrand.

Snow, C.P. 1963. *Two Cultures*. New York: Mentor.

Snow, C.P. *Two Cultures*. 1963. New York: Mentor.

Spencer, Herbert. 2015. *The Principles of Sociology*. London: Forgotten Books.

Spiegelberg, Herbert. 1984. *The Phenomenological Movement*. The Hague: Nijhoff.

Stafford, Thomas. *The Origin of Christian Science*. Crezte/Space Independent Publishing. 2017.

Stern, Jessica. 2003. *Terror in the Name of God*. New York: HarperCollins.

Stevens, Graham. 2011. *The Theory of Descriptions. Russell and the Philosophy of Language (History of Analytic Philosophy)*. New York: Palgrave.

Stewart, David, and Algis Mickunas. 1990. *Exploring Phenomenology*. Athens: Ohio University Press.

Svensson, Arne, and Otto Wendel. 1965. *Techniques of Crime Scene Investigation*. Second, Revised and Expanded American Edition. New York: American Elsevier Publishing Company.

Taylor, Charles. 1985. *Philosophy and the Human Sciences*. New York: Cambridge University Press.

Taylor, Charles. *Philosophy and the Human Sciences*. vol. 2. New York: Cambridge University Press, 1985.

Teilhard de Chardin, Pierre. 1965. *The Phenomenon of Man*. New York: Harper.

———. 1967. *The Divine Milieu*. New York: Harper.

Thaler, Richard H. and Cass R. Sunstein. 2009. *Nudge*. New York: Penguin.

The Spirit of Charvaka Lokayata. Lexington, KY: CreateSpace Independent Publishing Platform. 2017 .

The Spirit of Charvaka Lokayata. Lexington, KY: CreateSpace Independent Publishing Platform. 2017.

Thurow, Lester C. 1993. *Head to Head*. New York: Warner.

Tillich, Paul. 1957. *Dynamics of Faith*. New York: Harper.

Tillich, Paul. 1965. *The Courage to Be*. New Haven, CT: Yale.

Time. 1979, December 10.

Tonnies, Ferdinand. 1957. *Community and Society*. New York: Dover.

Ulich, Robert, ed. 1971. *Three Thousand Years of Educational Wisdom*. Cambridge, MA: Harvard University Press.

Varela, Francisco, and Evan Thompson. 1992. *The Embodied Mind: Cognitive Science and Human Experience*. Cambridge, MA: The MIT Press.

Velasquez, Manuel. 2014. *Philosophy*. Boston: Cengage.

von Bertalanffy, Ludwig. 1968. *General System Theory*. Boston: Brazillier.

von Humboldt, Wilhelm. 1993. *Limits of the State*. Liberty Fund.

Walzer, Michael. 1977. *Just and Unjust Wars*. New York: Basic.

Wang, Qi. 2017. "Five Myths About the Role of Culture in Psychological Research." *Observor* 30, no. 1 (January): 20–24.

Ward, Dane. 2017."Envisioning the Fully Integrated Library." *The Chronicle of Higher Education* LXIII, no. 20 (January 20).

Weber, Max. 1968. *The Sociology of Religion*. Boston: Beacon.

Weinberger, Caspar. 1990. *Fighting for Peace*. New York: Warner.

Weiner, Norbert. *The Human Use of Human Beings*. New York; Avon. 1970.

Weiner, Norbert. *Cybernetics*. Cambridge, MA: MIT Press: 1961.

Weiner, Philip P. ed. *Leibniz Selections*. New York; Charles Scribner's Sons. 1951.

Weitz, Morris, ed. 1966. *20th-Century Philosophy: The Analytic Tradition*. New York: Free Press.

Whipple, Christopher. 2018. *The Gatekeepers*. New York: Broadway Books.

Whitehead, Alfred North, 1964b. *The Aims of Education*. New York: Mentor.

Whitehead, Alfred North. 1958. *Modes of Thought*. New York: Capricorn.

Whitehead, Alfred North. 1964a. *Science and the Modern World*. New York: MacMillan.

Whitehead, Alfred North. 1964a. *The Aims of Education*. New York: Mentor.

———. 1964b. *Science and the Modern World*. New York: Mentor.

Wild, John. 1955. *The Challenge of Existentialism*. Bloomington: University of Indiana Press.

Wilder, R.L. 1982. "The mathematical work of R.L. Moore: its background, nature, and influence." *Archive for History of Exact Sciences* 26, no. 1 (1982): 73–97.

Wilson, Edward O. 1998. *Concilience*. New York: Vintage.

Winter, Gibson. 1961. *The Suburban Captivity of the Churches.* New York: Doubleday.

Winthrop, Henry. 1966a, January. "Institute of Intellectual Synthesis." *Educational Forum.*

———. 1966b, April. "Generalists and Specialists." *Journal of Higher Education.*

Wittgenstein, Ludwig. 1961. Tractatus Logico-Philosophicus. London: Routledge & Kegan Paul, 1974.

———. 1968. *Philosophical Investigations.* Trans. G.E.M. Anscombe. New York: MacMillan.

Wittgenstein, Ludwig. 1965. *The Blue and Brown Books.* New York: Harper Torchbooks.

Wolf, Stewart, and John G. Bruhn. 1993. *The Power of Clan.* New Brunswick, NJ: Transaction.

Wrubel, Robert. 1991. "GM Finally Fights Back." *Financial World,* November 26.

Zitarelli, D. 2001. "Towering figures in American mathematics." *American Mathematical Monthly* 108 (2001): 606–35 (available through EAF on CD).

Zitarelli, D. 2004. "The Origin and Early Impact of the Moore Method." *American Mathematical Monthly* 111 (2004): 465–86.

Zuboff, Shoshana. 1988. *In the Age of the Smart Machine.* New York: Basic Books.

INDEX

CPSIA information can be obtained
at www.ICGtesting.com
Printed in the USA
LVHW060454191218
600949LV00007B/32/P